Who Stole Jesus?

Who Stole Jesus?

By Paul D. Little

Romans Road Publishing

Atlanta, GA

2019

ROMANS ROAD PUBLISHING:
AN IMPRINT OF KING'S WAY PRESS

King's Way Press
4215 Jimmy Lee Smith Pkwy Suite 19-210
Hiram, GA 30141

The views and opinions expressed herein are those of the author alone and may not be shared by the publisher.
All Bible verses cited herein are taken from the 1611 Authorized King James Version of the Bible unless otherwise noted. Quotations from other works are duly cited in the "List of Citations" at the rear of the book and/or are used by express permission by the rights holders.

Published and printed in the United States of America

First Publication June, 2019

ISBN 9780998836751

www.stolenjesus.com

Cover Artwork Copyright © 2019 by Alex McVey

Cover Text Layout by Zach McCain

This book is dedicated to my Lord Jesus Christ. Without you I am nothing. Thank you for saving me and providing for my every need!

"Amazing Grace, how sweet the sound that saved a wretch like me, I once was lost, but now I'm found; was blind but now I see..."

Preface

When an author pens a non-fiction title, people will often ask of them, "Why did you write this book?"

In consideration of this question and in anticipation that someone holding a copy of this book might ask it; my reasons for writing this book are numerous. The most imperative reason spurring my decision to write this book was the sincere desire to set the record straight on who Jesus really *was*, who Jesus really *is,* and why that actually *matters* to us as a people, as Christians, and even as a nation.

False theories, false accounts, false teachings, and false characterizations of Jesus abound in today's world. In fact, a new theory on Jesus, and what He really meant when He said this or that, is seemingly hatched near weekly. It's really no wonder why so many people are confused as to what He stands for, what He's about, who He claimed to be, and what He'd do in the same daily situations that we're faced with in our modern society. With all the false information being disseminated today, it's very hard for a "young in the faith" Christian to know which Jesus is a false persona and which Jesus is true.

In today's society, the narrative of "who" Jesus is most often gets told by those who don't even know Him, or worship Him. Those who seem to know only as much as they can "Google" when it comes to His teachings, His life, and what the Bibles says about Him, usually lead the way. These "Google theologians" are the very same people who are usually the most adamant in speaking against Him. They're also the group who're wrong about Him more often than not.

You're more likely to hear who Jesus *was* from an atheist today, than you are to hear who He *is* from a Christian…and that's tragic on many levels. In the majority of cases wherein an atheist expounds upon who Jesus is, you're sure to be provided a great deal of false information. Sadly, this false information is often parroted by others, much of the time without rational thought or analysis; even by some professing believers.

Jesus has quite literally been stolen; kidnapped, held against His will, by those with ulterior motives. Comparable to the plastic baby 'Jesus' figures that pranksters frequently steal from outdoor nativity sets at Christmastime; He's been removed from His rightful position. He's being showcased by various political, social, and economic groups to support *their* own worldly agendas. Instead of His Father's mission of salvation, He now stands for whatever's most expedient to the people using His image to bolster their personal agendas and political aspirations.

He's being held captive by those who have less than pure motives in wanting to use His persona to justify *their* own personal beliefs, their own lifestyle choices, and oftentimes, their own twisted, perverse political and socioeconomic worldviews. Jesus is missing in modern America, as well as in the rest of the world. We need to find Him so that we can present Him to the world as He really is, rather than how the numerous groups with private agendas and self-serving motivations desire for Him to be.

So the two questions that beg asking are these: If Jesus, the *real* Jesus, is missing in the world today, how do we go about locating Him? And once we find Him, how do we go about presenting Him to the rest of the world so that *all* people may see Him as He truly is?

The simple answers, in a nutshell, are: The real Jesus can be found in the Bible. And once we read, pray over, and study the Bible, we will know how to best present Him for all to see.

But alas, these days, nothing is ever really quite that simple. Not when we have those who'd seek to change the meanings of even the most basic passages in the Bible to fit their own goals and worldviews. With countless, always emerging new English translations, and even the newest "LGBTQ friendly" Bible versions, even basic Bible study can sometimes lead to more confusion for the believer and the unbeliever alike.

If our starting point in this endeavor isn't based on solid footing, then how can we possibly succeed?

The Bible, the *real* Bible, accurately read and rightly divided, is where we'll find the roadmap to Jesus and where we'll find the truth as to who He is, and what His true characteristics are. Only after carefully and prayerfully studying the Bible can we determine who stole Jesus. It's then that we'll begin to uncover the lies and distortions about Him that are so prevalent in today's world. Only then, once we discover who has taken the real Jesus and left us with a cheap counterfeit, or actually a *bunch* of poor quality knockoffs, can we set the real Jesus free for all of the world to know.

That is my goal. If I can help show who Jesus really was and who He truly still *is;* if only one person gets the clarification that they need on this matter; if only one person gains a true understanding of the *real* Jesus, then I'll consider this work a success. It'll have been well worth the time and effort it took to research, compile, write, and present this book.

In introducing this work, I feel the need to make one point very clear to you, the reader. While political stances and political parties are mentioned early and often in this book, this work is not intended as an overtly political tome by any means. It's purely because of the warring factions of political classes and parties, and their desires to claim Jesus as a co-sponsor to their own worldly agendas, that this book *must* reference politics as part of a natural discourse of the subject at hand. This book is not intended to be about politics, however, politics and religion can't easily be separated. This is especially true when discussing America as a country. In America, politics and religion have *always* intersected and paralleled, often walking side by side, even hand in hand, since our founding. When it comes to discussing Jesus and politics, it's not so much about left and right; it's about what's clearly right and what's clearly wrong.

In truth, Jesus cannot be discussed honestly and earnestly without also examining the politics and the motives behind *all* of the groups who seek to use His name. Various groups from the farthest of the far right to the farthest of the far left have tried to co-opt the message of Jesus and make it their own; supplementing traces of the Gospel with their own personal biases and preferences that Jesus probably wouldn't share. It's for this reason that politics becomes a very natural part of the conversation when discussing Him.

It's my hope that you, the reader, will find the information contained within these pages to be helpful, insightful, possibly eye-opening, and genuinely informative. I know that for some readers the material contained within this book will be controversial and might challenge some of their long-held beliefs. Many other readers might find themselves nodding their heads with the facts as they're presented. Still other readers may have mixed feelings about what they read within these pages. Others reading this book might get angry or defensive about what's said within this volume.

That's all okay.

It's all normal and healthy to experience these emotions; especially about a topic that so emotionally charged. Any time material is presented that causes us to think outside of, or to closely examine, our deeply held spiritual beliefs, resistance to the message is certainly going to be a factor. The only thing that I ask of you, the reader, is to review and consider the information contained within this book with an open mind. Even more importantly, to consider what's presented with an open heart. A heart and mind seeking, and receptive to, truth will often find it.

By all means, don't take what I say as the unvarnished truth. Rather, take what I say with an open mind and a grain of salt, and then check my source, the Holy Bible itself. See for yourself what the Bible has to say about any and all claims that I make within the pages that follow. Pray about it. Seek God's face in deciding what's credible and what's not. If I've done my job correctly and effectively, you should see that the Holy Bible verses quoted within this work, as well as the Bible in its entirety, should complement and bolster any of the claims and arguments that I present to you. My arguments should line up with the Word of God in a way that is both clear and concise.

I hope you'll enjoy reading this book. If you do, my hope is that you'll share it with others who might need it, or those who might enjoy reading it all the same. Together we can not only restore truth to Jesus, but we can make the world a better place in the process.

In the end, I know that when our search for Jesus is finished, we'll find Him right where He is now and where He's always been…unmovable, eternal, seated on the right hand side of the throne of God the Father. Let's begin our search for the truth and may God bless you abundantly.

Sincerely,
Paul D. Little- 05/28/2019

Acknowledgements

No work of this sort is possible without people believing in you and supporting your vision. This book is no exception. The following people have not only had a profound impact on my life, but the book wouldn't have been possible without their prayers, encouragement, support, or input.

First, I have to thank my Lord and Savior, Jesus Christ, for without Him, this book wouldn't have become a reality. Without Him, this book would have no purpose or meaning.

The following people helped make this book possible: My loving wife, Callie Little, who was my sounding board and my source of inspiration when I faltered, as well as my better half in all things; my precious children, Titus, Samuel, Luke, and Silas, who showed great patience with their daddy while he worked tirelessly on this book; My mother, Glennis Little who, although in Heaven now, remains a source of inspiration and strength for me, the great men of God in my life who helped make me who I am today: My father, Thomas Little, a true preacher who walks the walk and talks the talk- a better role model could never be found; Bro. Darrell Hunter; Pastor Keith Lee; my dear friend, Pastor Robert Dilbeck; and all the Godly men at those churches I've been blessed to be a member of over the years; my brother and sister-in-law Ken and Maria Stratton; my mother-in-law, Betty Gluckman; my Christian friends who helped encourage me through the years: David Walker: my brother-from-another-mother who now resides with Jesus, Maria Ratliff, Rebecca Hughes-Peace, Rick Olsen, Marilyn Perkins

Hultquist, Carolyn Lynton Morse, Rita Daniels, Debbie Scheibly, Gary L. Metzger, Mike O'Conner, Daniel Peters, Micah Tate, Scott Jackson, Kathey Reed, Amanda & Rich Penkoski, Relly Bolton, Eddie Simolini, Ross Anate, JD Krause, Stephen Briggs, Stacey Miller, Robin Craven, Steve Ware, Nathan Noyes, Fred Nocito, and all those in our little corner of the net who push back against the encroaching darkness; Mr. Bobby Fischer, the best Sensei and mentor person could have; Mark Randolph Watters: who pushed me to keep going; my dear Aunt Ethel: who's like a second mother to me, Nancy Murray, the sweetest lady around, Mrs. Dixie Walker: who's also like a second mother to me, Julie Walker: the sister I wished I'd been blessed with, Tom and Nora Buttram: the best neighbors ever, the Dilbeck family, Wanda Cooley and Marge Sweeney: without both of whom I'd likely no longer be counted among the living, and Dr. Madhavi Rayapudi who had the courage to buck medical tradition to save a life.

There are many others I could have and probably should have included. Rest assured, if your name does not appear here, it's not an intentional slight…it's just the result of the failing memory belonging to a flawed man. I try daily to make sure those around me know they're appreciated. If you're reading this and we know each other, you're no exception.

I also would like to acknowledge The Christian Post, and Marriage Conservation, two excellent Facebook Christian forums wherein I first discovered the alternative world of apostate 'Christianity' and the myriad of false Jesus's within the comments sections. Anytime one of these outlets posts Biblical truth, the minions of the devil are there in the comments section sewing discord and disinformation. Without these outlets, I'd never have had the necessary starting point and inspiration for this book.

A special thank you to the KJV 1611 Facebook page for their unwavering support and firm stance on the Word of God. A greater source for Biblical truth would be hard to find.

Now, I would be remiss if I didn't include the following people. Not because they're friends or family. Not because they mean anything to me on a personal level. No, the following people must be acknowledged because they're either apostate little 'c' "Christians", or they're hostile atheists and unbelievers who spread lies and disinformation about Jesus, Christianity, and Christians, on multiple Christian forums. They deserve acknowledgement only because they provided me with a plethora of false Jesus's to debunk. Many of these people have also attacked me personally, either through mocking the death of my child, lying about, harassing or libeling me. They've attacked my wife, left fake negative reviews on my Christian children's books, and have accosted my friends; all because we possess the courage to stand up for the Word of God in a time when modern PC culture says that's not acceptable.

The following fall into those categories: Jeff Fuchs, Bill and Gloria Perrin, Allison Welch, Joshua Wineholt, Jessica Justice, Linda Ray, David Nelson, Dave Cothran, Traci Monroe, Tracy and William Dixon, Steve Piantedosi, Dawn Cowell, Tina McManus Frei, Robert Cunningham, Sean Kennedy, and all of their many multiple alts and fake profiles. I'm sure I left a lot of their tight-knit cabal out, but the rest know who they are. A special nod goes to Sean Hart, who was the first to share with me the false notions that Jesus said "people are born gay" and that Jesus "affirmed and blessed a gay couple". These slanders against Jesus were the final push that I needed to decide to write this book.

Introduction

In today's world, we encounter people of nearly every race, background, personality, ethnicity, and worldview conceivable on a daily basis. One factor in common that's seen among people today is that they tend to have completely disparate viewpoints on a wide range of issues; yet individuals on both sides of modern, contentious societal issues often make the claim that Jesus would side with *their* personal beliefs and stances. Obviously, Jesus couldn't possibly side with each and every viewpoint in regard to politics, religion, and everyday social policies and issues. In a country wherein close to seventy-five percent of Americans self-identify as Christians, we can't seem to get anywhere close to approaching that percentage when it comes to agreement on social, political, or even religious issues. We, as Christians, are deeply divided across all fronts. (1)

So who's correct?

Which side of the argument is presenting the *true* Jesus?

Where does He *truly* stand on these issues that divide us?

After all, if *my* Jesus is different than *your* Jesus, it only stands to reason that one of us has to be following a false idol...a counterfeit...a fake...a phony...a snake-oil salesman of historic proportions.

In a world where so many different viewpoints are presented as being "the truth", who's right?

All you need to do to witness this deep, cutting division is to read the viewpoints expressed in the comments section under any current online article. Especially those that deal with contentious modern day societal/political/religious policies; you'll be bombarded with a wide range of individuals…all presenting opposing viewpoints; all of whom claim to have Jesus on *their* side. So, from this dissension, many questions arise as to the true nature of Jesus.

Is Jesus the Son of God?

Or, was He just "a good teacher"?

Was He just a prophet?

Was He simply a mortal man who was delusional and fostered a massive God complex?

Was He a far left-wing, radical liberal bent on changing the world through "social justice"?

Was He a staunch, dyed-in-the-wool conservative?

Was He truly a socialist, as claimed by some today?

Is He alive?

Is He dead?

Did He ever even live in the first place?

Was He a fictitious invention of man, used to control the masses?

Was He married?

Was He single?

Did He speak against homosexuality?

Did He show support for homosexuality?

Would He support abortion?

Would He call abortion murder?

Would He support gay marriage?

Would He stand firmly against gay marriage?

Would He support the Democratic Party with their modern day liberal ideology?

Would He stand with Republicans and their conservative views?

What would He say about our modern society and where we're headed as a nation and as a world?

Would He say that we're growing closer to Him as a whole?

Or, would He say that we're rapidly getting farther and farther away from the very Gospel that He preached?

I've personally seen and heard all of the above claims and counterclaims, as well as a plethora of other opposing positions postulated about Jesus online, in person, in books, in newspapers, on television, and on radio. There's just no way that *all* of these claims can be true. Especially given that most of these points are entirely contradictory to one another.

I've seen the far right, the far left, and the middle of the political spectrum *all* claiming that Jesus is on *their* side... so they *must* be in the right with their own ideology and viewpoints. I've even heard some argue that standing against some of their most spurious positions puts you at direct odds with Jesus.

But, where in all of this heated rhetoric and white noise, does the truth reside?

Is and was Jesus a far left-wing political radical, as many on the far left would have you believe?

Or was He a hardline right-wing activist, as the far right also claims?

Is Jesus a centrist with both liberal and conservative traits, as the political middle would have us believe?

Can Jesus both approve and disapprove of hot-button, controversial social issues such as gay "marriage" and abortion at the same time?

It seems that both flanks, as well as the middle, of any hotly contested idea, moral issue, or societal debate often try to use Jesus to bolster their own personal arguments. There's even been a rash of bestselling books published in recent years wherein the author claims to know the *real, secret,* "truth" about Jesus...and these books are being written and presented to us by Buddhists, Hindus, Muslims, and other non-believers! Self-avowed atheists have also gotten in on the act by authoring books claiming that *they, and only they,* are the real experts on Jesus.

What's even worse?

People are buying these books, as if they'll discover within the pages of these volumes some hidden secret about Jesus that only the author knows! Something that's escaped discovery for nearly two thousand years. Some secret that only a handful of "enlightened" folks know. I mean, if *you* want to take counsel on who Jesus is according to a Buddhist or an atheist, good luck with that...I'd rather stick with the Bible and a Bible-believing, Bible-preaching church with a Godly Pastor.

So, who's right?

Which group really has Jesus on *their* side?

What would Jesus *really* do and say about these things?

Can we really trust the true portrayal of Jesus to be presented to us by non-believers and Christ-denying skeptics?

Can people who don't even believe in God become credible sources of information about His Son?

Why do so many of us search for a "Jesus" who fits in with our own personal views, despite those views being incompatible with what the Bible teaches us?

Why do we seek to conform Christ to *us*, rather than conforming ourselves to *Christ?*

In this book I've attempted to answer all of these questions. I've come to the conclusion that in order to ascertain who Jesus really *is*, we must first eliminate who He most certainly is *not*. I've found that the best way to showcase the one, *true* Jesus is to debunk the false and counterfeit versions of Jesus that are promoted as the "real deal" by others. To cut away and discard the dross until only truth remains. With this approach in mind, the following chapters will first detail the false Jesus's, or the misrepresentations of Jesus's character, His stances, and His teachings. The latter part of this volume will then focus on the *one* true Jesus, the very same Jesus who appears in the Bible...the Jesus who now sits next to God the Father on the throne of Heaven. The Jesus who is waiting patiently for the appointed day and time to collect and receive His bride.

Thank you for taking the time to read this book and the willingness to hopefully learn more about, or to reinforce your knowledge of Jesus in the process.

—Paul D. Little

Table of Contents

Part One:
The Counterfeits

Chapter 1:
"Tolerant Jesus"

I've never been one for extended formalities, so what do you say, let's jump right in with both feet and start debunking some of the most prevalent of the many false Jesus personas? I'm sure that this first chapter alone might result in getting me banned from entry into every "blue state" in the union, but as they say, the truth often hurts...most of the time, only because we aren't ready to accept it as truth.

The pervasive myth of the "tolerant Jesus" is one that is both equally absurd and abhorrent at the same time; not because "tolerance" doesn't sound nice, warm, fuzzy, and agreeable. Not at all. Rather it's because this mythical version of Jesus is regularly used to justify exceedingly deviant social behaviors and lifestyle choices. This counterfeit Jesus was created by those who wish to justify their own sins without facing criticism for living ungodly. Living without repentance requires a "tolerant" savior for it to be workable. The problem is that it's not "workable" at all. Salvation minus repentance isn't salvation at all. It's called a false profession of faith...but we'll get into that topic in depth later.

This fake "tolerant' depiction of Christ is frequently used to water down or pervert the *true* message of eternal salvation. In many ways he serves as a means of allowing people to remain in their sin-filled lifestyles without the need for repentance; negating the need for implementing necessary changes to our daily lives that the Bible and Jesus Himself demands of us all.

2 Corinthians 5:17 "Therefore if any man be in Christ, he is a new creature: old things are passed away; behold, all things are become new."

Now don't misinterpret that scripture. I've seen those wishing to justify living in sin twist and use this passage to mean that the old requirements to live righteously have passed away. That couldn't be further from the truth. This passage speaks of the new life in Christ and how we're to allow our old, sin-filled lives to be crucified on the cross with Jesus. How we are to allow him to mold us into the new creatures we're called to be. How we are to leave our old sins behind.

We most often hear about the "tolerant Jesus" when he's used in the context of political or social policy arguments in our postmodern society. I've often witnessed this mythical version of Jesus trotted out by those who wish to explain or justify their most mind-boggling assertions. Many of these assertions happen to stand in direct contrast to the Biblical teachings of Jesus, and the picture of the righteous, sinless Savior we see depicted in the Bible.

This "tolerant Jesus" seems to be an "anything goes" type of guy; which is a far cry from the *real* Jesus of the Bible. Jesus, the *real* Jesus, preached the need for Salvation…along with the *requirement* for repentance (or the turning away) from sin. Without repentance, there can truly be no salvation.

Why?

Because if you don't possess a repentant heart, you haven't truly realized that you're a lost, hell-bound sinner. You can't realize that you're without hope, other than hope in Jesus's saving power, until your heart is repentant. If you refuse to recognize your sins as sin, there is no salvation. Without repentance and the admission that our sins *are* sins, we make Jesus, and the Holy Bible, liars.

In fact, the word "repentance", or some form thereof (ie: "repent", "repented", "repenteth", etc.), appears in the Bible one hundred and ten times. Based upon the average page count of most standard-sized Bibles, that means the word appears roughly once on every eight to eleven pages throughout the entire Bible.

Think about that for a moment. Let that marinate for just a bit; turn that fact over a few times in your thoughts. I'd say this repetitive mention in the Bible means that repentance is a pretty important idea.

One that God chose to remind us about every eight to eleven pages on average in His Word.

Who could deny that this has to be an important concept to Him?

Jesus's first recorded words in the Gospel of Mark are those in which he preaches repentance and faith. If one wants to truly claim they have faith, they must also have repentance. One without the other is void. Mark: 1:15:

> "*14 Now after that John was put in prison, Jesus came into Galilee, preaching the gospel of the kingdom of God, 15 And saying, **The time is fulfilled, and the kingdom of God is at hand: repent ye, and believe the gospel.**"*

This theme of repentance is one that appears throughout the Bible, over and over again at regular intervals. It's almost as if God was trying to drive a crucial point home, huh?

Once, while preaching on this subject, I asked a rhetorical question, 'What do you think it means if your wife asks you to do something every eighth to eleventh time she speaks to you?' The question was quickly followed by some chuckles and some muttered responses. One response that stood out above the rest was this: "It means you better do it or she's gonna knock a knot on your head." Well said, sir. Well said. Do we think God's going to do any different?

Here's the thing, God wants us to repent! Sometimes, when we fail to do so, He'll chastise us, knocking a proverbial knot on our heads. Just as a reminder.

> *Acts 3:19 "Repent ye therefore, and be converted, that your sins may be blotted out, when the times of refreshing shall come from the presence of the Lord;"*

Did you notice one key, all important phrase in that passage?

"Repent...and be converted". Why is this key? Because it quite clearly shows that Jesus considers repentance the first step in salvation. No conversion takes place without a repentant heart leading the way.

▪▪

In further debunking the myth of the "tolerant Jesus", it's first very important to note that the word "tolerance", as used by those who'd apply this term to Jesus, does *not* appear in the Bible. Not only does the word itself not appear in scripture, the very notion in this context is also absent from the Bible. A very important distinction when discussing the nature of Jesus. If "tolerance" was an important aspect of Jesus's character or His ministry, the word would have likely appeared in the Bible several times. At least one would think so. Yet, it doesn't make a single appearance in the Word of God. That alone should tell us something. Juxtapose that fact with the one hundred and ten times that "repentance" appears in the Bible and we can easily see which concept is more important to God.

Let's further examine this word, "tolerance", for a moment. "Tolerance" as defined by the Webster's Dictionary is:

Tolerance: (Noun):

1. Willingness to accept feelings, habits, or beliefs that are different from your own. 2. The ability to accept, experience, or survive something harmful or unpleasant. 3. Medical: your body's ability to become adjusted to something (such as a drug) so that its effects are experienced less strongly.

Now, the "southern definition" of "tolerance", at least in the part of America where I'm from, is somewhat simpler. It can best be summed up as:

Tolerance:
1. Puttin' up with somethin'.

Nothing in either of the accepted definitions of the word "tolerance" exemplifies a characteristic of the *real* Jesus from the Bible. Jesus was *not* and is *not* a tolerant Savior, at least not in the purely secular sense of the word as used and intended by many today. Nor was Jesus known for "puttin' up with" much foolishness. When Peter stepped out of line, Jesus said, *"Get thee behind me, Satan: thou art an offence unto me: for thou savourest not the things that be of God, but those that be of men."* And, that wasn't the last time that Jesus rebuked Peter, one of his most ardent followers. If Jesus would so strongly rebuke Peter, what makes anyone think He'd be tolerant of nonsense from any of us? The myth of the "tolerant Jesus" is abject dishonesty at best; and the direct and willful, purposeful subversion of the Gospel at worst. (2)

Let me expound upon this: We must not confuse the notion of "tolerance" with the notion of "acceptance" when it comes to sins... and the sinners who commit them. In confusing or interchanging these two concepts, we change the meaning of the Gospel message in its entirety. There's a vast difference between the *sinner* and the *sin*...and a vast difference between *"acceptance of the sinner"* and *"tolerance of the sin"*.

These differences are deeply profound!

Jesus was (and still is) willing to "accept" any and all who'll come, seeking Him in repentance. All those who possess a repentant heart and come seeking the Kingdom of God by the shed blood of the Lord Jesus Christ will find it. It doesn't matter what station in life a sinner is from, how rich or how poor they may be, or what sins they've committed in the past. Jesus *accepts* all who'd come seeking the Kingdom of God to enter therein... as long as they first accept Him for who and what He is...with, *and this is an unwavering necessity*, a heart that is repentant. (I'll fully address this later.)

All that's really necessary for salvation is for a lost sinner to have repentance in their heart; the recognition that they're a lost sinner, apart from God and bound for hell, belief in Him (including his death on the cross, His burial, and His resurrection; all for the remittance of our sins), a willingness to call their sin what it is: sin, and a personal acceptance of Christ as their Lord and Savior. A repentant heart is a heart that recognizes ones sins as sin and feels a sorrow for having transgressed against God.

The error being preached and taught regarding the supposed "tolerance" of Jesus comes in the form of a fundamental misinterpretation, or willfully deceptive misinterpretation, of what Jesus and His "accepting" nature entails. While Jesus is more than happy to *accept* all who come seeking Him, He was not and is *not* "accepting" of the *sin* that they've been involved in prior to repentance and salvation. Jesus sees each and every sinner, regardless of their sins, as a human being first and foremost; a precious soul in need of salvation. In other words, He sees us the way God sees us, as disobedient children.

Children whom He still loves in spite of our sins…and in spite of ourselves. I had one person tell me once that "God loves me just the way I am!" I had to correct them by stating, "No, God loves you *in spite* of the way you are."

∎∎

I saw a Facebook post recently about students at a high school protesting the teacher's LGBTQ (rainbow) flag that she was proudly displaying in her classroom; the very same classroom where crosses and patriotic shirts are forbidden to be worn or displayed. (3)

In the discussion comments that appeared after the online article, I came across a commenter who said:

> *"One of my children had a homosexual teacher in high school. He talked about his boyfriend a lot. My child became rather sympathetic to this guy. I had to remind my child that his lifestyle was an abomination to God while telling her to respect the teacher anyway. I didn't take this to the school authorities but if I had it to do over, I would. This teacher's perverted influence was not okay with me."*

The very first response to this woman's remarks was from one of the "tolerant Jesus" followers. The response from this "tolerant Jesus" acolyte made me cringe a little on the inside while also wincing in painful disbelief. This is a person who claims to "follow Jesus", but obviously doesn't really know Him, or His righteous nature, at all.

Here's her reply:

> *"So your child learned the acceptance that Jesus taught? That's beautiful!"*

On so many occasions, I've had to walk away before commenting on articles like this. This time however, I felt compelled to make a comment. You see, these people don't really have a clue what they're talking about. Far worse than that, they're helping to lead others astray with the false Jesus personas and mischaracterizations they're promoting.

Here was my response to the second lady's comment:

> *"Jesus did NOT tell us to "accept" or view other people's sins as normal. Please show me where in the Bible we are told to accept the prostitute remaining a prostitute? Where are we taught that we are to accept the thief remaining a thief? Where did Jesus tell the alcoholic to remain an alcoholic...and for the rest of us to "accept" them as such? He didn't. He told sinners He came across to 'go, and sin no more.' The same thing He'd tell every gay person He met today."*

Of course, there was no response to my reply. That could be because she had no answer that would've made any sort of logical sense. Remember, the goal of these people is not sincere, honest discourse, but rather obfuscation and misdirection. The intent is to muddy the waters and create confusion as to what's true and what's not regarding our Lord Jesus Christ. Their goal is forced submission via attempting to shame us into accepting their views as "correct" and in keeping with Jesus's "tolerance".

■■■

Jesus loves us all. From the sweetest little old church lady to the vilest sinner among us, He loves us all. He longs to save us all.

That having been said, Jesus absolutely and wholeheartedly abhors sin...in all of its guises and formats. *All* sin. Great and small; Jesus detests all of our sins equally. This includes *every* sin, no matter how big or how small the offense may seem to us.

A point that cannot be stressed enough is this: sin is sin and *any* unforgiven sin will keep a sinner who hasn't accepted the gift of salvation out of Heaven. The only way to receive forgiveness and cleansing from sin is through the shed blood of Jesus Christ. Even if the only sin you've ever committed is a "little white lie", you won't see Heaven, the same as a person who's a murderer won't see heaven... unless they receive salvation and the free pardon of sin through the precious blood of the spotless Lamb of God.

Jesus doesn't "tolerate" sin. If you come to Jesus thinking He's going to be "puttin' up with your sins", then you need to think again. Jesus was quite clear in His teachings that salvation comes by grace through faith, received by a *repentant* heart. He's a forgiving Savior, but He's not, by any means, a tolerant Savior. In fact, Jesus said we *must* be born again. Being born again is a rebirth. A new start. A new life. We can't be "born again" if we've decided *not* to allow our old selves to die in the first place.

> John 3:3 *"Jesus answered and said unto him, Verily, verily, I say unto thee, Except a man be born again, he cannot see the kingdom of God."*

In every circumstance that we're given in the Bible wherein Jesus met a sinner and gave them the Gospel, He also left them with the clear admonition that they were to repent of their sins and attempt to live righteously. He didn't turn a blind eye to the individual's sin, nor did He ignore it, nor did He fail to recognize it for what it was. He never said, "Alright now, go on back to whoring, thieving, lying, cheating, drinking, and doing drugs."

To illustrate this point, let's examine the story of the adulterous woman who was brought before Jesus for judgment. This encounter can be found in John Chapter 8. In this account, we see a woman, caught red-handed in the act of adultery. A woman who's brought before Jesus by the Pharisees to see what He'd have done with her. These men wanted to tempt and test Jesus by forcing Him to either pronounce judgment and death upon this woman, or stand in defiance of the Law that stated this was the penalty that was due.

According to Law at the time, she was to be stoned to death for her sins.

> John 8: 1-11:

> *"8 Jesus went unto the mount of Olives.*
> *2 And early in the morning he came again into the temple, and all the people came unto him; and he sat down, and taught them.*
> *3 And the scribes and Pharisees brought unto him a woman taken in adultery; and when they had set her in the midst,*

⁴ They say unto him, Master, this woman was taken in adultery, in the very act.
⁵ Now Moses in the law commanded us, that such should be stoned: but what sayest thou?
⁶ This they said, tempting him, that they might have to accuse him. But Jesus stooped down, and with his finger wrote on the ground, as though he heard them not.
⁷ So when they continued asking him, he lifted up himself, and said unto them, He that is without sin among you, let him first cast a stone at her.
⁸ And again he stooped down, and wrote on the ground.
⁹ And they which heard it, being convicted by their own conscience, went out one by one, beginning at the eldest, even unto the last: and Jesus was left alone, and the woman standing in the midst.
¹⁰ When Jesus had lifted up himself, and saw none but the woman, he said unto her, Woman, where are those thine accusers? hath no man condemned thee?
*¹¹ She said, No man, Lord. And Jesus said unto her, Neither do I condemn thee: **go, and sin no more.***

Notice and take to heart those last five, very striking, very *clear*, and very unmistakable words that Jesus spoke..."*Go, and sin no more.*" Just as with every other sinner, in this account Jesus was "tolerant" only of the human being who stood before Him. In this case, a woman anxiously waiting on His decision as to her fate. The woman's accusers saw her as a person who'd committed sins that were vile and worthy of death; therefore they saw her as devoid of any further value. *He* saw her as she was: a helpless, hopeless, lost sheep. One in desperate need of a shepherd. A lost child in need of redemption from her sins. A precious soul that needed the cleansing power of the shed blood of Jesus in order to overcome death.

I've been told, more than once, by those who preach this "tolerant Jesus" that "Jesus didn't judge this woman's sins." However, that's patently false. It's not just a mistake to say this; it's an ignorant *lie!* Jesus *did* judge this woman's sins as sin...and He acknowledged them publicly and openly as sin. That's blatantly obvious by the very words He spoke to her. The fact that He rebuked her to "go, and sin no more" means that He judged her, and quite accurately so, as a sinner. And He judged her sin as sin. He didn't *condemn* her to die, either physically or spiritually, for her sins which is quite a different thing than "judging her". He showed the ultimate act of love in forgiving her of her sins. Something that the Pharisees and religious leaders didn't expect or believe would happen. They thought they had outsmarted Jesus, but He wasn't tripped up the way they'd expected. So while it's true that He didn't condemn the woman, He very much *did* judge her.

At the very same time He had compassion on her, Jesus was disgusted and disappointed by the actual sins that the woman had committed. He was not "tolerant" of her sin, nor was He okay with her persisting in the sins of adultery after His encounter with her. He fully expected her to repent of her sins, and turn away from the lifestyle and the sin that had nearly gotten her stoned to death in the first place. He made it a point to say so directly…upon telling her to "Go, and sin no more". He judged her for sure. This much is clearly evident.

It's likewise important to note that while we aren't given the exact details in the Bible of what Jesus wrote upon the ground during this encounter, it's my personal belief that it may have been a laundry list of all the secret sins that'd been committed by the men within this woman's group of accusers. Jesus most definitely knew the secret hearts of these men, and if anyone knew their hidden sins, He did. As Jesus wrote upon the ground, this group of men slowly dwindled and dispersed as the sins that they'd engaged in were written in the dirt at her feet. All of this is hardly a sign that Jesus was in favor of "puttin up with sin", as we'd say in these parts.

Whatever our Lord wrote upon the ground that day, when it was coupled with His spoken admonition to the accusers, the message was powerful enough to convict the men in their hearts of their *own* sins, causing them to turn away from condemning the adulteress to die. This was a woman who, by the law at the time, *was* deserving of death and *should* have been stoned to death for her sins. Many times, just like this woman's accusers, we're guilty of forgetting about our own unconfessed and unforgiven sins…while castigating others for *their* unconfessed and unforgiven sins. (You didn't know that small town-Georgia preachers knew such fancy words, did you?)

Something else that should be taken away from the account given to us in John 8, is that this woman also received salvation on that very same day, at that very same hour.

How so?

When she answered the Lord Jesus Christ, note that she referred to him as "Lord", not "master" or "teacher"; both of which can carry very different meanings. If your Bible has any word besides "Lord" in this passage, you should toss it out (but that's an argument for later on…or perhaps another book). She acknowledged Him as LORD.

When the adulterous woman acknowledged Him as "Lord", she knew and acknowledged in her heart that this was the true and living Son of God standing before her. The promised Messiah stood before her. The Savior who'd just saved her from the condemnation of physical death, could also grant her eternal life, thereby saving her from spiritual death as well. With this realization in her heart that she was a lost sinner, and with her acceptance of Jesus for who He was, He saved her soul from eternal death and the torments of Hell.

■■■

While we're on this particular passage of the Bible, I have to address a side note. This particular passage of the Bible is one that Christians and non-Christians alike are often fond of quoting, at least in part, when it suits their needs.

How often have you heard, a comment along the lines of: "Now, Jesus said don't throw the first stone!"?

It happened to me just yesterday. I was participating in a discussion on an online Christian forum, one that's overrun with atheists. I engaged in a conversation that went like this:

> *Me: "If a person is a Christian, they shouldn't be supporting any candidate who supports abortion."*
>
> *Atheist: "Jesus said not to throw the first stone."*
>
> *Me: "You don't understand the meaning of those words do you? It's not 'throwing a stone' to state a fact."*
>
> *Atheist: "You Christians just hate everyone who disagrees with you and you're throwing stones when you probably support things Jesus wouldn't support too."*

The rest of the conversation devolves, as it nearly always does with the atheists on this particular forum, into him attempting to smear

Christians, while painting atheists as "tolerant" and more "Christ-like" than the believers who actually worship Him. Typical empty rhetoric and attempts to derail the conversation on things that matter to those who follow Christ; with a healthy dose of ad hominem attacks thrown in for good measure.

Those who like to throw out the "don't throw stones" banal platitude sadly don't understand what that passage of the Bible was intended to illustrate. That passage wasn't about righteously "judging" sin as sin. Not at all. It wasn't given to tell us not to "throw stones" at others by speaking about their very real transgressions against God. It was given to us to illustrate two very powerful points.

The main reason for this scripture is to illustrate our lost and hopeless human condition without Jesus. Let's take a moment to consider this adulterous woman. Under the Law at the time, she was to be stoned to death for her sins. That was the penalty assigned by God for adultery. Had Jesus not been there at the time, she *would* have died; a very painful, possibly very long, drawn-out death. It was only through Jesus's presence there, Him being in the right place at the right time, as He always is, that this woman's life was spared. Jesus was the intercessor, the merciful Savior, who intervened and protected her from certain death.

No, the admonition against "throwing stones" is at best secondary to the greater point; and used incorrectly by most people even then. This passage illustrates our own personal need for Jesus. It illustrates how when we stand before God, guilty in our sins, we have no hope... other than the shed blood of our Lord and Savior, Jesus Christ. Just as that adulteress would have faced certain and painful physical death, without Jesus's intervention, *we* will face a certain, and painful, *eternal,* spiritual death...if we stand before God without Jesus.

This is why this passage exists in the Bible. God wanted to clearly illustrate the difference between having Jesus and *not* having Jesus. *This* is the main idea of this account. The same people who most often use the "don't throw the first stone" defense would also be the same people who reject the greater meaning of this passage.

The admonition that Jesus gave to the woman's accusers wasn't an admonition against calling sin what it is: sin. Not at all. Jesus Himself called it sin. The whole passage, including this admonition, serves to further illustrate a much, much more profound and larger point: that *all* are guilty of sin and need Jesus.

You see, those men were all guilty of some sin, even if no one else knew what their secret hearts were hiding. God did. And Jesus being God, knew all of their secrets as well. Probably all of those men in the group of accusers had sin in their lives that, if exposed, could have led them to the same place that they brought this woman to: a tribunal before man, to be punished by man. Possibly to even be sentenced to death themselves.

When those men heard Jesus's admonition and saw whatever He wrote upon the ground, they were convicted in their hearts of their own sins. They walked away from their condemnation of this woman, choosing to leave her un-condemned and alive.

The point intended to be made is that without Jesus, we *all* have no hope. No escape from the judgment and the deadly wrath of God because of our sins. No pardon for those sins.

These are truly the main points that God wanted taken away from the passage of John chapter 8. It's Satan who tries to blind the eyes of the lost to the truth and who promotes the false notion of "throwing the first stone" over the most *important* meaning of this all important Biblical scripture. Those same people who most often misquote this scripture are usually those who need to heed the deeper meaning therein.

(I also have to point out as an aside that "throwing a stone" literally means *throwing a stone.* As in trying to kill someone by stoning them to death for their sins. So, unless someone is literally lobbing heavy stones at your head because of your sins, no one has "thrown a stone at you" and accusing them of doing such is an exercise in biblical ignorance and bearing false witness.)

■ ■

Now, let's backtrack to the original point. Did Jesus leave it at saving this woman from both a painful physical death, and saving her soul from eternal death and the torments of Hell?

Did He just send her on her merry little way after He'd saved her life and granted her salvation?

Did He pat her on the back and tell her "You're okay now. See ya later. Keep on keeping on"?

No!

He left her with a very strict and stern admonition to "go, and sin no more". He didn't say "go on back to your lovers" or "go about your business as usual"; He fully expected her to go home and to make a serious change in her life and how she lived it on a daily basis.

Obviously, Jesus knew at the time, just as He knows now, that even a redeemed sinner *will* sin again, because the sin nature is an integral and indwelling part of each and every one of us. That doesn't mean that we'll necessarily commit the *exact* same sins again and again, but as humans with an indwelling sin nature, we *will* sin in some form or fashion. It's impossible for us to live for long without failing God and sinning in some manner. In fact, Jesus knew that this woman *would* sin again (not necessarily the same sin) probably before sunset on that very same day.

It's a fact that before you finish reading this book, that you'll have sinned many times, just as I'll have sinned many times before I've finished writing it. Sin is an inescapable fact of life for humans, although we should still strive to avoid sin in our daily lives. The way to do that is by maintaining a repentant heart, a repentant lifestyle, and daily prayer. Reading our Bibles daily also helps to overcome the sin nature within. Even the redeemed in Christ fall short and fail God daily, but we should always try our best not to.

So what then did Jesus mean by "go, and sin no more"? Since He knew that we *will* sin again, what did He specifically mean by commanding the adulteress to "go, and sin no more"?

Jesus was speaking specifically about the very sin that she was engaged in at the time, which was taking lovers to bed who were not her husband. He was also speaking of developing a repentant heart and mindset with the desire *not* to commit sin…any sins, again. While it's certain that we'll fail at times and sin again, when we do so it should give us pause. It should grieve our hearts and spirits immediately and cause us to once again seek the Lord for our spirits to be renewed, and for our fellowship with Him to be restored.

While it's not feasible to believe that Jesus thought that this woman would never commit *any* sin again; He did expect her to refrain from the sins of adultery and lust. He did expect her to try, honestly try, to live a righteous lifestyle. His admonition was for her to try to refrain from *all* sin, as much as is humanly possible, knowing that she would fail at times. This is an important distinction, because Jesus *does* expect for us to not only repent at the time of salvation, but to continue on in a repentant lifestyle *after* salvation as well.

After salvation, our intentional sins of rebellion should become fewer and fewer as we mature and grow in the Lord Jesus Christ.

■■

I'd be remiss if I also didn't take a moment here to point out a serious disparity in the repentant heart and the unrepentant heart. I've had this conversation many times with those who claim to be "followers of Jesus" yet who, at the same time, deny the need for repentance as a vital part of salvation. These folks are quick to point out things like this: "You sin every day. We all do."...While that's a factually accurate statement, the premise that the statement is predicated on is entirely wrong. They use this claim to justify own their desires to hold on to those sins that they don't want to repent of.

You see, we all *do* sin each day.

Even if it's a "tiny" sin. Even if it's what we'd all agree is a "minor" sin. The difference, however, between the unrepentant sinner and the repentant sinner is a profound matter of the heart. If you truly have the indwelling of the Holy Spirit and you're saved, you'll have a deep inner desire *not* to sin. To refrain from sin. All sin...even the one's we might consider "tiny". This desire leads to a noticeable change in your life, or it should. Your very sins should begin to change.

Now what in the world do I mean by that?

How does the very nature of our daily struggle with sin begin to change with salvation?

Let me see if I can explain this in a way that's simple and easy to comprehend. When we truly have the Holy Spirit dwelling in our hearts, our desire to sin becomes less and less with the passage of time. Instead of immediately giving in to the sins of the past, we actually wage war against those temptations. Sometimes, unfortunately, the flesh wins out. More often than not though, we're able to shake off those temptations that once tripped us up. The more we refrain from those old sins of the past, the easier it gets to turn away from them altogether. Soon, we're a changed person. Our very hearts are different.

When we do fail and give in to temptation, if we truly have salvation, we experience a deep shame and guilt. A nearly soul-crushing guilt that comes only from Holy Spirit conviction. We then have a burning desire to confess those sins to God and repent thereof. That's an explanation of the repentant heart in a nutshell.

When we possess a repentant heart, we'll begin to see a great difference in the way we live. You see, there are two distinct categories of sin for the purposes of this illustration. There are two distinct *types* of sins that we can fit all sins known to man into. (Now, don't misunderstand this point, I'm not "ranking" sin. All sin is unacceptable in the sight of God, and for the lost sinner, even the tiniest of sins will keep them out of Heaven, if not covered by the blood of Jesus. A lie is the same as a murder when it comes to sin, according to the Word of God.)

One of these categories of sin, I like to call the *"Sins of Commission"*. These are the things that we do when we give into temptation and do that which we know is wrong. We willingly *commit* one of these sins against God. Watching pornography, cheating on one's spouse, getting drunk, lying, stealing, doing drugs, these are all examples of *"Sins of Commission"*. As we mature in our walk as Christians, our *Sins of Commission* should recede like floodwaters after several sunny days with no further rain. These sins should rapidly begin to dry up and disappear from our lives. The longer we abstain from them, the more willpower we have to continue to refrain from them.

These sins are like smoking cigarettes. If you've ever smoked and tried to quit, you know it's hard, sometimes very hard, to kick the habit. Yet, with each passing day that you don't smoke, it becomes easier to deny that urge to smoke. Eventually, if you remain steadfast, the desire to smoke passes completely. Soon enough, even the smell of someone else's smoke will cause a reaction of revulsion in the former smoker. Sin is much the same. The more they're abstained from, the easier it becomes to deny these impulses and temptations. Eventually even the thought of such sins that you once engaged in will cause the same revulsions as cigarette smoke does to a former smoker.

The second category of sin is what I call *"Sins of Omission"*. To "omit" something means to "leave it out", oftentimes on purpose, but it can also be done without forethought.

So what exactly are *"Sins of Omission"?*

Well, for one, they're the more common sins among the truly redeemed. You see when we obtain salvation and the Holy Spirit sets up shop in our hearts, we go (or at least we should) from committing willful, defiant sins that we know to be wrong, to most often committing sins that are really *Sins of Omission*. Sins wherein it's not so much what we *did*, it's more of what we *didn't* do. We strive not to sin, but we always fall short of God's expectations. Most often, these failures are in the form of omitting, or failing to do, something that we know we should've done.

Some great examples of this type of sin: failing to help someone who needs it, failing to do something we feel God is leading us to do, and failing to do what's right in a given situation. For instance, if I see a man in need of help on the side of the road and I do *not* offer assistance (when I could have), that's a *Sin of Omission*. If I fail to witness to a person who I believe God is leading me to witness to, that's a *Sin of Omission*. The most common *Sin of Omission* that we make as believers is neglecting our daily Bible reading and prayer time. We also often fail to witness to those around us, fail to tithe, and fail to encourage our brethren. These *Sins of Omission* are the most common types of sin for the true believers, and they denote a marked difference between the repentant and the unrepentant sinner.

The unrepentant sinner is a person who, while they know they're sinning against God, they simply don't care. They're not concerned with the detrimental effects that their sins have on themselves, or those around them. Sadly, I come across many people each week who call themselves by the name of Christ, and yet are unrepentant in sin. They curse, drink, do drugs, engage in fornication, lie, steal, cheat, and more...without the slightest qualms or guilt. With their mouths they claim to know and love Jesus, yet their very hearts and actions tell a vastly different story.

Any person who can commit *Sins of Commission* without remorse, and without conviction in their hearts, likely hasn't ever truly obtained salvation. That's just a fact. If you're *not* a new Christian and your sins of *Commission* outnumber your sins of *Omission*, you might need to do a serious spiritual self-examination. Or you may want to speak to a Bible-believing and Bible-preaching deacon, elder, pastor, or preacher for clarity on this issue.

■ ■

The example we looked at in John Chapter 8, the one that people often use to justify a false Jesus, actually blows the myth of the "tolerant

Jesus" out of the water. The believers and followers of "tolerant Jesus" would have you to believe that "anything goes" as far as Jesus is concerned. They believe that repentance is an old and outdated notion. Those preaching a "tolerant Jesus" wouldn't see a problem with the adulterous woman continuing to commit the very same acts that got her into trouble with the law in the first place. In fact, they tell us that if we have a problem with this adulterous woman continuing on in that exact same sinful lifestyle, that it is *we* who are guilty of "judging" her. (Another Biblical misconception that I will address later on in this book). They claim that *we're* the ones being un-Christ-like by expecting her to change and repent from her previously wicked ways.

They simply couldn't be more wrong. I can find nothing in the Bible that shows that Jesus was supportive of, or would be "tolerant" of, a lifestyle that involves unrepentant, unconfessed, and unrestrained sin. I can find no example of Him telling a sinner to continue on in their sins, or telling them that they were not expected to repent.

∎∎

Let's study another example that disproves the notion of the "tolerant" and "anything goes Jesus". The incident in the Temple, as illustrated in Matthew Chapter 21 verses 12-13, which is often referred to as the story of "Jesus Cleansing the Temple". It's a perfect example of how Jesus did *not* tolerate or "put up with" sin:

> *"And Jesus went into the temple of God, and cast out all them that sold and bought in the temple, and **overthrew the tables of the moneychangers, and the seats of them that sold doves,** 13 And said unto them, It is written, My house shall be called the house of prayer; but ye have made it a den of thieves."*

Here is an example of one of the few times in the Bible that we see a picture of Jesus displaying some righteous anger. (Note: Anger is *not* a sin in and of itself, as long as it's righteous anger and doesn't lead one to sin. Jesus was incapable of sin, and His anger was very much righteous and justified.)

It was not with "tolerance" that He overthrew the tables and chairs of those who bought and sold in the Temple. It was with righteous

18

anger that He did so. Anger that Temple of His Father, which should've been revered as a place of worship, was being used as a common flea market...a place of corrupt commerce rather than a place of worship.

If you want to see just how "non-tolerant" Jesus was in this instance, just research the very same account in the book of John. You'll find that Jesus also used a whip to clear these buyers and sellers out of the Temple, thereby restoring it to its proper use.

If we are to believe in the "tolerant Jesus" as presented by those who follow him, He wouldn't have done such things. Driving the buyers and sellers out of the Temple with a whip and overturning tables and chairs isn't a very "tolerant" set of actions, is it? I'd say no, at least not by the measuring stick with which the left usually measures one's "tolerance".

After all, to some of the purveyors of "tolerance", even the simple act of citing a Bible verse is an act of intolerance. These same people who mistakenly castigate Christians for "judging" others would likely call Jesus's actions "un-Christ-like" and very "judgmental" as well. They'd likely consider this a hate crime if Jesus entered a church or synagogue and took the same actions today. Truth be told, it's badly needed in this day and age; many of our churches have become much worse than the temple Jesus cleansed.

This Biblical account of Jesus's actions destroys the narrative of the "anything goes" and "tolerant Jesus".

If I may be so bold, I think if the *real* Jesus walked among us in modern day America, the "tolerant Jesus" followers would be loudest voices in the crowd clamoring and screaming "Crucify him!"...while foam drips from their chins.

■■

Now, let's move on to a modern day example of how the believers in the "tolerant Jesus" have again taken the real Jesus, hidden Him away, and replaced Him with a cheap knock-off or counterfeit version: A recent AOL news story featured the harrowing tale of a woman who launched a lawsuit against her former employer, a Baptist church, for "unjustly" firing her. The article was clearly written from a viewpoint that was overtly sympathetic to the woman, and one that was also overtly hostile toward the church.

So, why did the church fire the plaintiff?

For violating their very specific code of conduct expected of church employees. The self-same code of conduct that she readily agreed to adhere to upon being hired. In her frivolous suit against the church, the employee claims that the church leadership engaged in "discrimination" and that she was "unjustly terminated".

So, what specifically led to her firing, and why does she feel that she has a valid legal case against this Baptist church on the spurious grounds of "wrongful termination" and "discrimination"?

The woman claims that she was fired simply because she refused to get married...and that the church wrongfully terminated her because of her living arrangements. She said the church was aware of her living situation at the time they hired her. The church however tells a vastly different story; one that involves her breaking their codes of conduct, not just once, but several times over.

On the surface, the woman's story sounds truly outrageous! Who in their right mind wants churches to be able to force their employees, or anyone else for that matter into marriage?

Right?

What person of sound mind thinks that churches should be allowed to dictate such a private, intimate, and personal matter?

I, for one, wouldn't be in favor of any such thing. It's downright un-American...and ungodly.

But, is that *really* what happened here?

Is this woman telling the truth? No.

No, she's not.

As a friend of mine's beloved mother used to say, "I smell something funky, and it ain't the collard greens cooking on the stove"...

Can you smell it?

I can.

Like with so many other of these types of stories that get eagerly reported, often with key details omitted, whenever Christianity or a church is involved, the reported "truth" and the *real* truth are often very divergent. It turns out that the *real* situation behind this conflict was this: This church originally hired the plaintiff knowing that she'd previously given birth to one child outside of wedlock. The church handled this matter of her prior sin in a very compassionate and very Christ-like manner. They didn't hold the previous mistakes the applicant made *before* her job interview against her. (Which was the righteous thing to do, as we've *all* made mistakes. We all have sins in our past. If a sin-free past was a prerequisite for church employment, churches would then have a very hard time finding qualified employees.)

At the time of hire, this woman was given an employee handbook that fully, and in great detail, explained not only the job expectations of the position she was seeking to fill, but also the lifestyle bylaws that *all* of church staff were expected to adhere to. She understood these rules and readily agreed to live by the biblical standards set forth by the church. She accepted this as a condition of her employment. These rules and bylaws clearly stated that any violations of these expectations were grounds for immediate dismissal…for *any* persons employed by the church, up to and including the Pastor.

That should've been the end of this story. Period. Employee breaks the rules. Employee gets fired. Simple as that. This woman knew the church rules and bylaws. They weren't secret. She can't claim ignorance. Since she willingly chose to break them, she *should* have been terminated. That's a no-brainer. However, like so many today, she's loathe to take responsibility for her actions, and must blame others instead.

So, this woman is hired, given the rules and bylaws governing all church employees, and agrees to these conditions by accepting the job offer. Now, let's fast forward a few months in time. The woman's happily working for the church. She's reportedly doing a very decent job by all standards. Soon however, it becomes obvious that she's become pregnant, yet again. (Without being married to the father of the expected child.) She's publicly stated that she has no plans to get married to the father of the expected child. Nowhere in the foreseeable future does she have plans to wed. Unbeknownst to the church, she's been cohabitating with the father of her previous child, who's also the father of the unborn child, since she was hired. She's thereby living in a perpetual state of sin. Her living arrangement (meaning living as married while not actually being married) was not disclosed to the church at the time of her employment. Cohabitation with a person she isn't married to, thereby openly committing the sin of fornication and adultery, is a flagrant violation of the rules that she agreed to as a condition of her employment.

When the facts concerning her living arrangements come to the attention of the church, she is counseled by the Pastor and a group of elders on this matter. She is advised that the situation of her living conditions, her cohabitation and out-of-wedlock pregnancy, was unacceptable conduct for a church employee. She was reminded of the rules and bylaws of employment that she'd happily agreed to as a requirement for being hired.

The leaders of the church go on to advise her that one acceptable solution, to her self-induced problem, would be for her to set a date by which time she'd marry the father of her children. She accepts this as a mutually agreeable, viable solution and agrees to get married, or at the very least, to set a date for an upcoming marriage, within the next few months. The church didn't even ask her to have her lover move out. (Which wouldn't have been an unreasonable thing to ask. It's more than reasonable for a church to ask an employee to cease sinful cohabitation immediately.)

I think the church was quite measured in the way they handled this dilemma. They could've fired her immediately, without affording her the chance to remedy the situation. Instead, they chose the compassionate route…and yet they were still punished for it.

Again, it bears pointing out that this lady *knew,* without any doubt, before accepting the job that the situation she'd put herself in was not one that would be compatible with her employer's rules. She knew this arrangement could very well result in her immediate termination. This wasn't something that should've come as a big surprise to her. Nor should she have been shocked that the church asked her to resolve this matter in a way that would be consistent with church and Bible teachings.

The church gave her a few months in which to set a wedding date. It's important to point out that the church leadership did *not* tell her that she had to be married within a few months, or even wed by a certain date. They simply wanted a concrete date that she could point to in the not-so-distant future, in order come into compliance with church bylaws and standards. They were more than reasonable and far more "tolerant" in their demands than many other churches would've been. I know my own church wouldn't likely have been this lenient.

Fast forward in time again to a point that's several months after an agreement between the church and the plaintiff had been reached. The woman *still* has not set a date by which she'll be married. Instead she's made it known that she's doubling down on her open rebellion against God. She's reversed course and adamantly states her refusal to get married...in opposition to her previous pledges to her employer to do so. The church is then forced to make the painful, although entirely justified, decision to fire her. She's continued to willfully violate the conditions of employment that she readily agreed to upon taking the position with them. The church just can't have that.

Once more, this should've been the end of a very unfortunate story. Employee accepts the rules; employee violates the rules; employee continues to violate the rules after reaffirming and agreeing to uphold the rules; employee then gets fired. Simple. It's a common sense scenario in most employment situations. If you refuse to work within the rules and framework of your employer, you get fired. Period. Not a difficult concept to comprehend for most people.

For a Baptist church to maintain a pregnant, non-married, and cohabitating employee on their staff makes that church look very bad. Especially when the same church teaches and preaches against these very same sins. The church, in this case, really had no choice but to terminate the employee given the unfortunate conundrum that she created by her actions. For them to do otherwise would've been to engage in abject hypocrisy. It'd also cause the church and the leadership therein to lose credibility in the eyes of their members.

■■■

Uh-Oh! Quick, call an attorney! Notify the ACLU! Someone has been victimized by a mean old, hateful, and intolerant church!

According to the followers of "tolerant Jesus", the Baptist church acted outside of the way *their* Jesus would've acted. They claim Jesus would've never fired this woman because of her situation. He would never be so unkind as to fire a pregnant woman! How intolerant!

Really?

So, regardless of the fact that this woman signed a binding agreement to comport herself in alignment with the Bible, and with church bylaws, she can't be held accountable for her actions while working for a church?

Even after being given several chances to rectify the situation that *she* created in the first place?

Even though her very lifestyle is in direct opposition to the church bylaws, the Bible, and the teachings of Jesus Christ Himself?

Who Stole Jesus

I guess the "tolerant Jesus" would have given hugs all around. Then he'd have admonished the church for daring to follow the Bible. He'd probably have come over to babysit while the lovely couple took some personal time to go clubbing, right? Or maybe he'd have brought over some beer and marijuana so that everyone could have a good time? *Sarcasm intended.*

Let's examine the claim that Jesus wouldn't have fired this woman. As I stated before, while Jesus was known for *not* condemning someone for their past sins; He *was* known for *admonishing* sinners not to repeat the same mistakes and sins of the past. He warned sinners not to keep engaging in the sins that they were *presently* involved in. So, for the sake of making this point abundantly clear, let's remove the Baptist church from the equation and insert Jesus in place of the church. (As the church is supposed to be an earthly representation of Jesus.)

> *So now, what we have is a woman coming to Jesus (the Baptist church) seeking a job. Jesus tells her that while He forgives her for her past transgressions (the previous child born out of wedlock and engaging in sex before marriage) that He expects her to follow His rules, behavioral expectations, and lifestyle from this point forward. Those are the conditions set forth in order for her to accept this job offer. The woman readily agrees to these expectations and takes the job. Then, instead of changing her lifestyle and holding to the agreement that she made, she continues to violate all the same rules and expectations over and over again. She engages in those exact same sins repeatedly. She further compounds the problem by cohabitating with her lover. Jesus confronts her after it becomes undeniably obvious that she's pregnant once again. Pregnant without a marriage. He gives her ample time to make the situation right by marrying her lover, who she lives with, as if married already. She agrees to do this, but does nothing to fix the problem for several*

more months. In fact, she then boldly announces to Jesus (the church) that she will not abide by her previous promises. That she wishes to continue to live in sin. She arrogantly states that she expects to remain employed with Him. Finally, Jesus realizes that despite His best efforts to reach this woman, to get her to change, the woman still adamantly refuses to repent. So, Jesus has to move on and part ways with her. She's fully rejected Him and there's nothing more He can do about it, without becoming a hypocrite Himself.

Those who believe in "tolerant Jesus" actually accept as true, and have vociferously argued, that He would've continued to allow this openly rebellious and defiant woman to keep defying Him for months and years on end. They trust that He would've allowed her to continue to make a mockery of Him and His Gospel for everyone in the church, as well as everyone outside of the church, to see.

How can a church teach others not to live in sin if one of their own employees is guilty of being deeply embroiled in sin herself? If a church employee acts this way without remorse and without the church even batting an eye about it, how can they teach against it? How can a pastor tell his congregants not to engage in the sins of premarital sexual relations and cohabitation if one of his very own employees is openly fornicating? Had he allowed this woman to remain employed at the Baptist church, the pastor would've faced allegations of hypocrisy…and those allegations would've been true. He would've lost credibility among his congregants. That's dangerous, because that's something that will destroy a church from the inside out.

Curiously, the online news story about this sad affair featured the following statement from the plaintiff's:

"While Kellam and Coalson said they understand the church's policy regarding morals, they added they're having a hard time understanding the reasoning behind Kellam's termination."

Well, isn't this just a stunning display of cognitive dissonance?

Okay, wait…the couple involved makes the claim to understand the church policy regarding moral standards? Yet, they also claim they "have a hard time understanding the reasoning behind her termination"?

Does that statement seem to directly contradict itself, or is it just my imagination?

How can you on one hand "understand the church's policy regarding morals" and on the other hand fail to understand being terminated for violating the very policy that you just stated you understood in the first place? Where's the disconnect here?

All aboard the crazy train!

Let me make it clear for Kellam and Coalson if they, or anyone they know, happens to be reading this book. She was fired *because* she understood the church's policy regarding morals and decided to openly *rebel* against that policy; standing in defiance against both the church and the Lord Jesus Christ.

There. Does that clear things up?

In fact, this quote alone should cause any reasonable judge to toss this lawsuit. She admits that she understood the policy and then broke it. Enough said. Case closed.

Jesus (the *real* Jesus) would have undoubtedly done exactly as this Baptist church and the leaders thereof did. He definitely wouldn't have tolerated this rebellious woman's actions forever. Not without taking some sort of stand against her. I can't find any teachings in the Bible that shows Jesus coming back to the same person over and over again asking them, nay begging them, to repent and change. At some point, at least in the examples God provided in the Bible, Jesus always moved on to others cities and other people who might accept, rather than reject, Him.

That's precisely what the church in this scenario was faced with doing. They took the same course of action that we can easily surmise that Jesus would've taken. (4)

■ ■

Many other examples of the disparities between "tolerant Jesus" and the real Jesus are spewed online daily. All one needs to do to hear, read, or learn all about the "tolerant Jesus" is to go online and read a current news story. Especially if that story makes any mention of polarizing social issues such as gay "marriage", transgender bathroom issues, abortion, politics, or religious issues. Read said article and then peruse the comments section at the end of any of these articles. You'll most likely be greeted with gleaming "pearls of wisdom" such as:

- *"Jesus wouldn't discriminate against anyone for loving someone else."* Or:
- *"So-called Christians don't share the same tolerance as Jesus."* Or:
- *"Jesus would be all for gay marriage."* Or:
- *"Jesus never said anything about homosexuality..."* Or:
- *"Jesus would've said to let these people use the bathroom of their choice."* Or:
- *"Jesus would not have condemned this woman for having an abortion."* Or:
- *"Jesus said people were born gay."* Or:
- *"Jesus allowed people the choice to sin, who are we to say otherwise?"* Or:
- *"Jesus affirmed a gay couple."* Or:
- *"Jesus didn't have anything to say about abortion."* Or:
- *"Jesus was a radical socialist."* Or:
- *"Jesus was the first radical liberal."* Or:
- *"Jesus didn't judge people for their sins, why should you?"*

Sadly, these are all very real, verbatim comments that I've read onscreen with my own eyes. And, the examples above are only the tip of a very large, very noxious iceberg. I've stared in utter dismay at my computer screen, while shaking my head in abject horror and disbelief, that so many people could be so woefully deceived. Especially when the truth is so readily available and easily accessible to all. Unless you live in a hut in the middle of a jungle somewhere, and have had no chance to hear the Gospel and no chance to read the Bible, there's just no excuse for this sort of nearly unimaginable, wanton Biblical ignorance.

SIDE NOTE: The internet can be a wonderful, efficient, and very effective tool when used correctly. There's no better way to quickly access information for research, school projects, general knowledge, fast fact-finding, etc. Used properly, the worldwide web can be a great blessing.

Used incorrectly however, the internet can be extremely destructive, even dangerous. The obvious pitfalls aside (access to pornography, temptation for spouses to locate and contact old flames, social media narcissism, using the net to harass others, etc.), the internet can be a wild-west horror show of misinformation and misdirection. When it comes to theology on the internet, this is often the case. Unfortunately the ease of access to spread and receive information online also makes the internet a fertile breeding ground for the spreading of misinformation and all-out lies. Especially where God, the Lord Jesus Christ, and the Gospel are concerned.

Christians, preachers, and pastors have a hard time attempting to undue all the harm that "Google theology" has wrought in this world. It's literally costing people their very souls. And, if you spend any time at all on any Christian online forums, you'll encounter "Google theologians" galore, in all of their misinformed and willfully ignorant glory.

■■

Particularly troubling are the "tolerant Jesus" followers who call themselves "real Christians", while attempting to cast doubt upon the salvation of others. They do this, all while stating these others aren't Christian, simply because they don't embrace the ideals of their mythical, leftwing, "tolerant Jesus". They castigate and scorn others for daring to believe in the real Jesus. The one who's portrayed in the Holy Bible.

The fact that these people actually believe that Jesus would support and "tolerate" deeply sinful things like gay "marriage", abortion, transgenderism, pornography, usage of foul language, multiple wives, open marriages, drunkenness, drug usage, and a litany of other sins, speaks to how far liberalism and general apostasy has encroached into our churches. That they believe that embracing these sins, and the sinners who commit them, as "normal" makes a person more Christ-like, truly baffles and boggles the mind.

In the words of a good friend of mine, if you subscribe to that belief system: "You just ain't right!"

What better proof do you need that these followers of the "tolerant Jesus" are following a counterfeit, than the Holy Bible itself?

Shouldn't it be the supreme authority on the matter?

Jesus Himself is the Living Word of God!

The Bible is very clear, throughout both the Old and New Testaments, that homosexuality is an abomination to God and a sin. Furthermore, the Bible proclaims that a man should not adorn and present himself as a woman, nor should a woman adorn and present herself as a man. The Bible states that God created them "male and female". It doesn't mention a hybrid of the two. Both the Bible, and Jesus Himself, make it abundantly clear that harming children is an extreme offense in the eyes of God. It's clear that those who do so endanger themselves to God's wrath. (And what could cause more harm to a child, than ripping a living one from the womb in order to kill it?)

How then could Jesus be "tolerant" of such things as gay "marriage", men being allowed to use the women's restroom while dressed in drag, and the murdering of unborn children in the name of abortion?

Who really believes that getting drunk, watching pornography, and cursing like a sailor are "godly" things to do?

Who in their right mind thinks that Jesus would "tolerate" all these sins and more…especially if these sins are running rampant among the redeemed?

If Sodom and Gomorrah were destroyed by God for their wicked and ungodly ways, homosexuality being chief among them, what makes anyone think that Jesus (who *is* God) would tolerate something like gay "marriage"?

By the way, a God who destroyed two cities because of their evil ways and the depth of depravity therein doesn't seem a very "tolerant" God to me. In fact, His destruction of Sodom and Gomorrah, as well as the worldwide flood in the days of Noah, would seem to be the very antithesis of the secular left's definition of "tolerance" or an "anything goes" attitude. God isn't tolerant of sin. He never has been. He never will be.

■■■

SIDE NOTE: While I try not to chase every rabbit and side argument that necessarily appears as a result of discussing these biblical topics, this is one I must address here and now: *Sodom and Gomorrah.*

The falsehoods peddled by the left pertaining to the Bible don't just stop at the slander of and mischaracterization of Jesus. No, nearly all aspects of the Bible come under attack from modern day "Google theologians"; many of whom fancy themselves valiant keyboard warriors for their own twisted versions of "the truth".

The account of Sodom and Gomorrah in the Bible is no exception. There's a false narrative about the demise of these cities that's gained popularity in recent years. The internet has only helped to spread biblical falsehoods that were once much more isolated and contained. Unfortunately, this pervasive lie has become an accepted "truth" (even though it's definitely untrue), even among some of those who call themselves Christians.

The rewritten story goes like this: Sodom and Gomorrah weren't destroyed because of rampant sin, homosexuality the chief among them. No. The new claim is one that's completely off the reservation of common sense. The new allegation is that these cities of sin were destroyed, not because of sexual sin, debauchery, and open rebellion against God, but rather simply because of them "being inhospitable".

Read that again.

According to the left, these cities were wiped off the face of the earth by God because the people just weren't friendly. Now, wrap your head around that. Does that make any kind of logical sense?

With all of the nations that have attacked Israel and the Jewish people around the same time, with all of the other injustices going on in the world at that time, God wiped out all of the men, women, and children of Sodom and Gomorrah for simply being unkind?

So, let me get this straight...they believe that God wiped out Sodom and Gomorrah for the "sin" of being inhospitable, yet He didn't destroy Nazi Germany for the extermination of more than six million Jews?

How could being "unfriendly" be worse than the wanton, brutal killing of millions of God's chosen people?

If God were going to destroy entire cities, and every man, woman, and child therein, for being inhospitable, why is Chicago still standing?

Paul D. Little

How can someone with an even partially functioning brain buy into this nonsense?

If God's standard for wholesale destruction was nothing more than being inhospitable, then pretty much every city in every nation would be in dire trouble and mortal danger.

So where do they get this deception they're pushing?

The same place as always: cherry-picked Bible verses that they lack the discernment, or spiritual insight, to understand. This is a favored tactic of the left: pick a Bible verse, quote it out of context, and twist it to fit their warped worldview. It's a highly favored tactic of Satan himself.

To arrive at this crazy conclusion, they base their falsehoods upon a passage in Ezekiel which names the sins of Sodom. Ezekiel 16: 49-50 is often quoted as a means of backing up the claim that homosexuality had nothing to do with Sodom and Gomorrah's downfall and destruction.

Ezekiel 16:49-50

> *"⁴⁹ Behold, this was the iniquity of thy sister Sodom, pride, fulness of bread, and abundance of idleness was in her and in her daughters, neither did she strengthen the hand of the poor and needy.*
> *⁵⁰ And they were <u>haughty</u>, and committed <u>abomination</u> before me: therefore I took them away as I saw good."*

Take a look at the underlined words above, *haughty* and *abomination*. The Sodom and Gomorrah deniers conveniently, either willfully or in ignorance, fail to comprehend that verse fifty of this passage specifically calls out the sin of not just homosexuality, but rather the sin of *prideful homosexuality*. Homosexuality *is* a sin; prideful homosexuality is a sin with extra relish on top. It doesn't get any clearer than that.

Further evidence exists in Jude 7 as to what was the real issue in these cities. This passage specifically calls out the sins of Sodom and Gomorrah as fornication, which is *all* sexual activity outside the union of man and woman in marriage, and "going after strange flesh"…which is undeniably the sin of homosexuality. It couldn't possibly be anything else.

To believe that Sodom and Gomorrah were destroyed because of an all too common "inhospitable nature", is beyond ignorant. It takes an abject fool to believe this.

Jude 7

> *"⁷ Even as Sodom and Gomorrha, and the cities about them in like manner, giving themselves over to **fornication**, and **going after strange flesh**, are set forth for an example, suffering the vengeance of eternal fire."*

■■

Back to business: On the subject of gay "marriage", in the Holy Bible itself, we see the definition of marriage as defined in Genesis 2:21-25:

> *"And the Lord God caused a deep sleep to fall upon Adam, and he slept: and he took one of his ribs, and closed up the flesh instead thereof; ²² And the rib, which the Lord God had taken from man, made he a woman, and brought her unto the man. ²³ And Adam said, This is now bone of my bones, and flesh of my flesh: she shall be called Woman, because she was taken out of Man. ²⁴ **Therefore shall a man leave his father and his mother, and shall cleave unto his wife: and they shall be one flesh.** ²⁵ And they were both naked, the man and his wife, and were not ashamed."*

The Word of God is decidedly and unequivocally against homosexuality, and it undoubtedly defines marriage as the union between a man and a woman before God. It would appear to me that a person would have to be completely bonkers to believe that Jesus, as The Living Word and as God Himself, would support an atrocity like gay "marriage". That just doesn't make sense. It's like adding two and two and coming up with ninety-seven rather than four.

Let me be clear here, because the followers of the "tolerant Jesus" love to paint any opposition to evil as "hate"; Jesus *loves* the homosexual just as much as He loves any other sinner. Let me repeat: Jesus absolutely loves the homosexual as much as He loves the rest of us; including the redeemed. The sin of homosexuality in and of itself, however, is an utter outrage in His sight.

So, what would the *real* Jesus do upon coming to a face to face confrontation with a homosexual person?

What would He say if He were asked about the homosexual lifestyle and agenda?

The only possible answer is very clear based upon the Holy Bible and the teachings and examples provided therein. If Jesus met a homosexual, His approach would be the same as when He met any other sinner during His ministry. He would lay the Gospel out for them, concisely and clearly, with patience and love. Then, after He'd presented the Gospel, He'd admonish the homosexual to "go, and sin no more". He would be unequivocal about their sins being sin, the same way He was unequivocal with the woman at the well about her sins being sin, and likewise with the adulteress woman mentioned in John 8. That means He would expect the homosexual to no longer engage in the homosexual lifestyle; to repent of *all* of the sins in his/her life.

■■

SIDE NOTE. I have to throw in a side note here, since I've mentioned the woman at the center of John 8 yet again: she is *not* Mary Magdalene. There's absolutely also not a shred of evidence that this woman was ever a "prostitute" either. John 8 says she was caught in the act of adultery, nothing more. We often hear that "Mary Magdalene was a prostitute" and that she was the woman mentioned in John 8. The Bible does not say that at all. What the Bible tells us about Mary Magdalene is that she was possessed by seven demons and that Jesus freed her from those demons and restored her sanity. That is the extent of what we know about her life prior to meeting Jesus.

It also bears noting, she was *not* Jesus's wife either. Jesus did not have a wife. (More on this later.) (5) (6)

■■

While Jesus is openly accepting of the *person* who comes to Him, He'd completely reject the teachings of those who follow the mythological "tolerant Jesus". Those who believe and profess that Jesus would be on board with a homosexual continuing on in that lifestyle after salvation, can't possibly know the *real* Jesus of the Bible. Those who believe that He'd allow and accept any person continuing on in the lifestyle of homosexuality (or any other repetitive, daily sin) are completely and totally wrong. They couldn't conceivably be more wrong if they tried. When the Bible tells us that we're to become new creatures in Christ, it means that we're supposed to strive to leave our old, sin-filled, pre-salvation lives behind us. Like Lot's family, we're supposed to leave our old, sin-filled lives behind without looking back; and like Lot's family, there are dire consequences for failing to do so.

See 2 Corinthians 5:17:

> *"17 Therefore if any man be in Christ, he is a new creature: old things are passed away; behold, all things are become new."*

While this Scripture encapsulates so much more, one meaning of this verse is that in addition to our sins having "passed away", through being covered by the precious shed blood of Jesus, we're also to strive to become a "new creature" in Christ. Our old lives, habits, mindsets, and actions should "pass away" as well. To "pass away" literally means "to die". To cease to exist. To become a relic of the past. In reference to human beings, someone "passing away" literally means that someone has died. We often hear this term when we receive the tragic news of someone close to us dying. "Uncle Bob just passed away."

So, we're told by God that our old self, our old person before Christ, literally needs to die. If you're in a Bible believing, Bible preaching church, this will sometimes be referred to as "being crucified with Christ"; meaning our old selves die upon receiving Christ. That it is symbolically crucified with our Savior, when we receive the free gift of salvation. If we do as the "tolerant Jesus" followers believe, we're literally refusing to let our old, sinful selves "pass away" by keeping them alive and well. There are those who'll do anything and everything to keep their old lives on life support...and that's the inverse of what should happen when we accept Jesus.

When we truly receive Christ as our Savior, we also receive the Holy Spirit, the third person of God, indwelling within our hearts. This helps facilitate, in fact it's the only way we can facilitate, the necessary changes that God expects in us. This is the beginning of the "new creature" that we're called to become. We should seek to remake and remold ourselves into *His* image through the help of the Holy Spirit.

Pay close attention to the statement above.

In fact, go back and reread it. If you need to, read it yet again. Why?

Because today, more and more people are trying to remake and remold Christ to *their own* image, rather than conforming themselves to *His* image. They find it far easier to attempt to twist and contort Christ to fit their warped needs and desires...because it requires very little effort on their part. Change isn't always easy, but it *is* not only possible, but probable if you're truly saved.

You can't do what the scripture says while holding fast to your sin. Sin and Jesus have the net effect of repelling one another. If you attempt to hold on to sin with your left hand and Jesus with your right, you'll either be ripped apart...or one will slip from your grasp while the other remains behind. All too often it's the sin that remains behind, while Jesus slips away from your grasp.

Why?

Because if the truth's made known, it's infinitely easier to hold on to sin, than it is to hold on to Jesus. Holding on to Jesus requires a much greater personal effort. It requires radical change on our parts. It can cause us to lose friends, family, and other loved ones. It causes us to give up many of the things that we once so enjoyed. It's takes effort.

When we start becoming that new creature in Christ, when we start saying "no" to sin, others around us will turn against us. When we no longer partake of the sins of our friends and family, often times they will reject us. This isn't a surprise. The Bible tells us this will happen.

Matthew 10: 34-36:

> [34] *Think not that I am come to send peace on earth: I came not to send peace, but a sword.* [35] *For I am come to set a man at variance against his father, and the daughter against her mother, and the daughter in law against her mother in law.* [36] *And a man's foes shall be they of his own household.*

The "tolerant Jesus" crowd tries instead to remake and mold Jesus to *their* image. Their Jesus, not surprisingly, shares an infinity for all of their favorite sins. He's convenient and stress-free to follow. He turns a blind eye to all of their sins and simply says to them: "I love you, don't change." Since He has no standards, there's not much for a person to do in order to please Him. No sacrifices, no restrictions, no change required.

He's an easy-go-lucky type of guy.

And when people profess to have this Jesus, their friends and family who are lost love them all the more. Because this Jesus has no standards, those who follow the "tolerant Jesus" are still able to go to the bars and clubs with their family and friends, still able to imbibe with them in drunken revelry, and still able to abide by their friends using foul language, whore-mongering, etc. Because their "tolerant Jesus" has no standards, they have no standards. Therefore their friends and family feel no pushback against their evil ways, so the enmity mentioned by the real Jesus in the passage above never comes to fruition. Were He the real Jesus, these same family and friends would begin to pull away from the new Christian, as that person begins to live for God.

The problem is, that He's *not* Jesus. Not the *real* Jesus anyway. And because of that, He was no power to save us. No redeeming power, no healing power, no power to help us. He's nothing more than a false front.

■■■

Let's take a deeper look at marriage itself now as it relates to the "tolerant Jesus" crowd. Jesus Himself, when asked about divorce and the sanctity of marriage, gave us the definition of marriage in the Bible (He reiterated the definition of marriage that's so clearly defined by God in Genesis).

See Matthew 19:4-5:

> *"And he answered and said unto them, Have ye not read, that he which made them at the beginning made them male and female,* ⁵ *And said, For this cause shall a man leave father and mother, and shall cleave to his wife: and they twain shall be one flesh?"*

It seems pretty clear as to what Jesus thought that marriage consisted of. Notice that Jesus didn't say anything about a man and a man, or a woman and a woman, cleaving to each other and becoming one flesh? He didn't give an alternate definition of marriage. No, He only spoke of a man and a woman. That's because that's what marriage *is*, at least according to God. The "tolerant Jesus" crowd makes the argument: "Well, that was because the social norms at the time were different than today."

Can you believe this incoherent theological garbage?

As if Jesus would've included same-sex couples, if that'd had been the "social norm" of the day?

I've news for these folks: Sexual deviancy wasn't unheard of at that time. There were sexual deviants back then, just the same as there are today. It wasn't as in the open as it is today, because back then, you were more likely to be punished for the sin in accordance with Mosaic Law. "Homosexuals" didn't exist as an identity back then, largely because to identify oneself as such would mean certain death. That doesn't mean the sin wasn't practiced in secret. Jesus absolutely knew of sexual deviants, in all of their guises, who practiced their sins behind closed doors.

My answer to this crazy assertion is twofold: #1: There's still no evidence to support the acceptance of sexually deviant behavior as a "social norm" in the US today, or really even as a "social norm" in the rest of the world for that matter; and #2: If you believe in the *real* Jesus, you know that as the Son of God, He could see across and down through time. He would've known what the "social and political climate" would be in this day and age. Had His proclamation of what constituted a valid marriage needed clarifying based on the "social norms" for a future generation, He would've done so at the time He spoke those words. Yet, He didn't because God *still* sees this sin as sin.

The position of the "tolerant Jesus" crowd suggests that God makes his laws willy-nilly and changes them on a whim…in accordance with the times. Yet, we see no Biblical evidence of Him ever having done so in the past. I've yet to see evidence that God has sent down any recent revisions of His Word to fit our current "social norms". There's no expiration date on Scripture. I can't find a single Bible verse or teaching that bears a label that says "Good until xx, xx, xxxx" date. Yet that doesn't stop the "tolerant Jesus" crowd from pushing the belief that Scripture is "fluid" and "changes" with the times. That God puts expiration dates on His Word.

■■■

Interestingly, as a side note, the same passage wherein Jesus addressed marriage also gives us an insight into the "transgender" issues that are becoming more and more prevalent today. In the same passage cited above, Jesus states that God "made them male and female." I've found no evidence in the Bible that God ever created a third gender, or a blending of the two. He did not create sixty-plus genders. He did not create "gender fluid" people. That means that transgenderism is a man-made problem and a man-made concept. A mental state that isn't of God. No third gender exists, much less dozens more beyond that. Transgenderism doesn't exist in nature and God didn't create it. It only exists solely in the minds of men. The very word "gender" has been hijacked to mean something that it never did before.

Since I began writing this book, the "tolerance" crowd has added more and more of what they refer to as "genders" to the mix. They're now claiming, at last count, that there are over sixty genders! Yet, there's no proof to back this claim up. What they now showcase as "genders" in reality aren't genders at all. They're actually mental states better described as "gender identities". The term "gender" has always historically been a grammatical term which literally means "sex; male or female". "Gender identity" is a mental issue wherein a person's gender remains static. It's what you are and can't be changed or altered.

In truth, if I had a dollar for every gender that exists, I'd have…a whole $2.

▪▪▪

Now back to our examination of marriage as it relates to this "tolerant Jesus", juxtaposed with the real Jesus of the Bible. If homosexuality is a sin worthy of death, according to the Old Testament, how could anyone expect that Jesus would bless or give His support to such an evil idea as a gay union being called by the name "marriage"? Yet, the "tolerant Jesus" crowd tells us that in fact He would support that which His Father calls abomination. They don't just stop at making the spurious claim that He'd support it, they actually push the ludicrous belief that He'd actually *celebrate* it.

Yep. That's right, they're actually gullible enough, or steeped in their sins so deeply, as to believe that Jesus would not only attend, but would *celebrate* a gay "marriage". I've actually had an alleged Christian tell me that Jesus would not only attend the "marriage" but that He'd officiate it! That's beyond insane to believe! Those who buy into this nonsense try to tell those of us who haven't lost our sanity that by standing against gay "marriage", and the mockery that the concept makes of the sacred institution of Godly marriage, that *we're* the ones going against the teachings of Jesus.

Read that last line again.

I know. It sounds as crazy on paper as it does when you hear it directly from a person's mouth. Trust me on that. I've heard some crazy things come out of the mouths of those who claim Christ, albeit usually the "tolerant Jesus". This insanity is chief among them. You have to wonder if these same folks also believe that vampires, werewolves, and zombies exist too.

The "tolerant Jesus" crowd are quick to point out that the word "homosexual" doesn't appear in the Bible. As if that matters! Of course it doesn't and it wouldn't. There's two reasons why that word doesn't exist in the Bible. We'll examine both.

#1: "Homosexuals" as a type of person, an identity, didn't exist when Jesus walked the earth. Oh, don't get me wrong, the sin existed. The acts existed. The secret life existed. But, people didn't openly identify themselves as such. If someone engaged in this sin, it wasn't part of a person's identity. It was a sin that mostly took place in secret.

Why?

Because the Bible commanded that people engaging in this sin be put to death in those days. Therefore, this sin was committed in secret and in private. "Homosexuals", as we know them today, identify so strongly with their sin, that it appears in many cases that their entire life is built around their bedroom proclivities. Yet that wasn't the case in Jesus's day. A "homosexual" as we know them today, didn't exist two-thousand years ago. So it only makes sense that the Bible would not reference something that didn't exist.

#2: The word "homosexual" didn't exist at the time that the Bible was first translated into English. However, there are plenty of words that concisely describe both homosexuality, and homosexual sex acts, in the Bible. These descriptions make it clear that homosexuality is indeed the subject at hand in several passages of God's Word. This false talking point, "the word 'homosexuality' doesn't appear in the Bible" is a wholly ridiculous argument. It's a red-herring argument meant to derail a much greater point. It's nothing more than the act of petulant children raking all of the chess pieces off the board because they're losing the game...and then claiming they won the match.

The claim that the Bible doesn't speak against "homosexuals", because the word didn't exist at the time, is akin to claiming that because the illness now known as "influenza", which was first named by the medical community in 1918, didn't exist as a *named* disease before that year, that the disease itself didn't exist either.

That's crazy right?

Even though the official name for the disease we now know as "influenza" didn't exist until 1918, medical history shows us that people suffered, and even died, from the flu as far back as we can research in history. To say that the disease didn't exist historically, and that it wasn't described in other terms prior to 1918, simply because the word we now call it didn't exist until that time is extremely ignorant.

See the point here?

We can't claim that something didn't exist prior to us naming it...unless it's something that we newly created ourselves.

Denying that the Bible speaks out against homosexuality because the word "homosexual" didn't exist in Biblical times, and didn't exist when the Bible was first translated into English, is intellectual dishonesty at its very finest. It's a juvenile argument that requires the person making the argument to set aside their brain.

Romans 1:26-27 clearly speaks of something that can only be what we now call homosexuality:

> *"For this cause God gave them up unto vile affections: for even their women did change the natural use into that which is against nature: [27] And likewise also the men, leaving the natural use of the woman, burned in their lust one toward another; men with men working that which is unseemly, and receiving in themselves that recompence of their error which was meet.*

I have to add here that the fallacious argument often used by the left that the above verses pertain only to "acts of prostitution in pagan temples", is patently ridiculous. This instruction was not given to a select, limited group of people, nor were the proscriptions against homosexuality given only to "pagan temple worshipers". If Paul were speaking only to pagan temple worshipers, he'd have had a lot more to say than what he did.

Those making this false claim would do well to read verse seven of the Romans 1, which contains a reference indicating the scope of this verse.

Romans 1:7 reads:

> *"⁷ To all that be in Rome, beloved of God, called to be saints: Grace to you and peace from God our Father, and the Lord Jesus Christ."*

Take note of the salutation in verse seven.

Had these verses only applied to a select group of people who worshipped pagan gods and practiced deviant sex in pagan temples, it wouldn't have been addressed "to all that be in Rome". Now, this expression of "to all that be in Rome" needs further examination. What did Paul mean by that? Did he mean only the city of Rome proper? And if he did, was he speaking only to a minority of people who frequented Roman pagan temples and took part in the sexual debauchery there?

The first thing that we must notice, is that the context of Romans 1, and the way it was written, makes clear that it was written to believers. That's right. This letter was written to the redeemed in Christ; but it was also meant as a guidebook to the lost to show their need for Christ. The second thing that bears noticing is that the salutation in verse seven makes clear that Paul is speaking not just to Rome proper, but to all those who resided in Roman controlled territory. The Roman Empire at the time stretched from Britain in the northwest, to Egypt in the southeast, and encompassed all points in between. Most of the known world at this time was under Roman rule. That means that Paul was literally addressing the world as a whole. So, we see that not only was Paul addressing the entire known world, he was addressing specifically those who were already redeemed in Christ, not a handful of Roman pagan temple worshippers. Therefore to attempt to limit the teachings in Romans 1 to a limited group of people is sheer ignorance.

Notice also that there's not a single word about temples or prostitution in any part of Romans 1 either. The raw truth is that this chapter in the book of Romans outlines nearly thirty broad sins, possibly more depending on how you count them, and that homosexuality was specifically and purposefully included among them. It's concisely and clearly called out as a sin, in both male and female versions thereof.

Those making the claim that Romans 1 doesn't speak to homosexuality fail to understand the main purpose of the book of Romans in the first place. The book of Romans was given to us by God for a two-part purpose. The first part of that purpose shows us our lost and hopeless condition outside of Christ. The huge list of sins mentioned in Romans 1 are general headings under which most of the other sins known to man will fall. If we're honest with ourselves, the sins listed in Romans 1 are things we're all guilty of. Everyone in the world has committed at least one sin on that list (and likely up to a half-dozen or more). This chapter shows us our dire need for Jesus.

The second part of this book was given to us to show us what we need to *do* about our lost condition. Often, this outline of salvation in the book of Romans is referred to as "The Romans Road" or "The Romans Road To Salvation". The book of Romans in a nutshell is this: first we are shown by God the problem (our sins) and then we're shown the solution to that problem, which is salvation in the Lord Jesus Christ.

∎∎

Among the many general categories of sin listed in Romans 1 are idolatry, homosexuality, gluttony, whore-mongering, fornication, lying, envy, maliciousness, murder, needless arguing, gossiping, meanness, two-facedness, hating God, despitefulness, disobedience to parents, pride, boastfulness, inventing evil things, imagining or dwelling on evil things, lack of compassion, deal or covenant breakers, failure to love others, being implacable, being unmerciful, taking pleasure in evil, being unthankful, being vain, denying God, and worshipping God's creation above God Himself.

If we're honest with ourselves, at one time or another, we've all committed sins that fit into one or more of the above categories…and that's exactly the point. Without Jesus and His sacrifice on the cross, we'd all be lost because we're all sinners. That we all sin in different manners from each other in no way changes the fact that we've all sinned and come short of the glory of God. This is what Roman's shows us…our sins and the remedy for our sins. Attempting to remove any sins from this list based on our personal beliefs and biases is a sin in and of itself...and that includes the sin of homosexuality. God didn't remove it from the list, so it's still sin, like it or not.

■■

The "tolerant Jesus" crowd also likes to drop this pearl of "wisdom" on us: They claim that Jesus Himself "never said anything about homosexuality in the Bible..." or "If homosexuality was so wrong, Jesus would've mentioned it by name..." This is commonly used as an argument for not only excusing the sin, but as an argument in favor of condoning gay "marriage".

Technically, they're correct on their first point, but only in the strictest of literal senses. Since the word "homosexual" didn't exist as a word in Greek or Hebrew when Jesus walked the earth, and neither did "homosexuals" exist as a type of person, and "homosexual" didn't exist in English when the Bible was first translated into English, Jesus couldn't have used that word. The word didn't exist in Hebrew, Aramaic, or Greek at them time either. In making those spurious arguments though, it truly shows how willfully ignorant some people are, or rather how blatantly dishonest they are, concerning God's Word and the teachings of Jesus Himself. While Jesus never used the specific word "homosexual" in the Bible, He did provide very specific guidance that makes it clear that He'd never support or accept such abominations as the sins of homosexuality or gay "marriage".

Jesus had a lot to say about righteousness. He spoke often about keeping the Commandments. He spoke often about repentance. He spoke often about sexual immorality.

See Mark 7:21-23:

> *[21] For from within, out of the heart of men, proceed evil thoughts, adulteries, fornications, murders, [22] Thefts, covetousness, wickedness, deceit, lasciviousness, an evil eye, blasphemy, pride, foolishness: [23] All these evil things come from within, and defile the man.*

Underline those three key words in the above passage, "fornications", "adulteries", and "lasciviousness". All three of those words speak directly of sexual immorality. *All* sexual immorality, including the sin of homosexuality, is included here. It seems pretty clear to me that Jesus *did* in fact speak against homosexuality in addressing sexual immorality. Here's all the evidence you need that Jesus *did* in fact condemn homosexuality: fornication and adultery. He spoke on both at length. Let's again revisit His definition of marriage: Jesus defined marriage as the union of a man and woman. He also defined adultery. He said that if a person even looks upon another person to whom they aren't married to with lust (meaning sexual desire), they've committed adultery with that person in their heart, despite having not ever physically touched them.

Let's look at Matthew 5:28:

> *"28 But I say unto you, That whosoever looketh on a woman to lust after her hath committed adultery with her already in his heart."*

Now, before someone even goes there, I'll address this here and now: this passage is not intended to be specifically limited to a man lusting after a woman. Jesus spoke it this way because He was addressing a group of men. It applies to all, including those who lust after others of the same sex. It likewise includes women who lust after men they aren't married to. In a nutshell, He defined adultery as even *looking* upon anyone with sexual desire when you aren't married to them.

So, what we have here is Jesus saying that the act of looking upon *someone* you aren't married to with lust *is* a sin. It's the sin of adultery. What some people refer to as one of the "Big Ten", meaning that it's one of the specifically mentioned sins of the Ten Commandments. This means the very act of any homosexual looking upon another person of the same sex with sexual desire *is* adultery…and Jesus absolutely *did* speak against that!

Now let's look at fornication as well. Fornication is defined as *any* sexual act outside of the confines of marriage. Again, if you consult Jesus's definition of marriage, it includes *only* a pairing of man and woman. That means by definition *any* homosexual sex act *is* fornication, since Jesus, God, and the Bible do not recognize a homosexual union as a valid "marriage". Jesus spoke directly against the sin of fornication and the sin of adultery when He taught against sexual immorality. Those making the claim that He never spoke on the topic of homosexuality are guilty of peddling complete and utter falsehoods. Falsehoods that are aimed at excusing the sin.

Let's pick apart, break down, and examine the "Jesus never said argument..." even further. Not only is it a pretty juvenile premise in the first place, it just doesn't make a lick of sense.

Would anyone from the "tolerant Jesus" crowd argue that beating your spouse is a good idea?

Or argue that it's okay with God to do so?

Why not?

After all, using their own special brand of what they pass off as "logic", Jesus also never *explicitly* said "Don't hit your wife", did He? That statement doesn't appear in my Bible.

Does it appear in yours?

Of course, I can't see anyone advocating for such an atrocity under the same spurious "logic", can you?

Why?

Because we *know* it's not right. We have the God-given common sense to know that not beating your spouse is covered under the more general topics of sin that Jesus addressed and forbade.

Do unto others comes to mind, right?

Nor does the Bible directly mention thousands, upon thousands of other specific, common sense scenarios that we easily recognize as sin. Many of these acts don't appear to have been addressed directly by Jesus in the Bible either...if we're arguing from a strictly literal and technical standpoint.

So again, applying the "logic" of the "tolerant Jesus" followers, all of these terrible things must be okay, right? Because, you know, "Jesus never said..."

Is that really what they want to argue?

Do we want to live by what "Jesus never said..." as a society?

No.

Not at all. In fact, as I've said in the past, "If you lived one day of your life by doing all of the things that 'Jesus never *specifically* said...' you'd be in jail before nightfall."

Think about that for a minute.

I have several questions for the "Jesus never said..." crowd, such as:

1. Is embezzling from your boss okay?

2. What about raping someone?
3. Child molestation?
4. Physically abusing your children?
5. Beating up random people on the street?
6. Breaking into your neighbor's house?
7. Keying your neighbor's car?
8. Slicing your enemy's tires?

Why would all of these things be wrong if we apply the same argument as the "Jesus never said..." crowd?

After all, Jesus never *specifically* said *not* to do all of the above things did He?

Did Jesus ever expressly use the word "rape" in the Bible?

Isn't that the exact same argument that the "tolerant Jesus" crowd is attempting to make regarding homosexuality?

Their point seems to be that if Jesus never said something against a certain sin, specifically calling it out by name, then that sin must be okay with Him. Is this really the logic we want to base our faith or our society on?

Is this the kind of logic we want to base our belief system as Christians on?

If so, we're in for a lot of trouble!

Of course when you ask the believers in the "tolerant Jesus" these things, they come back with: "But, but...all those things are illegal! Being homosexual isn't illegal." This kind of response is called "moving the goalposts" because the logic is always shifting. No one argued that homosexuality is, or even should be, illegal. Although, it should be noted that at one time, in the not-so-distant past, it actually *was* illegal in the US to engage in homosexual sex acts. The statement that "homosexuality isn't illegal" is obfuscation, pure and simple.

The question at hand wasn't whether it's legal, but rather whether it is *sinful* or not. The answer to that question is a resounding yes! It's every bit as sinful as any of the other examples above. That it's not against the laws of man, does not mean that it isn't against the laws of God. Killing your unborn offspring isn't against the laws of man either, yet it does go against the laws of God. There are a lot of things that man has made legal, but that God still considers sin.

The unvarnished truth is that the imagination of man is far more devious, far more morally bankrupt, and far more depraved (and getting worse every day), and far more corrupt, than any one person can even begin to comprehend. With the exception of the Almighty God, no one can understand the true depths of depravity and evil that man is capable of. God knows how depraved the imagination of man could be, and He warned us of such:

> *Genesis 6:5 "And GOD saw that the wickedness of man was great in the earth, and that every imagination of the thoughts of his heart was only evil continually."*

> *Genesis 8:21 "And the LORD smelled a sweet savour; and the LORD said in his heart, I will not again curse the ground any more for man's sake; **for the imagination of man's heart is evil from his youth**; neither will I again smite any more every thing living, as I have done."*

> *Romans 1:21 "Because that, when they knew God, they glorified him not as God, neither were thankful; but **became vain in their imaginations, and their foolish heart was darkened.**"*

Let's think about this twisted and contorted logic of "Jesus never said…" for just a moment longer. If Jesus had to specifically name each and every conceivable, evil act of sin that man could possibly imagine or commit, the Bible itself would be so massive as to make it virtually impossible for anyone to read. Even within an entire lifetime we couldn't come close to finishing it.

We're talking about trillions of pages instead of the few thousand pages that we now have in most Bibles. In fact, it would've taken Jesus several additional years, if not entire decades, of His ministry to name each *possible* sin or variation thereof… all while speaking without pause. This would have severely hindered His work and would've taken away from the main focus of His ministry.

When God gave us the Bible, He intended for us to use another valuable tool at our disposal in conjunction with it. To help with comprehending and understanding His Word, He blessed us with common sense. It's what's lacking when we make the "Jesus never said…" type of arguments. These arguments serve only as pathetic attempts to excuse and justify our own sins and shortcomings. God intended for us to use our common sense, in conjunction with the written Word, in order to live according to His commandments and expectations. God expects us to use righteous discernment along with the Bible, to know what He expects of us. When we have the Holy Spirit residing within us, this isn't a challenge for us at all.

God also gave us yet another indispensable tool with which we can know sin and recognize it for what it is: our conscience.

As Christians, when we sin, don't we know it?

Don't we feel that guilt, that nagging sense of "wrongness" in our souls?

Of course we do.

That's what ultimately leads us toward the path of salvation in the first place. It's that *knowing*, that sureness that we're lost sinners that causes us to seek God. When we hear the Gospel and are convicted of our sins, that's when our conscience begins to eat at us even more. Our conscience will always tell us when we've strayed, especially as a child of God…that is unless we've so hardened our hearts to the truth that we no longer hear our conscience crying out when we sin. If we're not careful we can build a wall around our conscience with our sin. One that can become impenetrable, so that we no longer hear it crying out when we transgress against God.

What we can ascertain is that the *general* categories of sin and guidelines for avoiding sin that we've been given in the Bible, and by Jesus Himself, cover a multitude of more *specific* situations and sins. Using the examples I've provided above as *specific* things that "Jesus never said…" I'll show you how when common sense is applied, we can see that Jesus actually *did* speak against these things. Even if they were addressed in a more generalized sense.

For example #1: Anyone possessing even a modicum of common sense knows that embezzlement falls under the "Thou Shalt Not Steal" commandment. Jesus shouldn't have to address each and every way that "stealing" can be accomplished by man. It's enough for most people that we know that theft, in any guise, is a sin. It doesn't really matter that Jesus didn't *specifically* say "Don't rob a bank" or

"Don't take from the cash drawer at work", or "Don't shoplift from Walmart" or "Don't defraud someone". Most of us are intelligent enough to realize that "Thou Shalt Not Steal" encompasses everything from taking your neighbor's prized power tools without permission, to robbing a bank, and everything else in between. We shouldn't have to look for Jesus to speak on each and every specific form of stealing. If it's not yours and you take it by force, by deception, by fraud, or simply without permission, it *is* stealing. And Jesus *did* speak against it...whether He named the exact manner of theft specifically or not!

Likewise, let's examine example #2: Child molestation is covered by several general Biblical guidelines. It's addressed even more specifically when Jesus said of anyone harming a child, "it were better for him that a millstone were hanged about his neck, and *that* he were drowned in the depth of the sea." This makes it pretty clear that harming children is not something to be tolerated... regardless of how that harm comes about (something for pro-abortionists to consider). It would've taken Jesus years to compile an entire list of all the many ways that a child could possibly be intentionally harmed. (7)

Abortion? Check.
Physical abuse? Check.
Sexual abuse? Check.
Mental abuse? Check.
Neglect? Check.
Malnourishment? Check.
Failure to properly discipline? Check.
Failure to teach a child right from wrong? Check.
Failure to love and nurture them? Check.

These are all forms of intentionally "harming" a child. Does Jesus really need to address each and every way that you could harm a child for us to know that these things are *all* wrong?

Common sense would dictate that Jesus *did* speak against these things, even if He didn't call them all out by name.

For example #3, let's examine rape. Jesus never *specifically* mentions rape in the Bible, either. Suffice it to say that rape is also covered by a lot of the other teachings of Jesus. General teachings in the Bible, including the verses in Deuteronomy which require death for the rapist, also make known where God stands on this sin. We clearly know that it's *not* right for someone to rape someone else. (8)

Why would we expect Jesus to have to give us specific instructions on this matter?

Anyone with even a modicum of common sense knows that it's wrong to harm someone else in this way. Do unto others? Anyone?

For example #4, we look back to child molestation, the same teachings of Jesus apply.

For example #5, let's look at harming others. It goes without saying that "Do unto others..." applies here. Jesus's teachings on how to interact with others tells us all we need to know about this.

Examples #6 through #8 deal with destruction of another person's personal property. The examples of property crimes above are also not *specifically* mentioned by Jesus, but there's enough evidence in the Bible that any person with an IQ over fifty can clearly see that it's morally wrong to do these things...without our Lord and Savior having to specifically state for us *not* to break into our neighbor's house, *not* to key the neighbor's car, or *not* to slash our enemy's tires.

An old substitute teacher that I had dozens of times throughout my high school experience used to share some really funny pearls of wisdom. She'd drop these sayings on the class every once in a while. It's a real wonder that she kept her job, even back then, because of some of her more bombastic witticisms. For sure, she wouldn't remain employed for long in today's politically correct and overly sensitive climate.

Her #1 pearl of wisdom that she liked to share with problem students?

"Don't be an idiot."

Concise, to the point, and straight to the heart of the matter.

Her #2 most commonly shared pearl of wisdom?

"God gave you a brain. Try using it!"

Both of her favorite phrases could readily be applied in the case of those proffering the "Jesus never said..." argument.

We have the Bible, God's Word, on these matters.

We shouldn't need anything else. But even so, God also gave us cognitive abilities, reasoning skills, and a conscience to guide us. For those of us who are saved: the Holy Spirit dwelling in our hearts should guide us. We know right from wrong, or at least we have no excuse for not knowing the difference.

■■

We shouldn't even need to address the rest of the sins that the "tolerant Jesus" is said to be okay with. Only someone intent on proving that they possess the poorest of reasoning skills and, without question, almost no comprehension skills would think that Jesus would be okay with things like pornography, foul language, drunkenness, and all of the other sins that people try to excuse in the name of "tolerance". If I were to address all of the sins that the "tolerant Jesus" crowd says He'd support, this book would be much, much longer than it is now.

The fact that Jesus Himself is the living Word of God, the Word made Flesh, along with the very fact that the Word so clearly lays out what sin is, should be enough for most people to understand that Jesus would never "tolerate" or "wink" at our sins.

There's a huge difference between a Savior who "tolerates" and winks at sin and the unrepentant sinners who commit them, and a Savior who accepts all who would come to the Throne of Grace, but who also expects for them to approach the throne with a repentant heart. A heart that's ready to choose Jesus and Heaven over their sins, is a heart that's broken upon the altar of repentance and shame. With salvation, that broken heart doesn't just get healed, it gets transplanted with a new, fresh beginning.

The Jesus that demands repentance and obedience is the *real* Jesus. The Jesus who tolerates and participates in your sin is nothing more than a very cheap and poorly constructed counterfeit.

Who Stole Jesus

Chapter 2
"Married Jesus"

Here we have another modern day, entirely mythological, "Jesus" persona. More and more people try to suggest, and unfortunately there're those who actually believe, that Jesus was married. Specifically, that He was married to Mary Magdalene. These people couldn't be more wrong…even if they intentionally tried. There's truly not one credible shred of evidence whatsoever to support this outlandish "married Jesus" claim. Yet despite that fact, people still seemingly *want* to believe in this idea.

Why?

Because, it fits in with their own selfish narrative and motives. Not only is this claim outrageously false, there's a mountain of evidence to show otherwise. All Biblical evidence points to Jesus having never been married. Jesus was not sent here to seek out a secular life for Himself. That alone should be enough to discourage this line of thought. Yet there are many people who're more than willing to be deceived by modern-day revisionists in both history and theology. Even many staunch believers have bought into this nonsense.

Some see this as a misguided, romantic notion. One woman I spoke with spun this fiction to me as the "ultimate romantic tragedy". She artfully spun the tail of the redeemed prostitute, who although considered by her fellow man to be one of the worst of the worst sinners, finds redemption in Jesus. She then falls in love with the sinless son of God. They secretly marry and a forlorn Mary is the first person her "husband" appears to before revealing Himself to His disciples and others, and ascending back to Heaven.

The problems with this account are multiple. Not only is there no evidence whatsoever in the Bible that Mary Magdalene was *ever* a prostitute, but we also know that this story doesn't fit with any of the facts that we know about Jesus and His ministry. (We're told that Jesus cast seven demons out of Mary Magdalene. She apparently was also woman of considerable wealth, when prostitutes were not known for being wealthy. Most prostitutes became such because they were *poor*.) In other words, it's an entirely fictional "romance"...because it never happened.

Hopeless romantics aside, there are two distinct camps of "married Jesus" followers and promoters. The first are the easily deceived, the second are those who have a more nefarious intent: to plant subtle seeds of doubt about the Gospel accounts of Jesus. The latter are the more dangerous of the two camps. If they can get you to doubt the Word, then all bets are off.

If Jesus was in a secret marriage, and possibly begat a secret bloodline, what else in the Bible are we being misled on?

This is the question the second group wishes to subtlety plant in your head. More importantly, they desire to cause you to ponder this question *in your heart.* Satan's never more successful at misleading and damaging us than when he the plants subtle seeds of doubt in our hearts. That's what he did with Eve in the Garden. He planted the seeds of doubt and envy, watered them, and watched gleefully as they grew into full-blown rebellion against God. This isn't any different; his methods haven't changed since the dawn of time.

This "married Jesus" mythology, although it did not originate with the fictional book *The Da Vinci Code*, was certainly made more popular and gained more notoriety through the sensational, overwhelming success of this book. In the plot of this entirely *fictional* book, Jesus supposedly begat a secret bloodline through children with His alleged wife, Mary Magdalene. The book then goes through a complex plot line detailing how the Catholic Church would do anything, and go to any lengths, to guard and cover up this earth-shattering secret.

This desperation included, but was not limited to, murdering those who would expose the "truth" of Jesus's secret "bloodline". As the story unfolds, we're led to believe that the artist Leonardo Da Vinci supposedly hid multiple hints to this wild conspiracy theory within his most famous works of art. A "code" of sorts to be discovered later and decoded by a future generation. Thus the title, *The Da Vinci Code.*

The book conveys the idea that one of the most famous paintings of all time, *"The Last Supper"*, is proof that the disciple to the immediate right of Jesus in the painting (to the left hand side for those viewing the painting) is actually Mary Magdalene. A woman, hidden in plain sight, rather than one of the twelve *male* disciples who we're familiar with from the Bible.

While artists have always been known to take artistic license with their works, I doubt that Da Vinci purposefully intended for this figure to be Mary Magdalene. Even if that *is* what he intended, it hardly matters at all, because the fact remains that this piece of art is nothing more than merely a painting. It's only oils and dyes on a canvas. An artist rendering of an event that happened well before his time. One that he was not an eyewitness to. This painting doesn't even have what the Mona Lisa has going for it, in that the Mona Lisa is a *portrait* that was rendered with a live model posing for the artist. The Mona Lisa wasn't painted by an artist fourteen hundred years after she lived, as *The Last Supper* was.

The Last Supper is only a painting. Nothing more. An artist's personal interpretation of an event long past. It's *not* a photograph. It's *not* a snapshot in time. It's certainly *not* to be considered conclusive "evidence" of any sort of cover up or conspiracy by the Catholic Church. That's an important distinction that bears not only pointing out, but remembering as well. A painting produced by an artist is *not* conclusive evidence that would ever be considered valid "proof" of anything. At least not to any person with a developed sense of logic.

Can you imagine if, in a court of law, a prosecutor tried to enter a painting of this sort into evidence, aimed at proving that a person was guilty of murder…or some other heinous crime? Unless the painting was actually used in the commission of the crime, or used as a murder weapon, it would have no evidentiary value to the criminal case at hand.

Can you imagine, the state trying to prosecute a defendant on the grounds that a painting *might* suggest the suspect's guilt…but *only* if you looked at it through just the right perspective?

Not to mention if the painting in question was produced much, much later, after the actual crime occurred, and was painted by someone who only held secondhand knowledge of the event in question?

A ridiculous scenario, right?

It'd never happen.

Yet that's the same logic that those who choose to believe in what I call "the Da Vinci Deception" employ to suggest that Jesus *was* married. This belief is based largely on this painting and a flimsy, wacky, conspiracy theory put forth by an author of a work that's entirely fiction.

The Last Supper is certainly a masterpiece, although the painting was created by an artist who never laid eyes on either Jesus or His disciples. An artist who held a personal grudge and an agenda against Jesus, the Bible, Christianity, and the Catholic Church itself.

It's disheartening that so many people have bought into the satanic lie of *The Da Vinci Code*. Make no mistake, that's exactly what it is too: a lie intended to cast doubt upon the divinity of The Lord Jesus Christ. It's an attack on the very veracity of the Bible itself. It's nothing more than a trick of the devil. A fiction with the primary purpose of misleading those who'd follow Christ. Remember, Satan pulled this same sort of trick on Eve inside the Garden of Eden when he caused her to doubt God's Word. He caused her to question what God said about the forbidden fruit of the Tree of the Knowledge of Good and Evil.

Casting doubt upon God and His Word is one of the most effective tools in Satan's arsenal. It's one that he's used pretty convincingly, from the dawn of time, to present day. He attempts to use "logical reasoning" to accomplish his goals; and it seems to work very well on those who're only too willing to allow themselves to be deceived. For those desiring to disbelieve God, Satan is all too willing to give them reason to do so.

I can only imagine a very similar conversation taking place between Adam and Eve when she presented the idea of eating the forbidden fruit to Adam. Did she use the tactics of "logical reasoning" to get Adam to take a bite of the fruit, thereby going against what he *knew* was right?

It would appear so. Satan loves to entice us through appealing to our sense of "logic" and "reason". It's part of human nature to seek knowledge. We want to make sense of our world. It's when the pursuit of knowledge becomes reckless that we get ourselves into trouble.

Don't get me wrong. Knowledge is a very good thing. Healthy examination of our knowledge and our world is a good thing. But when the pursuit of knowledge becomes an idol, it becomes a destructive force in our lives. Many people have allowed this relentless pursuit of knowledge to drive them away from God. The Bible warns of this.

We are to seek Godly knowledge…while being careful not to chase after worldly knowledge, which often leads away from God. It's also imperative that we not confuse "knowledge" with "wisdom", which are two entirely different things. You may possess a wealth of knowledge while still being bereft of wisdom.

1 Timothy 6:20-21

> *"²⁰ O Timothy, keep that which is committed to thy trust, avoiding profane* and *vain babblings, and oppositions of science falsely so called: ²¹ Which some professing have erred concerning the faith. Grace* be *with thee. Amen."*

■■

I happened to work for a large chain bookstore during the height of *The Da Vinci Code's* popularity. The staggering amount of people claiming to be Christian who not only bought the book, but also bought into this concept of a "married Jesus" was both truly amazing and deeply depressing at the same time. Being in a position to be able to discuss the book with customers, I heard all manner of nonsense. People would tell me how convincing the author's words were. They shared how much "sense" the concept of a "married Jesus" made to them. Many were seemingly enthralled with the concept.

I would often find myself reminding these customers that there's a very good reason this book was shelved in the "Fiction" section of the store. Because that's what it is: a work of pure fiction and nothing more. It was nestled right there in the section where it belonged: among all the other fantastical tales of mythical creatures, fantasy kingdoms, improbable suspense stories, and volumes describing all manner of terrifying plots and perils. I dealt with more than one customer who was perplexed when I explained that the book simply isn't true. That it isn't an autobiography of the main character. Rather, that it's in fact a work derived *solely* from the author's imagination.

When considering for yourself whether there's any credibility to "the Da Vinci Deception", you must first consider the facts that we already know to be true. Consider this nugget of truth for example: Da Vinci began his work on *The Last Supper* over 1460 years *after* Jesus ascended back to Heaven. No one living at the time Da Vinci painted *The Last Supper* would've had any real clue as to what Jesus really looked like. Da Vinci painted Jesus to appear as he, Da Vinci himself, envisioned Him. In fact, many historians and theologians believe that, just like we know that God created man in *His* own image, Da Vinci created Jesus and the disciples in *his* (Da Vinci's) own image for the purposes of this painting.

There exists strong evidence to support the assertion that Da Vinci harbored a very strong and not-so-secret hatred for the Catholic Church. It's a certain fact that Da Vinci was *not* a Christian, not by any stretch of the imagination. At least not by the real definition of what it actually means to *be* Christian. Historians and theological scholars believe, based on the evidence, that Da Vinci was in fact a militant homosexual. A man who despised the Catholic Church and everything about Christianity. It's a historical fact that he was tried in court, on charges brought by the church, for sodomizing a male prostitute…not once, but *twice*.

Da Vinci was known to often try to disprove the parts of the Bible with which he disagreed, or found to be inconvenient.

Why would anyone consider someone who's not a Christian, and who clearly demonstrated open hostility toward Christianity and the Bible itself, to be a credible source of evidence or information about our Lord Jesus Christ?

Why not just ask Satan himself for his opinion and views on Jesus and the Bible? After all, any enemy of Christ's teachings would be just as credible in their claims and beliefs as Da Vinci was with his own.

In further efforts to debunk the claim that *The Last Supper* painting holds any evidentiary credibility regarding Jesus or His disciples, let's consider what the Bible has to say about men having long hair.

1st Corinthians 11:14 states:

Paul D. Little

"Doth not even nature itself teach you, that, if a man have long hair, it is a shame unto him?"

This Scripture would seem to be a clear indication that Jesus wouldn't have walked around rocking the long-haired, unwashed hippie look, yet Da Vinci painted Jesus and His disciples with long, flowing locks of hair. Lustrous manes that most women would be envious of...(sarcasm intended). If Da Vinci, whether done purposefully or whether done in ignorance (I believe it was purposefully done to show his contempt for the Church), made such major a mistake in an all-important matter regarding the appearances of Jesus and His disciples, why would anyone trust him on any other details regarding our Lord and Savior? Even if it *was* his intent to claim that Jesus was married, and begat a super-secret bloodline, why would anyone believe someone who couldn't even get a basic aspect of Jesus's appearance correct?

Let me ask you this: If I told you that two plus two equals five...and I didn't just tell you this, but I *swore* it to be true, would you trust me to tutor you in Algebra?

Probably not. Case closed.

Why would we allow someone who's a lost sinner to teach us about Christ?

Go back and read that Bible verse pertaining to long hair again. There's a key word in that Scripture that you might skip right past without realizing how important it surely is.

Notice that word "shame"? Now think about this for a minute: when does "shame" occur in our lives?

Anyone?

What causes shame?

Shame only occurs where *sin* is present.

It's sin that causes shame. If it's a shame for a man to have long hair, then that can only mean one thing...that it's a sin. Since Jesus was the only man who ever lived without sinning, He couldn't have had long hair. It's as simple as that.

Da Vinci got it wrong.

Period. So, now that we know that Da Vinci's *The Last Supper* painting depicts a group of men who looked nothing like Jesus or His disciples, we can cast that away as any sort of evidence regarding Jesus.

Now back to the "married Jesus" myth.

Consider that if Mary Magdalene *had* been married to Jesus, it would've been nearly impossible for them to cover up that marriage. It'd have been even harder to cover the birth of a supposed child of this illicit union. (As *The Da Vinci Code's* main premise alleges that there were offspring born of this fictional relationship.) One would think that those responsible for crucifying Jesus would be *very* interested in His child, if in fact He'd had one.

Could you imagine the imminent and lifelong danger such a child would have lived under?

He'd have been a fugitive his entire life, having to remain furtive and hidden from the world. This would've been no easy task as the Jewish people were well known for keeping meticulous records on births, deaths, and personhood. A child with no known origins would have raised some serious eyebrows.

A child of Jesus would have been a threat to both the ruling government *and* the religious leaders of the day. The child would've made for a very powerful, symbolic persona and would have been a rallying point for all who opposed the ruling class. He would have been a threat to religious leaders at the time because he would've continued his father's legacy. That wouldn't and couldn't have been tolerated by either the Jewish priests or the Roman authorities.

Not to mention there would have been those who would've sought to use the child for their own personal gain; they would certainly have made the existence of such a child known. Do you not think that the followers of Christ would have presented this child as the "God-child"? He or she would have become an instant celebrity and likewise would've had a substantial bullseye painted on them at the same time. Likewise, just as Judas was all too quick to betray Jesus for thirty pieces of silver, how much more would the temptation be for someone to report the existence of this child for financial gain?

Surely we would've heard about this child at some point in human history?

Surely there would have been accounts of people trying to either: locate and destroy the child or to find and worship him?

Surely he would have been promoted as the Son of Jesus?

It's an almost certainty that even the most secret of documents, whispers, and legends pertaining to this child would've come to light within the last two thousand years.

Do you really think that a secret as *huge* as the Son of God, Jesus Christ, having a child via a secret marriage is one that could have been covered up for over two thousand years?

Only to come to light because a marginal author of a fictional book managed to crack "The Da Vinci Code"?

If that's what you believe, I have a rather large statue that sits in a very scenic harbor just outside of New York that I'd be glad to sell you at a very affordable price. If the price is right, I'll even throw in some prime beachfront property in Arizona as well.

■■■

I still remember a news story that first surfaced in the early 1990's that related how a group of archaeologists purported to have found the "burial crypt of Jesus" and how they found bodies of a "Mary", a "Jesus", and a "child of Jesus and Mary" within it. The names were found inscribed on some of the crypt markers within said tomb. The writer of the article was near ecstatic at this finding. This story has been pointed to as "proof" of Jesus's "marriage" and His alleged parenthood with Mary Magdalene.

The one very important, nay vital, piece of contextual information that was conveniently left out of this "earthshattering" news story?

The fact that the names "Mary" and "Jesus" were both as common, in what is now the nation of Israel, as the names Mary and John are in modern America and other countries. I can only imagine that if you searched cemeteries throughout America that you'd find many, many graves for married couples with the names of Mary and John.

In fact, a simple, thirty second Google search performed today netted hundreds of results for couples named Mary and John, as well as multiple references to a historical ship that was named *Mary and John*. I'd venture to say that many of these couples probably also have children who may be buried near them. This "find" in Israel is hardly credible proof that Jesus was married. It's quite ludicrous actually. In fact, I wouldn't be surprised if many more tombs of a "Mary and Jesus" were found in Israel and the surrounding areas at some point in the near future.

Pointing to this information as "earthshattering" and proof of Jesus's "marriage" is less credible than most reported Bigfoot sightings.

■■

Next in deciding if a "married Jesus" makes sense, we must consider Jesus's mission here on earth. Jesus wasn't sent here by God to marry, to become a father, or to become a regular member of society. He wasn't sent here to pursue the wants and desires of mortal man. Nothing about His thirty-three years on this earth was about pursuing a "normal" life.

Jesus was sent here to preach God's Word and to die on the cross for the remission of our sins. He had a much larger purpose than that of any ordinary man of those times. Having a wife and a child would have seriously hampered both His ability to travel and His ability to effectively preach His Gospel. Also, in my personal opinion, getting married, while knowing that He faced certain death on the cross, would've been an exceedingly cruel thing to do to a wife who was carrying your child.

I've heard a lot of people these days proclaiming how Jesus being married "just makes sense" because "it would've been strange and usual for a Jewish man in His thirties to be walking around unmarried at the time."

Is that really what these people want to argue?

I've heard better arguments for the existence of vampires and werewolves than this lame attempt at "logic".

It makes me wonder if these people really think things through before they mindlessly parrot stuff like this.

Um, hello?

While it's true on the surface that *most* Jewish men would've been married well before the age of thirty, we must consider this information in the actual context of who Jesus *was* and *is*.

Here's an actual conversation I had with someone who's convinced that Jesus was married and promotes this fiction as "truth":

> **Him:** *"Well, it just makes sense that Jesus would've been married."*

62

Me: *"Oh, how so? I can't see that it makes any sense at all."*

Him: *"Well, you obviously haven't studied Jewish culture or you'd know that it would've been very odd for a Jewish man of His age to be walking around Israel, unmarried."* (I love the arrogance here. The "well you haven't studied" approach to arguing a point is a pretty common trait among the left. It's an attempt to ridicule someone into submission from the start by basically starting the conversation with "Well, you're stupid, so let me educate you…")

Me: *"Oh, is that so? So, it was unusual for a Jewish man in His thirties to be walking around Israel, unmarried?"*

Him: *"Exactly. It would've made Him a social outcast and He would've stuck out like a sore thumb."*

Me: (Trying and quite nearly succeeding to suppress my laughter) *"Oh, okay. So…I guess it would've been normal for Him to be walking around Israel, curing the blind, healing the sick, and raising the dead? I guess it would've been perfectly normal for a Jewish man to do these things? To challenge the Jewish priests, the Pharisees, and the political leaders of the day? To walk around claiming to be the Son of God, and in fact, proclaiming that He was God Himself? Just so long as He was married, right? I'm sure He wouldn't want to appear odd or anything…"*

Him: *"Well, we have no evidence He did any of that. Or that He even lived in the first place. I'm done with this conversation!"*

(Needless to say, I left the conversation, walking away while shaking my head. Here's a person who's obviously an unbeliever…yet he's pushing the narrative of a married Jesus?? To what end?? What's his goal in doing so? And true to form, once the argument gets blown out of the water, they want to take their ball and go home...)

If you can't see the agenda here, you aren't paying attention. It's obvious the reason this unbeliever and other unbelievers, as well as gullible Christians, around the world push the married Jesus...because if they can cause you to believe Jesus was a married, normal human man and nothing more, they've won the battle. Planting seeds of doubt is what this is all about.

As pointed out in the conversation above, it was also rather "strange and unusual" for a man to be walking the around claiming to be the Son of God, at that time in Israel. I'd venture to say that it was more than just a little strange to see a Jewish man performing miracles like healing lepers and causing the blind to see, causing the dead to rise again, and casting out demons.

All of Jesus's miracles would've been out of place at the time. Why should the fact that He wasn't *married* matter?

Only a person with some serious flaws in their reasoning abilities could come to this conclusion.

Can you imagine?

I can almost see it now. Let's travel back in time and witness a group of four Jews standing around in a wheat field, conversing about Jesus. I can almost see the following conversation taking place:

First Man: *"Have you heard about this Jesus guy?"*

Second Man: *"Have I? Of course I have! The whole village is talking about nothing but this guy. He's being talked about across the land. My brother told me he even witnessed Jesus raise a man from the dead! Can you believe that?"*

Woman: *"I know! It's amazing! My cousin heard about Him casting demons out of a crazy man. He caused them to enter into a herd of swine and the man is now as sane as you or I."*

First Man: *"Yeah. They're saying that everywhere He goes, He's performing miracles of all sorts. He's developing quite a large following, that's for sure."*

Third Man: *"Yeah. He's definitely something else. I mean, He's raised people from the dead, cast out demons, caused the blind to see, and much more. We've never seen anything like it before, that's for sure."*

First Man: *"He claims to be the Son of God. The prophesied Messiah."*

Woman: *"Well, He's making a convincing case for Himself. I'll give you that."*

Fourth Man: *"Yeah...but you know what really bothers me about this guy? I mean it really nags at me...The man's thirty years old and He's not married! Talk about strange! What a weirdo!"*

Ridiculous, huh?

Yet people actually make this argument and don't see the fallacy thereof.

A man going against the Jewish religious establishment was also very "strange" at the time. A man who taught the things that Jesus taught about compassion and love (especially loving our enemies) was very strange at the time. It would've likewise been strange for a man to allow Himself to be beaten, spit upon, tortured, and killed because of His claim of being the Messiah. In fact, it's the very oddities of Jesus's life that lends credibility to the fact that He *is* the Messiah, The Christ, and the only begotten Son of God. That He *is* God. I've never understood the "it would've been strange" argument to justify the belief in a "married Jesus".

Out of all of the "strange" things that Jesus did with His life, His actions, His teachings, and His miracles, why do we think that He'd be concerned about being perceived as "strange"?

Wasn't that kind of the point?

I'd argue that God commanded Jesus to come here and to be "strange" for our benefit.

Otherwise what would've set Him apart from all of the other religious figures at the time or throughout history?

Sadly, so many people willingly believe this "married Jesus" deception. Make no mistake, the goal of the "married Jesus" camp is to cast doubt upon the truth of Jesus and who He is. After all, if you believe that we've been deceived for all of these years and that Jesus actually had a secret family, that He fathered a secret mortal bloodline, what else might we have been misled about?

Was He truly the Son of God, and God Himself?

Or was He just a prophet, a teacher, and a good man, as some would have us believe?

If Jesus had a secret family and secret bloodline, then we were lied to in the Bible. If not directly, it would have been a *huge* lie of omission, but a lie nonetheless if Jesus had led a secret double life. If we were lied to about Jesus being married; if Jesus harbored this sort of secret, then we must ask: Can we trust the Bible at all?

Why should we believe any of it?

These would be valid questions if the myths about "married Jesus" were true.

Be careful what you believe. Once you start down this road of doubting what the Word says, especially because of an unfounded theory of man, you tread on very dangerous ground. You stand in danger of doubting what you should *know* to be true.

And that my friend, is the goal of those putting forth this fiction of the "married Jesus". Just as Satan planted the subtle seeds of doubt in Adam and Eve regarding what God said in the Garden regarding the forbidden fruit, he seeks to do the same by casting doubt upon God's Word in any way that he can. Be careful that you don't allow such poisonous seeds of doubt to take root in your heart…or you might likewise find yourself in similar open rebellion against God.

Chapter 3
"Buried Jesus"

Here's another mythological Jesus for us to examine. This chapter is a logical follow-up to the "married Jesus". Why? Because the allegation of the "buried Jesus" is used to justify the existence of the "married Jesus". The difference between the "buried Jesus" and some of the other counterfeits, is that the goal here isn't even vaguely disguised or veiled. There's not even the slightest attempt to obscure their goal in promoting this counterfeit Jesus. It's quite obvious that the "buried Jesus" crowd has an open agenda of discrediting the Divinity of Jesus, as well as the Biblical account of His resurrection and ascension, by trying to prove that His earthly remains are here on Earth, buried in a grave or within a crypt.

If the body of Jesus can be found here on Earth, within a crypt or a tomb, then obviously He couldn't have ascended to Heaven as described in the Bible. Listen long enough and you'll hear some people argue, "Well, couldn't He have just ascended in spirit, the same way that we do when we die, leaving His body behind?" The problem with this argument is that it goes contrary to what we're told in the Bible regarding His ascension and resurrection. Jesus didn't ascend to Heaven in strictly spirit form. He rose again as a living, breathing, flesh and blood human; a human who was also God. He picked up His life...*and* His body again after willingly laying it down for our sins. He did *not* leave a physical body behind. No empty vessel was cast aside as He ascended to Heaven.

Also, consider this, if His body still lay in a tomb, what reason would the masses have for believing in the resurrection? All we would have is the word of a few women and the disciples who claimed to have seen Him after He arose. Had His body remained in the crypt, the resurrection account would forever be tainted by the cloud of doubt a body remaining behind would have created. Simply put, if people could have viewed His lifeless body lying in the tomb, no one would believe He'd risen from the dead.

By casting doubt on the ascension and resurrection, they cast doubts upon *all* other Biblical claims. This includes the claims regarding Jesus being the Son of God and the risen Savior. It'd be foolish to believe in a Savior who was dead and buried. Yet, that's the end goal of those who present us with the false "buried Jesus".

I touched on this briefly in the previous chapter where we looked at and debunked the "married Jesus". In this short chapter, we'll address this fictional Jesus head on. Recently an old article resurfaced after a book was written on the subject of Jesus being married. Part of the "evidence" for this claim was the fact that a "new" crypt was found in Israel with graves belonging to a "Mary", "Jesus" and "The son of Jesus". I'll repeat, what was left out of this account was the commonality of those names during that time period, and in that region. Jesus and Mary were as common as "Mary" and "John" are today in modern America. It's hardly surprising that *a* "Jesus" and *a* "Mary" were a couple in ancient Israel; and that this same couple also had a child.

■■

Let's examine the "buried" Jesus and see if this notion makes any sort of sense on a purely intellectual level. The Bible tells us that the religious and government rulers of the day were in a panic once they discovered that Jesus's body was not in His tomb. The Jewish religious leaders paid the Roman soldiers who were watching over Jesus's tomb to lie about the situation. They were told to say that they fell asleep while standing guard. This excuse was used to surmise that the disciples must've taken Jesus's body, secreting it away to some hidden burial tomb, while the Roman guards were sleeping. Let's just take their argument on merit for a moment. Let's say that we believe that the body was taken.

They can't have it both ways.

If the disciples had stolen Jesus's body in order to fake the resurrection and ascension, why would they allow Jesus's body to later be entombed?

Even if they believed that the disciples took Jesus's body and allowed Him to be entombed, why would the disciples allow the grave to be marked as such? Why would they clearly mark the grave with His name?

Wouldn't that have defeated the purpose of stealing His body in the first place?

Surely the disciples weren't that stupid.

Most of them were learned men. Most were far better educated that many of their peers of the time period. If they would've gone through all the trouble to steal the body, why would they allow it to be buried for anyone to find later? This would have been a monumental oversight. A mistake of epic proportions.

It doesn't make the slightest bit of sense.

I can almost see it now:

Disciple #1- *"Hey, we need to steal Jesus's body to make it appear that He rose again. That way people will believe what He said and taught."*

Disciple #2- *"Cool idea bro. Let's do it."*

Disciple #3- *"Yeah, between all of us, we have enough muscle to move that massive stone blocking the tomb. We can get in and take Him."*

Disciple #4- *"You bet. The eleven of us can pull this off for sure!"*

Disciple #5- *"I'm game."*

Disciple #6- *"Let's go!"*

Disciple #7- *"This is really going to freak those religious and political leaders out when they see His empty tomb."*

Disciple #8- *"You bet it is!"*

Disciple #9- *"How are we gonna deal with those Roman soldiers though? We can't kill them, that'd destroy the ruse."*

Disciple #10- *"We'll wait until they fall asleep! I'm sure they won't notice the noise of us rolling away a stone that weighs two tons. How much noise could that possibly even make, right?"*

Disciple #11- *"Great plan! And when we're done, we'll bury Him in a clearly marked, entirely easy to find crypt. I mean there's no need to try to hide His body or try to obscure His burial location, right? I'm sure they'll just believe He rose again. We can even label the crypt with His name."*

Can't see this conversation taking place?
Neither can I. Yet that's what we're being asked to believe by the "buried Jesus" camp. Not only do the people who push the idea that Jesus was just a mortal man want us to believe that Jesus's body was stolen by the disciples, they also expect us to believe that the same people who went through so much trouble to supposedly take, and then hide, His body were also stupid enough to then allow Him to be buried in a *clearly marked* grave.

A clearly marked grave. Think about that.

Right there, in the open for any and all to find. Even the most gullible of persons would have to see the glaring holes in this argument and this "logic" if you will. It simply doesn't add up.

Again, many of the disciples were well-educated men by the standards of their time. These men were definitely of above average intelligence; smart men who possessed the ability to read and write, as evidenced by the Gospels. Such men wouldn't have been so stupid as to leave Jesus's body buried in a *marked* grave. At best, if they wanted to conduct such a ruse, they would've taken the body and hid it in an unmarked grave, so as to preserve the idea that He had resurrected. Or, even more likely, they would've destroyed the body so that it could never be found. At the minimum, they would've smuggled the body to a location far, far outside the area and would've buried Him in an unmarked grave. One that no one would ever connect with Jesus had they stumbled upon it.

If you truly believe in the "buried Jesus", there's really no hope for convincing you of the truth of who Jesus is. A "buried Jesus" would indicate that He did not ascend to Heaven.

Furthermore, if the Biblical account of His resurrection and ascension is not true, then virtually nothing else in regard to Jesus really matters. Without Jesus having defeated death and having risen again on the third day as He promised, *we* have no hope of salvation and eternal life.

If Jesus was a mere mortal, one who is now dead and buried, our hopes for eternal salvation are gone as well...dead and buried along with Him. That makes the "buried Jesus" far worse than most of the other false "Jesus" figures that we encounter today. Believing in this "Jesus" can lead you straight to eternal damnation.

Belief in "buried Jesus" means unbelief in the *real* Jesus of the Bible. Unbelief in the real Jesus, the Jesus of the Bible, means that a person cannot receive salvation. No salvation means eternal spiritual death, separation from God, and suffering. That makes the "buried Jesus" one of the most dangerous counterfeit Jesus's of all.

Chapter 4
"Left-wing political Jesus"

Anyone with a firm grasp and comprehensive understanding of American history knows that politics and religion have always shared an intertwined and virtually inseparable relationship in this country. That includes religion and politics going hand in hand within our government. Despite what modern day revisionists of American history would have us believe, our Founders very much intended on God, and faith, being an integral part of our lawmaking processes.

It *is* accurate to say that they didn't want the government to have the power to make *participation* in any *specific* religion mandatory, as had happened previously in Europe and elsewhere in the "Old World". With that said, they conversely truly believed that God held a very important and profound role in our daily governance. They believed that seeking God's wisdom and guidance was a *necessity* before making decisions of profound importance.

The Founding Fathers made multiple references to God in many of our founding documents. What's more, Benjamin Franklin even proposed a resolution, one that was passed by the first Congress, which made prayer before daily sessions of Congress *mandatory*. Read that again…mandatory prayer sessions seeking God's guidance for wisdom in running this country was instituted by our Founders, the same men who atheists and revisionists now claim tried to keep God out of government.

Who Stole Jesus

Have you ever wondered why the Senate and House still pray before the start of their respective daily sessions? Especially in this current political climate that is so openly hostile toward God?

There's your answer. *It's law.* Of course, participation is no longer *mandatory* for our lawmakers in these overly-sensitive and politically correct times. However that doesn't change the fact that the law remains on the books to this very day. The tradition of prayer before daily sessions of Congress still survives today because it was made mandatory by our first Congress.

I'd be negligent in addressing this subject if I didn't also emphatically state the fact that there's no concept of "Separation of Church and State" in the Constitution of the United States of America. No mention of that phrase whatsoever occurs in any founding document. This concept and that very phrase we hear so often bandied about, usually by the left, comes from a letter written by Thomas Jefferson to a Baptist Church organization. In that letter, Jefferson explains that the reason the First Amendment, specifically what's known as the Establishment Clause, is written the way that it is was to provide a "wall of separation between Church and State" at the federal level.

This "wall of separation" was meant to keep the *government* from controlling the *churches*. That's right. It was never about keeping God out of the government. It was never meant to be used as it's commonly applied today!

The letter to the Danbury Baptist's appears here in its entirety:

To messers. Nehemiah Dodge, Ephraim Robbins, & Stephen S. Nelson, a committee of the Danbury Baptist association in the state of Connecticut.

Gentlemen

The affectionate sentiments of esteem and approbation which you are so good as to express towards me, on behalf of the Danbury Baptist association, give me the highest satisfaction. My duties dictate a faithful and zealous pursuit of the interests of my constituents, & in proportion as they are persuaded of my fidelity to those duties, the discharge of them becomes more and more pleasing.

Believing with you that religion is a matter which lies solely between Man & his God, that he owes account to none other for his faith or his worship, that the legitimate powers of government reach actions only, & not opinions, I contemplate with sovereign reverence that act of the whole American people which declared that their legislature should "make no law respecting an establishment of religion, or prohibiting the free exercise thereof," thus building a wall of separation between Church & State. Adhering to this expression of the supreme will of the nation in behalf of the rights of conscience, I shall see with sincere satisfaction the progress of those sentiments which tend to restore to man all his natural rights, convinced he has no natural right in opposition to his social duties.

I reciprocate your kind prayers for the protection & blessing of the common father and creator of man, and tender you for yourselves & your religious association, assurances of my high respect & esteem.

Th Jefferson
Jan. 1. 1802.

Notice that this letter does not indicate in any way that God is to be kicked out of government or the public square?

There's no hostility toward God mentioned within this letter at all. What's clear in this letter is that Jefferson and his brethren only sought to keep the government from interfering in the personal beliefs of American citizens with regard to God. Today's proponents of kicking God out of all things government would probably be aghast to learn that Jefferson mentioned God in a very personal manner to these Baptists.

What's often omitted when the left cites "Separation of Church and State" is that Jefferson went on to close the letter with a brief mention of God and reciprocal prayers. He would also later explain in other writings and speeches that this "wall of separation" was to protect the *Church* from the *State*, not vice-versa. The true intent of the First Amendment, specifically the Establishment Clause, was to keep the churches and religions free *from the government* interference. It was *not* designed to keep the government free from religious input, nor free from the influence of God.

This argument is lengthy and I'll save most of it for a separate book and a later date. Let's move on to the kidnapping of Jesus by political leftists and the "separation" crowd.

∎∎

Okay, so we see that the hijacking of Jesus begins with partisan leftists and their attempts to ban Him from the public square. Specifically by perverting the Founder's original intent of the Establishment Clause. To better understand how the political left has tried to hijack Jesus and His legacy, we need to examine what the left *claims* that they stand for. Then we must compare and juxtapose those claims with what they *really* stand for. Because what they claim to stand for and their actual record on the issues are most often at odds with one another. We can then try to match these true ideals up against what we *know* that Jesus Himself stands for. This compare and contrast of ideals versus reality will allow us see how the ideology of the left actually stacks up against reality...particularly when they put forth the notion that their ideals *are* aligned with Jesus.

On the surface if you look at the ideas and the values that the political left espouse, and claim to advocate for, one can see how someone might be confused or duped into thinking that Jesus might approve of their entirely worldly agenda. Taken at face value, their stated goals and beliefs are concepts that all Americans should value and support. But...is the agenda they hold up as their "values" really the truth?

Are these things really the ideals they champion?

Or is it all a thin veneer hiding the truth?

A façade?

Smoke and mirrors?

A pack of lies polished up to look like something it's not?

Let's take a look at the politics of the left and then compare those policy positions with the character and the teachings of the *real* Jesus of the Holy Bible.

Here are the basic policy platforms and stances that the modern leftwing politicians claim to embrace and fight for:

1. Religious Freedom
2. Helping The Poor
3. Women's Rights
4. Civil Rights
5. Equal Opportunity For All
6. Freedom Of Speech
7. Socialism (a more recent development)

Most of those things, with the exception of #7, sound pretty great, right?

Well, on the surface at least, the kneejerk answer would have to be a resounding, yes!

I mean, who could be against any of those first six points, at least at first glance?

However, with politicians and political parties alike, often what they "say" they stand for and what their *real* agendas happen to be are two completely separate and wildly disparate things.

In order to best illustrate the differences in the "left-wing liberal Jesus" and the very *real* Jesus of the Bible, I am separating each one of the policy points previously listed into two unique subsections. These will be headed as sections titled *What Would The DNC Do?*, followed by sections titled *What Would Jesus Do?*

Let's begin our in depth analysis.

What Would The DNC Do?:
Religious Freedom

Let's look at point number one on this stated policy list: Religious Freedom. A pillar of America's foundation. One of our most recognized, spoken of, and revered freedoms.

So what does religious freedom mean to you?

Most people, and indeed the Founding Fathers included, would say that religious freedom is the right for one to worship the God of their choice, in accordance with their own beliefs; free from coercion or government interference, or undue government influence.

Religious freedom means that if we want to worship any God, any object, any person, or even nothing at all; then that's our sacred right. The American people have the right to make that choice for themselves as individuals. And our government is supposed to respect and protect that right.

It also means that the United States government cannot hand one a Bible and demand that they must now worship the Christian God. Or hand one a yarmulke and demand that they must adhere to the Jewish faith. Or hand one a prayer blanket and force them to worship Allah as a newly minted Muslim. What religious freedom does *not* do is insulate a person from ever coming into contact with those who worship a different God. Or insulate them from hearing about a God that is not their own.

It does *not* ban the Ten Commandments from a courthouse wall.

It does *not* ban prayers in public school.

It does *not* ban God from the inner workings of government.

What does religious freedom mean from the viewpoint of a left-wing politician?

It means freedom *from* religion. All religion. This belief in freedom *from* religion is *not* anywhere close to true religious freedom. In fact, it's the antithesis of religious freedom. It means that anyone who doesn't share someone else's religious viewpoint must be shielded from any and all exposure to another person's beliefs. Under the guise of promoting "Religious Freedom", the left has been quite successful in getting prayer, the Golden Rule, the Ten Commandments, and any other references to God removed from our schools, our courthouses, and most of our public venues. The left has been very successful at stifling true religious freedoms in this country wherever they're found. That's their true goal in this fight. Despite their stated goal of religious freedom, they want freedom *from* religion instead. They view God as a threat and they don't want any mention of God to sear their consciences or to make them feel guilty.

The political left is constantly on the lookout for any use of God in the public square. It doesn't matter if everyone in attendance at an event supports and shares the same faith. Religion is to be stamped out wherever and whenever it may be found. This is especially true for anything involving the Christian faith. To those opposed to religious freedom, there's no situation wherein God is acceptable in the public arena. They've even tried to remove groups like the Fellowship of Christian Athletes and other wholly *voluntary* faith-based groups that meet outside of school hours, albeit on public school campuses, from being able to assemble on the school grounds.

On the one hand, they say that they promote religious freedom, on the other hand, when it comes to a Christian trying to actually exercise their Constitutional right to freedom of religion, the left literally goes nuts. They insist that no such freedoms exist for the followers of Christ.

You want to pray in public? No way!

You want to have a Christmas play in a public school? Absolutely not.

You want to hold voluntary private prayer with likeminded individuals at a high school football game after it's over? Think again!

We've even seen college professors threatening students with receiving poor grades over the use of the phrase "God bless you" when someone sneezes in class. You read that right. There're college professors who have banned the common phrase, "God bless you", from the classroom. Some students who say "God bless you" after someone sneezes actually do so at risk to their academic careers. (9) (10) (11)

Could this be any more nuts?

There're actually groups of people on the left who seemingly walk around actively *looking and seeking* to be offended by anything that's even remotely Christian. Whatever happened to the "live and let live" spirit in America?

For example, look at the recent uproar about roadside crosses for police and military men and women who've died in the line of duty. Since most of these men and women were Christians, their families are Christians, and those who put the crosses up are Christian, you'd think 'What's the harm in roadside crosses to commemorate these fallen heroes?' Well, honestly it shouldn't be an issue at all.

What harm could a roadside cross actually *do* to anyone?

What level of emotional distress could seeing a wooden cross by the side of the road actually cause someone?

How fragile must a person be to become so traumatized at the sight of two small pieces of wood slathered with some white paint that they must demand that it be taken down immediately?

Especially when they know that this cross provides some small measure of comfort to the families and friends of the person it was placed there for?

Well, to the anti-religious freedoms zealots of the left, *any* victory over Christian believers is to be welcomed and celebrated. It's another step in their overall goal to "protect" us all from God; in reality meaning to stamp Him out of public existence as much as possible. The distress that they feel at seeing the cross is *not* because of the cross itself, nor even what the cross represents, but rather the fact that the cross reminds them of the ugly darkness within their own hearts and souls.

To be brutally honest, part of the reason that those who're opposed to religious freedom in America have gained so much ground, and have had so many successes, is that those of us who *do* believe have *allowed* them to. We've let them have so many small and easy victories that have added up to big wins for their side over time. Some of these battles were won without even a metaphorical shot being fired from our side. While we as Christians, Jews, and other religious folks have taken the "live and let live" approach to these things, they've adopted the "seek and destroy" mentality against us. Had we fought all of these small battles harder, or in some cases had we fought these battles *at all,* we could've won more of these important smaller battles. The power of those wishing to impose their intolerance upon us would've been diminished, rather than strengthened. Each small defeat that we've allowed ourselves to suffer in relative silence has now become a series of lost battles that have likely cost us the entire war for religious freedom.

Ask any historian who's studied war throughout history and they'll tell you that the small battles really *do* matter. They matter a lot. Often, it's the small battles that have been able to turn the tide in war. Every war in America was fought and subsequently won based upon small victories that had combined effects of changing the momentum of the entire war.

Never let anyone tell you that the small battles don't count.

∎∎∎

Let's take a cause that was championed by the left and see how their stance on this issue stacks up to *true* religious freedom. Let's talk about gay "marriage" for instance.

Let's say you:

- *Own a bakery that offers wedding cakes.*
- *You're a Christian who regularly attends church.*
- *You have sincere beliefs and deeply held religious convictions regarding marriage and sexual sin.*
- *You wish only operate in peace without being dragged into the middle of someone else's sin.*

According to the majority of the Democratic Party and radical left-wing, anti-religious freedom zealots, too bad for you!

They want to *force* you to participate in something that goes against a foundational belief of your faith. A belief that you hold sincerely and deeply. A belief that if you participate in this event, that you are standing in direct opposition to your God. Whether you wish to participate or not, they believe that your religious freedoms should take a backseat to the beliefs and wishes of someone else. They encourage and pass laws or ordinances that allow bakers and other business owners to be sued, fined, or both for refusing to take part in the sins of their customers.

They don't comprehend the position of someone who loves their God and wishes to refrain from dishonoring Him. They can't perceive that it's *not* about hating anyone. It's *not* about "discrimination". It's about standing in solidarity with their God. They don't accept or understand the realities of faith and principle. Or rather, they don't care about the feelings and religious freedoms of the Christian business owners.

They believe that the *beliefs* of one must be invalidated if it conflicts with the *disbeliefs* of another.

How is that "protecting religious freedoms"?

It's not.

Period.

Can you imagine the Founding Fathers and what their reactions would be if we told them that we wanted to use *their* words and *their* ideals to force a believer in Christ to participate in something like gay "marriage"?

Especially against their will?

That we'd force a Christian baker to participate in the sins of others by forcing them to bake a cake for a celebration of something that goes against God and what He said marriage was?

They wouldn't be happy, I can tell you that with all sincerity and honesty. They'd never have stood for such nonsense. In fact, they'd probably have taken some sort of action against anyone proposing such a thing. I believe if we could travel back through time and visit the Founders, and a liberal told these noble men some of the things that the left has justified using their words, that he/she would find themselves swinging from the nearest tree rather quickly.

If I could ask a question of our former President Barack Obama, Nancy Pelosi, Harry Reid, Bernie Sanders, or any other high-ranking leader inside the Democratic Party, I'd ask "How exactly is *this* approach 'religious freedom'?"

Of course, in response they'd likely proffer the twisted, and wholly illogical argument, that they *are* in fact championing and protecting religious freedom!

WHAT?

Would they really say that? And could they really be serious if they did?

Unfortunately in their own minds, *they* truly are the heroes and champions of religious freedoms. I've had this very argument thrown at me several times over the past three years. Many liberals actually believe that forcing Christian bakers to bake cakes for gay "marriages", or forcing a Christian bed and breakfast to host a gay couple overnight, *is* protection of religious freedoms.

Sounds crazy, right?

Well, to everyone else it *is* crazy, but not to themselves.

That's right...they actually believe that they're *protecting* religious freedom by their actions. How you may ask, is forcing someone to go against their deeply held religious convictions protecting or promoting "freedom of religion"?

How is invalidating ones religious *beliefs,* so that another person can have their *disbelief* validated, an act of championing and furthering religious freedoms?

Their "logic" goes something like this:

In their sick and perverted version of "reality", they *are* protecting religious freedoms...the religious freedoms of the gay couple. They believe they're protecting the religious freedoms of the couple who demands that a Christian baker provide a wedding cake for their "marriage".

Yep, you read that right.

They think that the Christian business owners are the problem.

Why?

How?

Because by refusing to make the gay couple's "wedding" cake, *they* are trying to impose *their* religious views on the gay couple, thereby endangering *the gay couple's* religious freedoms.

Come again?

I know, you must think that you've misread that. Or that I've completely lost my marbles. However, I'll repeat it again: By virtue of the Christian baker refusing to bake a cake for a gay "marriage", the leftists say that the Christian *baker* is violating the religious freedoms of the *gay couple*. That *he/she* is attempting to impose *his/her* religious beliefs upon *the gay couple.*

Huh?

Still scratching your head on that one, aren't you?

Don't worry, you're not alone. I'm still trying to wrap my head around how anyone can view that convoluted attempt at logical thought processes as anything reasonable.

Bear in mind that the bakery owners in the now infamous Oregon case never tried to proselytize or convert the gay couple. They were not rude nor disrespectful to the couple in any way. They never said, "Hey, if you convert to Christianity we'll make your cake." They never said that they wouldn't bake birthday cakes, retirement cakes, graduation cakes, or any other type of cakes for homosexuals. In fact, they'd previously made birthday cakes, and other cakes, for this same couple...all while fully knowing that the couple was gay. They simply declined to make a cake for their gay "wedding"...because doing so would go against their deeply held religious beliefs.

In the case of Jack Phillips in Colorado, after declining to use his talent to custom design a cake for a gay "marriage", he even went as far as to offer the couple a generic cake that they could add their own cake toppers or decorations to. He simply stated that in accordance with his faith, he couldn't use his artistic talent to custom decorate a cake for a union that would be an affront to God. Of course he'd also previously refused to make a Halloween cake for the exact same reasons.

None of these bakers have discriminated against any gay couples. Not in the least. The couples themselves weren't the issue. They weren't ever the issue. The *event* that the cake was for was always the issue. These customers weren't turned away because they were gay. They were turned away because they wanted a cake for an *event* that would've made the bakers complicit in the sins of the couple.

So what's the difference in the cakes? Why is it okay for the bakers to provide graduation, retirement, birthday, and other cakes for a gay customer, and not a cake for a gay "marriage"?

Easy...it's the event the cake is for.

You see, it's not a sin to feed someone. It's not a sin to provide a gay person with a birthday cake that celebrates their birth. Being born isn't a sin. Celebrating being born isn't a sin. It's not a sin to provide them with a graduation or retirement cake either. Graduation is not a sin. Celebrating graduation is not a sin. Retirement is not a sin. Celebrating retirement is not a sin. Gay "marriage" *is* a sin. Celebrating gay "marriage" *is* a sin. That's why these bakers only refused service when the type of *event* became the issue. Those claiming that the bakers "discriminated" against the couples obviously don't know what the word "discrimination" means. The couples themselves weren't the problem. They never were. What the couples do in the privacy of their own bedrooms wasn't the problem. It never was. The *event* and only the *event* was the problem. And you can't discriminate against an event, because an event is not a person.

All these bakers are "guilty" of is politely declining to make a cake for something that's an abomination according to their religion, their closely held religious beliefs, and God. All the bakery owners wanted to do was operate their business in relative peace. They wanted to privately honor their commitment to God and the Lord Jesus Christ. Instead, enter the liberal politicians and activist judges who threaten their very livelihoods by trying to force them to choose between earning a living and setting aside their deeply held religious beliefs. All in order to refrain from offending someone else. The owners in Oregon were forced to close their business. In a ruling that defies sanity, they were ordered to pay $135,000 in "damages" to the gay couple for "discrimination". Discrimination that never occurred. (12)

Thankfully, Jack Phillips just received justice in his case with the Supreme Court finding in his favor. Colorado was openly hostile to his faith. Hopefully the Klein's will eventually find similar justice if their case makes it to the SCOTUS as well. (13)

In truth, the only rights that were trampled on in these cases are the religious rights of the bakery owners. The only discrimination in these cases was the discrimination that occurred *against* the bakery owners. Discrimination that was sanctioned and perpetrated by the government. And that's exactly what the SCOTUS found in the case of Jack Phillips. Unfortunately, a Colorado lawyer set Phillips up again by purposefully requesting a "transgender celebration" cake…one that he knew Phillips could not make for the same reasons. He attempted to order a cake that was pink on the inside and blue on the outside and expressed that the cake was to celebrate his "gender transition". Phillips declined on the same grounds that he declined the order for the gay "marriage". Again he was targeted for "discriminating". (14)

■■■

SIDE NOTE:

Thankfully, just last month, the state of Colorado dropped their fake "discrimination" suit against Phillips for declining the "transition" cake. It seems that new evidence come to light that would have once again caused the Supreme Court to find that Colorado was openly hostile to anyone invoking their religious freedom rights. (15)

■■■

It can't be said loudly enough: These bakers *never* engaged in discrimination! Not in the least. A fact that's been lost in this story and that was never reported by liberal leaning news outlets is that these same bakers have histories of refusing to participate in the baking of other cakes, for other people, when baking those cakes, or rather the purpose behind those cakes, also went against the baker's religious beliefs. Jack Phillips had expressly turned down decorating and baking Halloween themed cakes prior to this incidence for example. For the same reasons. He felt doing so would violate his religious conscience.

Was it the customer who was the issue in his rejection of a Halloween cake order?

Nope. The *event*, the very type of cake itself, was the issue with the order...not the person behind the order.

Sadly, divorce parties are becoming a fad in America. As crazy as it sounds, people are actually throwing parties to celebrate getting divorced. (Just another sign of how wicked we've become as a nation that we'd celebrate the dissolution of the wedding vows we make before God.) This very same Colorado baker, Jack Phillips, had previously also refused to bake a cake for a straight man who requested a cake for his divorce party. This occurred well before the gay "wedding" cake debacle. In neither case were the *people* ordering the cake the issue. The *event* the cake was for was the issue in both cases. (16)

You see the Bible says that divorce is a sin also. (With very limited exception.) All this baker did was refuse to make the divorce party cake, in the same exact manner that he later turned down the gay "wedding" cake. The decision to decline the orders in both cases had nothing to do with the sexuality of the couple or person ordering the cake. Nor did it have anything to do with the actual *people* behind the orders for the cakes. In both instances, the *purpose* of the cake, the *event* itself, the *event* the cake represented, was the problem. Discrimination did not enter into the picture in either case. It's just that one group of people are wrongly treated as a "protected class" by our government (a class solely based upon behavior vs an innate quality) and if Christians don't bow down to their every whim, they're falsely accused of "discrimination" and "hate".

I recently flipped the script on a liberal atheist who was arguing for shutting down bakeries wherein the owners refused to bake cakes for gay "marriages". I presented the following scenario to them. It was amazing to see their stunned face as the realization dawned on them that morality and deeply held personal beliefs *do* in fact matter. And that it's no laughing matter when someone forces you to go against your moral compass. Here's the conversation in a nutshell.

Me: "So, incest is legal in two states."

Them: "And?"

Me: "So, let's say you operate a bakery."

Them: "Okay. And?"

Me: "I think we can all agree that incest is morally reprehensible."

Them: "Yes...and?"

Me: "So in walks a man with his eighteen year old daughter. He says they are marrying each other and they want you to bake a cake for their incestuous marriage. Would you bake the cake?"

Them: "No! That's sick. It's gross. It's WRONG! I couldn't bake that cake in good faith!"

Me: "Thank you! You just stated exactly how the Christian bakers feel, with one exception. Not only do they feel the same way about it morally, they also believe it would be slighting their God to bake the cake as well. Do you see the point?

Them: "..." (Vacant stare as crickets chirp in the background.)

After recovering from their initial epiphany and shock, then they tried dissembling by claiming "Well incest is illegal in most states and it is morally wrong so..." You could hear the crickets chirp again when I informed them that homosexuality is also morally wrong and that until just a few short years ago, it too was illegal in all states in this country.

■■

Now take a look at the flip side of such situations. Notice that the same "logic" isn't applied equally when the scenario is reversed. In order to make a point exposing the hypocrisy of the left on this issue, a Christian customer sought to have three bakers who support homosexuality and gay "marriage" bake two cakes in the shape of open Bibles. The Bible cakes were to feature Biblical scripture that condemns homosexuality across their surfaces. The bakers in this instance likewise refused the requests. Citing their own deeply held personal beliefs as the reasons for rejecting the orders, the bakers politely declined the orders.

The customer who attempted to place the order filed a complaint with the *same* Colorado commission that'd previously ruled against Jack Phillips. The reasons for declining the orders were the *exact same* in both cases. One bakery refused to bake the cake for a gay "marriage" because doing so would violate their deeply held religious beliefs; the others refused to bake the cakes in the shape of the Bible with scripture that condemns homosexuality on them. In both instances the orders were refused on the basis of deeply held personal beliefs. (17)

Do you think that the person ordering the Bible cakes received the same ardent support from the folks on the left?

Why not?

It should've been a slam dunk decision for the customer based on the precedent and standards set forth in the first case. The situation that the second customer created was an exact reversal of the roles in the former complaint. Yet, once again, with their full hypocrisy on display for everyone to see, the same group of leftists who imposed heavy fines, and in effect tried shut down the business of Jack Phillips in Colorado, refused to support a man who simply wanted to order a cake that was consistent with *his* lifestyle.

If the first scenario was found to be "discrimination" why wasn't the second scenario found to be "discrimination" as well?

What's the difference in these two scenarios?

Nothing.

Literally not the slightest bit of difference. Except for the reverence with which the left views homosexual issues, and the disdain with which they view Christianity.

Did all of the same politicians who proclaimed to be the saviors of "religious freedom" come to this Christian man's aid? After all, if the bakers who refused to bake a cake for a gay "marriage" were accused of trying to impose *their* religious beliefs on the gay couple by refusing to bake them a cake, wouldn't it follow (according to the same illogical liberal arguments) that the bakers who support homosexuality and gay "marriage" and who then refuse to bake cakes with Biblical scripture on them are likewise trying to impose *their* religious beliefs (or lack thereof) upon this Christian man?

Why is it that an argument that applies to one side doesn't apply equally to the other?

After all, wasn't the claim of the gay community and their supporters that they only wanted "equality"?

Why's there a double standard for Christians when it comes to religious freedoms?

If liberal Democrats weren't the hypocrites they are, the answer would be "yes", that both cases are examples of "discrimination". Or "no" that neither case involves discrimination. It can't logically be a split decision. The scenarios are the exact same, with only the positions and beliefs of the bakers reversed. Given the standard that they applied to the first case, the same council should have supported the Christian man as well. Yet, they didn't. They found that the bakers were within their rights to refuse the Christian man's orders.

Sadly this case shows that their rules only apply when it benefits themselves, their supporters, or one of the "sacred cows" of liberalism. The liberal "protectors of religious freedom" not only didn't support this Christian man; they have spoken out vociferously *against* him. Some parties close to this case have resorted to calling this man a hate-monger and a homophobe publicly…solely because of his actions in trying to make a very valid point for his side.

■■■

All of this tyranny and hypocrisy occurs under the guise of protecting "Freedom of Religion". They've even twisted the Founding Fathers' original intent with the First Amendment, as it applies to religion and religious freedoms. They've contorted the meaning of it to arrive at the exact opposite of what the Founders intended at the time it was written. The original intent of the First Amendment, and what's known as the Establishment Clause, in regard to religion was to protect the *church* from the *state,* not vice-versa. One only need to look at the relationship between religions and governments around the world in their time, and in past history, to see why the Founders thought this to be an important distinction.

Throughout the history of the world, governments have had a penchant for first infiltrating a religion (just as liberals have infiltrated modern day Christianity), and then under the guise of that religion, harshly ruling the people, or committing atrocities against their citizens in the name of that religion. The regrettable events in the history of early Christianity were nothing more than the result of corrupt government infiltration of the religion itself. The Roman government took over the Catholic Church and used it as an excuse to commit crimes against her people, and people in other countries as well. It wasn't the "religion" or the "church" committing or condoning those acts, it was the *government* committing these acts under the guise of the religion. Certainly those atrocities laid at the feet of Christianity have no root in either the religion itself or the teachings of Jesus Christ. They have nothing to do with Jesus or Christianity at all.

What would happen in days of old was this: A tyrannical ruler or ruling party would come to power in a certain country. The ruler would then appoint his own leaders over or within the existing church or major religion of that country. These men, who were appointed over the church, were usually loyal to their ruler only. In many cases they weren't even religious men themselves or even followers of the religion that they were appointed to preside over. Some were appointed to high positions within the church ranks, or as figureheads of the church or religion itself. Then these corrupt rulers would use the guise of said religion to commit crimes and atrocities that benefitted the government, or specific ruler of that country. This was all done under the guise of the church or religion in question. We saw this happen with the early Catholic Church, Islam, and other major world religions.

For that very same reason the Founders sought to protect the *CHURCH* from the *GOVERNMENT*, and thereby protect the citizens of the US and their religious freedoms. The First Amendment was given to us to keep the government from mandating how, where, when, and what God a person may worship. In times gone by, in the Old World, the government could hand a person a prayer mat and tell them that they must now worship the god of Islam, or hand them a yarmulke and a Torah and proclaim that they must now follow the Jewish faith, or hand them a Bible and tell them that they were now going to be a Christian. The First Amendment expressly forbids "forced" worship of a *state mandated, obligatory* religion.

What the First Amendment does *not* do however is ban God from the public square. Nor does it disallow the Ten Commandments from hanging on a courthouse wall. Nor does it disallow prayer in public schools. The argument of those who say that it does these things is beyond ridiculous. Having a plaque displaying the Ten Commandments hanging on a courthouse wall does not force anyone to obey them; nor does it establish a state-mandated, obligatory religion. No one has ever been forced into practicing Christianity or Judaism simply because the Ten Commandments hang inside the foyer of a government building.

In fact, if spotting a display of the Ten Commandments on a courthouse wall, or hearing a prayer said in one's presence during a meeting at city hall, causes a person such deep emotional distress, then that person needs a therapist...and they need help sooner rather than later. I pray that these folks get the mental health help that they so desperately need if a simple wall hanging can create such angst.

Those trying to claim that the Establishment Clause forbids the exercise of religion within the confines of the government need to go back and take a deeper look at our nation's rich religious history. They'd also benefit from taking a tour of our nation's first government buildings. These folks would probably be surprised to see the Biblical scripture that's engraved over the doorways and in the arches in many of those historical buildings. There are many examples of how deeply religion played a part in our nation's founding that are still visible to this day on

Capitol Hill. All one must do to see the truth in how important God was to our founders, and what an integral part He played in our early government, is to open their eyes and actively seek the truth.

For those wanting a very good reference on this subject, you might want to check out the DVD, or read the book titled *Rediscovering God in America* by Newt Gingrich. It richly details how deeply God played a role in our nation's founding.

■■

Another example of the left's egregious distortion of the concept of "protecting religious freedoms" comes in the form of gay "marriage" legislation. Gay "marriage", or really the government's intrusion into marriage at all, is an example of *exactly* what the Founding Fathers meant to keep from happening when they wrote the First Amendment. Specifically, their narrow intent in writing the Establishment Clause is countermanded by this government intrusion into marriage. Legislating what constitutes "marriage" is a deep intrusion of the federal government into the realm of the church. It's literally the rewriting of a major church tenet by the government.

The government's role in rewriting and redefining marriage, in opposition to deeply held religious beliefs and tenets, is a direct conflict with the Establishment Clause of the First Amendment. Especially when that definition of marriage is rewritten for the express purposes of including pairings of people who were always precluded from taking part by the definition thereof. To understand the heart of this argument, you must first look at the *entire* history of marriage, especially the history of marriage within the United States. The government of the United States is only 243 years old, at least as a separate nation, as I near completion of this book. Conversely marriage is a religious tenet that has existed and endured for the last several *thousand* years. Marriage existed as it stood, before the entirely wrongheaded SCOTUS decision of 2015, long before the Bible was written and long, long, long before the United States of America ever existed as a nation.

For the sake of this argument we'll use the Bible as a timeline reference. Marriage is defined as between one woman and one man in the book of Genesis.

Genesis 2:24 states:

> *"Therefore shall a man leave his father and his mother, and shall cleave unto his wife: and they shall be one flesh."*

Why does this Biblical definition of marriage matter?

Because the book of Genesis is widely accepted to have been authored between 1440 and 1400 BC. This means that somewhere from between 3419 to 3459 years ago, marriage was known to have been defined by God as the union between one man and one woman. Basically, the concept of marriage as a religious tenet for Christians and Jews alike dates back to at least 3176 years *before* the United States government was formed as a country.

Now, let's look at the history of the United States government's involvement with both regulating and officially recognizing marriage. Marriage wasn't recognized in any way in US federal law until the passage of the Revenue Act of 1913. This was the first instance of the federal government formally recognizing marriage in law. It wasn't until ten years later, in 1923, that the US government started sanctioning marriage nationwide when they adopted the Uniform Marriage and Marriage License Act. By 1929, every state in the union had adopted marriage licensing laws. The passage of these laws constituted a huge act of overstepping the First Amendment, even back at that time. Specifically, we're talking about a violation of the Establishment Clause. The government now began to place itself in the middle of the marriage contract. A contract that was previously entered into solely between the man, the woman, and God. (18)

Now, fast forward from 1923 to current day. Today, the US government is once again overstepping its bounds, and is in direct violation of the true intent of the First Amendment's Establishment Clause, when it seeks to invalidate the religious rights of millions of Americans by legislating the wholesale redefinition of marriage.

Why is this a violation of the First Amendment's Establishment Clause?

Because the government is getting involved in, what is for most people, deeply held religious beliefs. A religious tenet with deep meaning between them and God. They're attempting to tell us that we can't hold these beliefs any longer. That our beliefs are invalid. That the Bible is invalid. They're literally rewriting the definition of a major religious tenet. First the government usurped the authority to govern marriage, and then, perhaps not surprisingly, only 102 years later, they redefined marriage altogether.

By legislating that a man can "marry" a man or that a woman can "marry" a woman, the government is in effect saying "It doesn't matter that for thousands of years marriage has been a tenet and pillar of your religion. It doesn't matter that marriage has *always* been defined as literally the union of man and woman. We're now informing you that you must accept that homosexuals can be 'married' to each other, the same as you and your spouse...and that your religious beliefs are invalid, null and void. Furthermore, we're redefining the term 'marriage' to include a group of people that the very *definition* of the word has always precluded." They think that your religious beliefs hold no value to anyone but yourself and that you need to just "get over it".

The usurpation of the Biblical and religious concept of marriage that first began in this country in 1913 is now complete. The First Amendment's Establishment Clause was meant to stop this sort of government takeover. This redefining, and control of religion and religious tenets. The Founding Fathers are probably rolling in their graves at this tragic turn of events. They could never have imagined an evil such as this being thrust upon the American people, largely against their will. Especially not employing *their* words, twisted from the Founders original meaning of course, to support that which they would never have supported themselves.

Ironically, again, the same Democrats who pushed for and promoted gay "marriage" are proclaiming it as a victory for "religious freedom". They say they're protecting the "religious rights" of all those homosexuals from the big, bad, mean, old Christians and other religious groups who're trying to push *their* religious beliefs on the homosexuals. Never mind that the redefinition of marriage is upending 3400+ years of religious beliefs and religious history. Even one of the Supreme Court justices, Justice Kennedy, who was the pivotal swing vote on this terrible decision, openly questioned whether the Court had the authority to change the longstanding, in fact millennials old, definition of marriage. Especially given the deep religious ramifications of doing so. Ultimately and tragically, Justice Kennedy caved under the immense political pressure of a small, albeit very vocal minority. One also has to wonder if he didn't have eyes on the historical legacy that he had to know that his decision would create. Many would call Kennedy's historical legacy tragic…and it truly is.

■■■

The very basis of the left's arguments on this issue isn't predicated on anything even remotely factual. They claim they were fighting for "marriage equality" when in truth there never existed "marriage inequality", in this country or anywhere else. The term "marriage equality" is a sham. A fraud. A huckster claim. It's snake-oil salesman terminology. A total scam of epic proportions.

All people in the United States of America have always had the ability to marry…within the definition thereof: including, but not limited to, consisting of the union of two parties of opposite sexes, of certain age, and not closely related to each other. What the left argued for and ultimately got, at least for now, wasn't marriage at all, but something else entirely. Something that can't be marriage by the very definition of marriage.

It's not as if gay "marriage" is something that had always existed in this country, although the left readily pushes that false notion. It's not as if some group suddenly tried to stamp it out in the name of religion. It's quite the opposite. There's never been a "right" for anyone other than a man and a woman to be joined together in marriage. And, even then, it was never really a "right" but rather a privilege; and a privilege requires that the conditions for obtaining said privilege be met. The privilege of marriage in this country has always been defined as the union of man and woman; in legal terms, secular terms, and religious terms.

It's a simple as that.

Homosexuals don't fit the criteria for marriage. That's not discrimination. That's not hate. That's not bigotry. That's just undeniable, incontrovertible fact. Simple. Indisputable. Fact. There never existed such a thing as "marriage inequality" (The entirely false label that the homosexual lobby applied to being blocked from participating in a privilege that they didn't meet the criteria for in the first place) since *any* homosexual has always been allowed to partake of marriage…so long as they qualified for marriage by marrying the person of the opposite sex, of their choice. A person who is of legal age and not closely related to themselves. In other words, they could always marry within the actual definition thereof.

Claiming that something called "marriage inequality" existed because gays couldn't "marry" each other is akin to claiming "vehicular inequality" exists because Lamborghini won't allow Toyota to use the Lamborghini name and emblems on their vehicles. Or that "food inequality" exists because a restaurant can't advertise their steak dinners and then sell customers a waffle promoted as a "ribeye".

It's a fact that in the secular definition, legal definition, and the religious definition of marriage, homosexuals have always been precluded from marrying members of the same sex by the very definition thereof. In secular terms, legal terms, and in religious terms marriage has always been defined, at least in this country and most others, as a union between a man and a woman. The very legislation that gave the federal government the right to recognize marriage, also defines marriage as the union of man and woman.

Simply put, the union of two men or two women has never met either the religious, legal, or secular definitions of marriage.

The 1828 Webster's Dictionary defines marriage as:

> "*MAR'RIAGE*, noun *[Latin mas, maris.] The act of uniting a man and woman for life; wedlock; the legal union of a man and woman for life.* marriage *is a contract both civil and religious, by which the parties engage to live together in mutual affection and fidelity, till death shall separate them.* Marriage *was instituted by God himself for the purpose of preventing the promiscuous intercourse of the sexes, for promoting domestic felicity, and for securing the maintenance and education of children."* (19)

This definition endured until the year 2003, when upon caving to political correctness, Webster's removed the gender requirements for marriage from the definition.

Why does this matter?

This definition of marriage endured with very little changes to it until the last few years. In fact, the first dictionary to change the definition of marriage, The American Heritage Dictionary, did so in the year 2000, eventually caving to political correctness and extreme pressure from the homosexual community. It wasn't until 2003 that the definition of marriage, which always specifically spelled out that marriage was the union of man and woman, was changed by Webster's to include gay "marriages". Again, this change coming only as the result of political correctness and immense political and social pressure by a vociferous minority. (20)

As stated earlier, the very legislation that gave the federal government the right to legally recognize marriage, also contains language that makes it clear that marriage exists only between two parties of the opposite sex. It's clearly spelled out in the Uniform Marriage and Marriage License Act of 1923. (21)

Earlier in this chapter we explored the Biblical definition of marriage, which also precludes homosexual pairings. The definition of marriage in the Bible is the oldest written definition of marriage known to man.

Combined, these three resources show it's a no-brainer that marriage is, and always has been, the union of a man and a woman. (At least in these United States of America.)

■■

Sadly, since I first started writing this book, the Supreme Court of the United States has issued the second worst ruling in the history of the esteemed judicial body. The marriage ruling in the summer 2015 is second only to the establishment of abortion as a "right" in its place in history as one of the most wrongheaded, and most contentious, rulings ever. The SCOTUS decided by a very narrow, razor-thin margin to invalidate the religious rights of millions of Americans by allowing the passage of gay "marriage"; thereby redefining a concept they had no jurisdiction or right to redefine.

The justices who voted for this atrocity have finished tearing the concept of marriage away from God and the houses of worship, where it belongs. The usurpation of marriage by the Federal Government that started in 1913 is now complete. Despite fierce opposition, these unelected, partisan justices chose to redefine a word and religious concept that millions of Americans hold dear. Thus they created a never before heard of "right" to gay "marriage"; despite that the very definition of marriage precludes same-sex pairings from taking part.

Can it be fixed?

That remains to be seen.

We now have a President, in Donald Trump, who's been courageous enough to nominate Supreme Court justices who'll adjudicate (as *is* their job) rather than legislate from the bench (as is *not* their job). With the most recent appointments of Neil Gorsuch and Brett Kavanaugh, the Supreme Court has been restored to a 5-4 balance. Before the death of Justice Antonin Scalia the court had a 4-1-4 split, (and with Scalia's seat temporarily unfilled a 4-4 split) which is what led to this unfortunate ruling. With a looming retirement of one, possibly two more justices, either by choice, by age, or by natural causes, we might just see some truly positive major changes on the religious freedom front in the coming years.

■■

Paul D. Little

What Would The DNC Do?:
Helping the Poor

Now let's examine the claim that liberal politicians make when they say that they, and their party, stand for "helping the poor", along the same lines of what Jesus taught in the Bible.

Again on the surface this claim seems like a great and noble goal, right?

Who wouldn't want to help the poor?

Certainly Jesus advocated for us to feed, clothe, and shelter the poor and downtrodden. To provide comfort to those in need. That's not arguable. No one can dispute this point with any sort of credible counterpoint. He definitely appointed us as our brother's keepers.

Now, let's take a look at what the left-wing politicos really mean when they say they're all about "helping the poor" and examine this claim to discover if it actually holds water.

Isn't this simply another political ruse?

First, something important has to be addressed and noted right out of the starting gate. It's been proven time and again that on a personal level, liberals are far *less* generous than their conservative counterparts when it comes to overall charitable giving. Now, we're not talking about giveaways from the taxpayers via the government. That doesn't count when it comes down to a personal level. It's been shown that conservatives are far more generous with their *own* money; from their own pockets. Conservatives out-give liberals by large margins at *all* levels across the income spectrum when it comes to charitable giving.

From rich to poor, liberals give less out of their *own* pockets when it comes to helping others than conservatives do.

This is just simple, unvarnished truth.

Let that sink in a minute. Those who trumpet their self-aggrandizing claims to be the most compassionate and most caring, have been shown time and again to give the *least* to help others. They fall well short of their contemporaries on the other side of the political divide...across *all* income levels. This can't be stressed enough. Rich liberals give less than rich conservatives. Middle class liberals give less than middle class conservatives. Poor liberals give less than poor conservatives.

Liberals like to claim they're generous, but what they really mean is that they're generous with *other people's money*. It's those with conservative leanings who actually give higher percentages of their *own* income to the less fortunate. This trend has been shown to be true in multiple studies.

Did Jesus say for us to take money from Peter to give to Paul? Or did He say for us to give freely from our own pockets? Did He want us to say "I pay my taxes.", when it comes to taking care of the poor? Or did He expect us to pay our taxes *and* give to the poor freely, from our own personal funds? That's easy. Jesus told us to pay our taxes when He said, "Render therefore unto Caesar the things which are Caesar's...". He also expected us to take part of what was left after paying our taxes and help those around us.

I don't expect you to take my word on this matter. In fact, as I said in my introduction, I don't want you to take my word for *anything*. A smart person trusts...but verifies. A fool believes what's told him without confirmation or verification. I want you to take any of the claims I make in this book, question them, and then seek the truth for yourself. I'm confident that what I state within this pages will withstand even the most astute scrutiny.

I'll even provide you some starting points for your research. The *New York Times*, a very far-left leaning newspaper to say the least, posted an article written by a self-professed, dyed-in-the-wool liberal author, titled *Bleeding Heart Tightwads*. This article details just how disparate this gap in charitable giving between the political ideologies truly is. The article also references a great book on the subject by the title *Who Really Cares?* by Arthur Brooks. (22)

■■■

The truth of the matter is that when the left says they favor "helping the poor", what the left-wing hardline politicos really mean is that they favor the heavy use of ever-growing and expanding entitlement programs. Entitlement programs that double as vote-buying apparatuses for the left. These are often cited to create the illusion that the left cares for "the poor". However this is all just an elaborate illusion. A game of smoke and mirrors for the gullible and easily confounded.

It's early December as I'm wrapping up the final rewrite of this book. I've just finished watching the movie adaptation of Charles Dickens' *A Christmas Carol,* the 1984 version starring George C. Scott, with my boys. I was struck by one scene in particular. I hadn't paid much attention to it before, outside of it revealing what a miser and miserable man Ebenezer Scrooge had been prior to his life altering epiphany. But the scene, the *words* uttered by Mr. Scrooge in the scene in particular, encompasses the liberal mindset regarding their fellow man. Especially when it comes to the poor. When one of the two solicitors for charity approach Scrooge in regard for a donation to help the poor and hungry, he alludes to the government programs that are already in place to help those in need.

Failing to catch the not-so-subtle hints that Scrooge proffered in his initial response for their request for a donation to benefit the poor, the solicitor asks him: *"What shall I put you down for?"*

Scrooge replies, rather emphatically, *"Nothing!"*

The total cluelessness of the solicitor is strikingly evident when he replies: *"So you wish to be anonymous?"*

To which Scrooge rather tersely replies: *"I wish to be left alone!"*

Scrooge then states that he doesn't make merry at Christmas and doesn't have the money to make others merry either. But, what really struck me was the last line uttered by Scrooge in this unfortunate exchange:

"I help to support the establishments I have mentioned -- they cost enough;"

And there we have the typical modern-day liberal mindset when it comes to helping the poor. Succinct and direct. "I pay my taxes, I shouldn't have to do anything else!" This is the liberal mindset. Just tax "the rich" in ever-increasing higher percentages and allow the government to take care of "the poor" with those taxes. Don't worry about lifting a finger on a personal level, right?

To a one, when discussing helping the poor with liberals, they've all stated they do their part with taxes, while abstaining from personal giving. Then they offer scorn that conservatives don't believe that ever-growing, bloated, fraud riddled, entitlement programs are the answer. Just like Ebenezer Scrooge, they view their contributions from their income tax withholdings to be sufficient "help" for the poor. That view is as cold and callous in real life as it is in this classic Christmas tale.

■■■

Democrat politicians don't really care about inner-city, impoverished minorities and poor whites as much as they care about *the votes* of these impoverished voters. The *vote* is what matters, rather than the very real person standing behind that vote. Instead of trying to ensure that the poor in these poverty stricken areas have access to better education, increased employment opportunities, and greater economic opportunities, it's far easier (from the liberal mindset) to hand them free housing, free food, free healthcare, and free money. All in exchange for blind party-line votes for Democratic Party political candidates. If these same voters were ever lifted out of poverty, it's far more likely they'd vote for the *other* party instead. And Democrats can't have that…even at the expense of those they claim to have a burning desire to help.

When election time rolls around every couple of years, the Democratic Party spends millions, sometimes billions, of dollars on reminding these voters who's handing out their food stamps, free housing, Medicaid, and welfare checks. They caution these voters that "the mean old Republicans" are the ones who want to take it all away. That the GOP makes them poor and keeps them poor.

Their campaign ads are akin to telling kids that Republicans want to kill Santa Claus…and in their own way, these lies are usually just as effective. Imagine if the same amount of money these career, lying politicians spend on reelections each cycle were to be spent on improving schools and revitalizing the neighborhoods in their constituent's districts. That would amount to substantial change. Alas, since it would drastically reduce the need for the very programs that Democrats use to buy votes, that's not going to happen any time soon.

In the meantime, nothing much changes for these impoverished voters. They're still subjected to substandard education via public schools, substandard living conditions, and substandard opportunities for personal or economic advancement. This especially holds true for impoverished minority communities.

But hey, as long as they keep voting straight party-line tickets for the Democratic Party, who cares right?

The same people who're all but forgotten by the very party they usually vote to elect; unseen and unheard by their elected officials, day in and day out. Suddenly, these voters finally matter when the polls get ready to open in an election season. That's quite convenient if you happen to be an out-of-touch politician. *Ignore the plight of your people, until you can once again rook them into voting for you.* This seems to be the Democratic Party mantra.

Evidence that the left's claims of helping the poor are false can be seen by anyone willing to take an honest look at who it is that runs the cities in America that are the poorest. Those with the largest and often most impoverished populations. It's not even hidden. It's in plain sight for all to see, yet goes largely unnoticed.

Atlanta?

Controlled by Democrats for over 130 years! The last Republican mayor left office in Atlanta in 1879.

Chicago? Under rule by Democrats since 1927!

Detroit? Presided over by Democrats since 1957!

What do all of these major cities have in common?

They all have very high rates of poverty, crime, unemployment, and poor living conditions (in some cases almost third world living conditions). Especially among the large populations of minorities residing there. These cities have highest rates of failing schools. They have highest rates of murder and violent crime. They have highest rates of incarceration among young minorities. They have astronomical rates of unemployment among their general population. Not to mention that unemployment rates among their minority populations that are double, sometimes nearly triple the national unemployment averages. (23) (24)

The very same groups of people who the Democratic Party claims to be helping reside in *all* of the areas where Democrats have remained in power for decades. These same constituents go unnoticed decade after decade, despite the campaign promises that "help is on the way". Frequently repeated, but never delivered on. Despite the promises of the politicians they elect, the voters in these areas become more and more impoverished with each passing year, while the areas they live in become more and more run down…and more dangerous day by day.

Coincidence?

I don't think so.

The very policies of the far left are the same policies that help to keep these voters poor, largely uneducated or undereducated, and virtually unable to change their personal situations. Yet the concern of the Democratic Party for these constituents ends once their votes are cast at the polling stations. The promises of brighter futures, better schools, safer neighborhoods, better opportunities, and gainful employment never materialize.

Still, despite the trail of broken promises from the last election to the current election, you can bet the same promises will be trotted out yet again. Usually by the very same failed politicians who broke their previous commitments to their constituents. Anyone who starts to wise up and wonder where the rainbows and unicorns they were promised are, and why those things they were guaranteed during the previous election cycle never materialize, gets handed the age-old DNC fabrication:

"Hey, we really, really wanted to help you, but those mean old Republicans blocked us."

Then the whole cycle of deception, false promises, and vote-buying begins anew.

Anyone who objectively studies politics for just a moment has to realize that the Democrat politicians' own resumes are often the best argument for why they should be voted *out* of office.

Detroit?

Over sixty years of complete Democratic Party control. Things continue to worsen there year after year. The same can be said for almost all of the cities that have been managed by the very same Democratic Party and corrupt career politicians for such a long time. The fact that these same career politicians keep getting elected over and over again, while nothing ever changes for the better, should lead people to see that the people they've elected, and believed in for so long, are failing them more and more with each passing day.

In the real world this kind of job performance wouldn't be tolerated for long. Outside of the insular bubble of American politics, no one else gets away with daily failure on such an epic scale.

Can you imagine an employer keeping an employee who exhibited such a dismal record of failure, year, after year, after year?

Politics for some inexplicable reason seems to have its own set of rules regarding success and failure. We have some of the same politicians in office today who've had stunning careers of abject failure; failure that span decades. Yet, incredibly, they're still in power. And they're doing nothing to help "the least of these", despite their grandiose claims otherwise. What's perhaps even more stunning is that these con artists manage to somehow trick their constituents into continually voting against their best interests.

Ghettos, Section 8 Housing, Food Stamps, Welfare, and other entitlement programs are by no means what Jesus meant when He commanded us to feed, clothe, shelter, comfort, and care for the poor among us. I wouldn't call dangling government entitlement spending in front of the poor, in exchange for political votes, the same thing as "helping the poor".

I highly doubt that Jesus would either.

■■

Paul D. Little

What Would The DNC Do?:
Women's Rights

Women's rights?

This is one of the *biggest* political platform issues that's been trotted out by the left each election cycle for the last forty years. "Come and join us! We're all about protecting your rights!" They enthusiastically proclaim this to women everywhere.

But, is what the left claims to stand for regarding "women's rights" really true?

And, are their beliefs truly in line with the teachings of Jesus?

"No" is the factually correct answer to both of these questions.

What they claim to stand for isn't true. Not even marginally true. Nor are what they consider to be "women's rights" actually in sync with the teachings of Jesus. Like most spurious claims of the left, this claim is a misrepresentation at best; an all-out brazen lie at worst.

So what do they mean when they say they're for "women's rights"?

What constitutes a woman's "rights", when viewed through their tainted political prism?

And who, precisely, is attempting to deny any woman their true constitutional rights, in the United States?

Well, it's pretty straightforward in truth.

No one is seeking to deny any woman her rights in America.

So, if no one is seeking to deny any women their rights, what exactly are we talking about when the term "women's rights" is invoked?

109

Liberals generally mean a couple of very distinct things that aren't really "rights" at all. At least not in the same vein of what the Founding Fathers intended when they designed our Constitution and our Bill of Rights. We're not really talking about rights at all.

The top rung, the big one, the main thing, the golden calf of the left if you will, their true meaning when they say "women's rights" is really nothing more than protecting access to the horrendous, life-ending procedure known as abortion. This is second to none in the agenda of the left when it comes to "women's rights".

The secondary meaning of this snazzy little catchphrase is protecting the self-proclaimed, contrived "rights" of women. Rights that don't exist as true rights at all. And, of course by "women", they in effect mean liberal women *only*.

Let's start with abortion.

What they mean most often when they invoke the term "women's rights" is their number one cause: protecting unfettered and unrestricted access to the legal means by which to murder an unborn child. They claim abortion as a "right", and they'll fight to protect it, no matter what the consequences may be. If you happen to be a woman who thinks that ripping a living baby from your womb and murdering it, by some of the cruelest means imaginable, isn't a "right", but rather an act of barbarism; then *you* are considered a threat to leftists. You *will* be singled out for verbal abuse, shaming, and more. Including, but not limited to, threats of rape, mutilation, and even death. In their minds, you lose *your* rights when you stand against anything *they* hold dear.

Don't even get me started on how you'll be treated if you're a man and you happen to voice your opinion on abortion. That's simply not allowed. I had a woman once tell me: "Not your body, not your business". Ironically this type of comment is often thrown out by people who routinely get involved in other causes that don't "directly" affect them. Typical leftist hypocrisy.

One vocal abortion advocate, a woman who constantly trolls Christian Facebook forums, is known for replying to men who comment on any discussions of abortion with: "Get a vasectomy!" When it was my turn to be on the receiving end of this pithy invective, I pointed out that I don't need a vasectomy as I don't engage in sexual relations with anyone but my wife, and that we'd welcome any child God graced us with. In turn, I reminded her that if she married and did the same, she wouldn't likely feel the need to murder her offspring to avoid the consequences of her casual sexual relations.

The left has been known to wish violence upon, and even in some cases to threaten rape, mutilation, and murder upon women who strongly and vocally oppose abortion. Any woman who does not support abortion quickly ceases to deserve *her* rights (in the eyes of the left) and then becomes a target. She's considered and cast as a traitor to *all* women in the eyes of many on the far left. *Her* rights cease to matter as soon as she fails to toe the line of the liberal agenda. Some have openly postulated that such women should be put to death, raped, or maimed because *they* are part of the problem that's holding the majority of American women back.

Ask conservative actress turned political commentator Stacy Dash about the record of "women's rights" and the far left. When she publicly stated that she was supporting Mitt Romney in the 2012 Presidential Election, some on the far left not only hurled racial insults at her; she was faced with death threats also. One of the more vocal voices on the left actually called for her to be raped. People are on record saying that "someone should rip out her womb"…all of this vitriol and hate simply because she supported a Pro-Life candidate for the Presidency. She advocates for life, rather than the culture of death and abortion, and that just can't be allowed to happen. Not according to the left. It's a sacrilege. Some of the more radical voices on the left suggested that she be murdered as "revenge" for her political stances. Some postulated that she should kill herself. (25) (26)

Can you imagine that?

Why all of this hate for simple espousing an opposing political viewpoint?

Because she's a woman who doesn't support the radical agenda of the left. That's really all it takes to engender such hatred and vitriol. Opposition can't be tolerated, ironically, by the party of "tolerance".

What about her individual rights as a woman?

What about her individual freedoms?

Judging by the amount of hatred and vitriol that's been spewed in her direction, simply for expressing her opinion, you'd have thought that she'd announced plans to publically drown a litter of puppies in a bathtub, rather than simply stating who she was supporting for President.

None of these so-called "champions of women's rights" even bothered to ask her why she's so vocal in her opposition of abortion. They don't know her backstory. Many are unaware that in years past Mrs. Dash was raped. She became pregnant as a result of that terrifying assault. They don't know that she strongly considered aborting the baby, but instead made the courageous decision to let the baby live. She kept him, raised him, and loved him; the ultimate act of turning a negative event into a positive outcome. They never bothered to ask how her decision to keep this baby changed her life forever...in a very positive and uplifting way.

They don't care about those details, because those details don't fit with their narrow, predetermined narrative.

As you, the reader ponder these words, let me ask some rhetorical questions to the women among you:

Do you happen to be a conservative woman?

Are you a woman who (gasp!) believes in the Biblical precepts of marriage?

If so, you're a disgrace to the left. You're the embodiment of all that's wrong with life for women. (According to the hard leftwing politicos.)

Are you a woman who believes that being a stay-at-home mother and a homemaker happens to be God's will for your life?

If so, you're a moron. (According to the left.) You're someone worthy to be shamed and scorned. You've obviously fallen for the tricks of the evil man who you've married. You've subjugated yourself to a man whose only desire is to keep you ignorant and pregnant. You're not worthy of "protection" or "rights" in the eyes the self-proclaimed champions of "women's rights".

How dare you not possess enough personal drive and ambition to make a career and a name for yourself?

How dare you rely on a man for emotional, financial, and material support?

What an embarrassment you are to all womankind!

Sadly, you can't make this stuff up. I've seen such comments directed toward women by liberals and atheists on Christian forums. My own wife has been referred to as a "Stepford Wife" simply because she believes in the model of family given us in the Bible.

Paul D. Little

Are you a woman who opposes employers being mandated to provide free abortive contraceptives, as well as abortion procedures, to their employees because of personal, deeply held religious objections?

If so, then you are a hateful, mean-spirited woman who sides with the evil men who only want to control women and women's bodies. You're a traitor. An enemy within. You're pure scum to the left. They'll deride you, asserting that you must be lacking in education, self-confidence, and self-worth.

And, you're selfish to boot!

How dare you desire to force your wacky religious beliefs on the "emancipated" women in the US?

When Democrats say "women's rights", you need to make sure that you know the term for what it actually is. It's code for "we care about liberal women only". If you oppose their viewpoints, their stances on abortion, or if you hold traditional marriage views in regard to marriage roles, or believe in marriage itself as a union of man and woman, then you aren't worthy of either "rights" or "protections" under the law. You're no longer entitled to the very same "rights" that the left-wing politicos claim to champion. In fact, you just might be worthy of death in their eyes.

This is what the left unfortunately seems to believe. One only need observe their disturbing, antisocial behaviors to see this.

What could be more restrictive of a woman's rights than to try to silence her from voicing dissent by utilizing threats, intimidation, name-calling, and humiliation against her?

Where is Jesus to be found in any of these beliefs?

■■

Paul D. Little

What Would The DNC Do?:
Civil Rights

Civil rights?
Oh boy, here we go again!
Another huge platform issue for the left. One that, like most of the rest, really isn't what it appears to be on the surface either. Here we have another game of smoke and mirrors. A con reminiscent of the old shell game. All is well as long as you "pay no attention to that man behind the curtain!" (27)

What do the left-wing politicos really mean when they say they want to "protect civil rights"?

What group, or groups of people, or politicians, who desire to take away your civil rights are they supposedly locked in an epic battle with?

What specific civil rights encroachments are they trying to defend or protect against?

In truth, they don't actually mean *real* civil rights at all, when they raise the notion of "civil rights". Much like many of the other policy stances they take, the left's *stated* values and their *true* values are not even remotely related. Not when it comes to this issue. Furthermore, there's no political party, no politicians, and no individuals who are opposed to "civil rights" in this country. Barring a few outliers who are relics of the past, that is. There's hardly anyone who opposes "civil rights" these days. At least not by the true meaning of the phrase...unless it's these same self-proclaimed champions of "civil rights" themselves.

115

So what does the left mean when they invoke the term "civil rights", as they often do in conjunction with their efforts to get elected?
How do they define that term?
What does it mean to them?

Typically when the left invokes their favorite catch-all phrase "civil rights", they usually mean virtually *any* imaginary "right" they can come up with in their convoluted, addled minds. To the left, a "right" is often something that's not necessarily found in the Constitution or the Bill of Rights; rather it usually means anything their hearts desire at any given moment in time. It's closer to what rational people would call a "want" rather than an actual right.

Their belief seems to be, *"If you can imagine it, then it must be a right."* The traditional definition of a "right" gets replaced by their new definition. An ever-shifting and evolving definition. A definition that in truth equates to "a desire", rather than the accepted definition of what constitutes an actual "right".

Certainly many of these assumed "rights" were never envisioned by our Founding Fathers. I daresay they'd be rolling in their graves at some of our assumed "rights" that have come about in recent history. A prime example of mistaking what is "a desire" for what is "a right" comes in the form of gay "marriage".

Honestly, tell me, when did marriage become a "right"? There's no mention of marriage as a right anywhere in the Bill of Rights. There's no mention of marriage in the Constitution of the United States. The Founding Fathers never mentioned marriage at all in *any* of our founding documents. In fact, throughout most of the history of the United States, marriage was something that the government stayed out of completely.

Why?

One reason is because marriage belonged almost exclusively to houses of worship. They saw no reason for the government to get involved in, or interfere with, marriage. A second reason is because they obviously did not view marriage as a Constitutional right. Simple as that.

In reality, it's *not* a right; it's a privilege instead. And our Constitution and Bill of Rights don't usually regulate or bestow optional privileges upon American citizens. It's imperative to point out that there's a distinct difference between these two different concepts, when it comes to rights and privileges.

(Note: Since I began writing this book, the second worst Supreme Court ruling in the history of the storied institution was handed down. Unfortunately this mockery of marriage has been made legal, at least for the time being.)

■■

So what differentiates a "right" from a "privilege" you ask?

That's easy. There're profound differences that makes it pretty simple to tell the difference. A "right", at least for Americans according to our Constitution, is generally something that one inherits from *birth*. You don't buy it. You don't sign up for it. You don't have to work for it. You don't have to beg, borrow, or steal to obtain it.

The right to "freedom of speech" is a prime example of a genuine Constitutional right. It's something that's inherited from birth. There's nothing that one must do to obtain this right; it belongs to a person by virtue of their birth inside these United States of America. One does not have to fill out any paperwork; there are no forms to be signed, or documents to be filed. There's no collateral involved. There's no conditions to be met. There's no application process to qualify for this right. There are no fees involved; no personal costs incurred. No legal loopholes or requirements to obtain.

It's a right.

It's automatic and free.

Period.

Another example of a genuine Constitutional right is the "right to privacy". Again, this is a right one is born with; a right enshrined in our Constitution. One doesn't need to apply for it, one doesn't need to fill out paperwork to obtain it. One doesn't need to meet any specific qualifications or prerequisites to receive it. It doesn't cost us anything on a personal level. It's a right in the truest sense and meaning of the word.

It simply *is*.

These are both examples of true, constitutionally granted and enshrined, protected, and authentic rights. You won't find more widely recognized and agreed upon rights within the US than these two examples...except for possibly the right to bear arms.

A "privilege" on the other hand is something that usually requires one to have met a precise, specific set of criteria or attributes in

117

order to be eligible for whatever the privilege entails. It's *not* automatic in the same way that a "right" is.

Usually, a privilege involves some amount of paperwork. Often an application or qualifying process is involved. Privileges require the meeting of certain specific obligatory conditions, restrictions, or rules. Driving is a prime example of a privilege. In order to drive legally, within most states in the USA, you must meet the minimum standards for the privilege. These include: American citizenship, meeting certain age restrictions, passage of visual and written comprehension tests, and the passage of an actual performance test. There's an application process. There are fees to be paid. One can be denied the privilege for failing to meet any of the requirements above. One can be denied the privilege to drive for any number of other reasons. If one fails either the written or performance exams, or if one fails to meet any of the requirements thereof, they won't be eligible to participate in the privilege of driving.

All of this means that driving *can't* be a right, because it's a privilege.

See a distinct difference between rights and privileges yet?

Unlike a right which can't be taken away (at least in most cases), a privilege *can* be revoked once it's been granted. If one secures the privilege to drive, yet racks up too many traffic violations or accidents within a certain period of time, their license to drive can be suspended by the issuing agency. If one gets convicted of DUI, their license can be revoked for a period of time…possibly indefinitely upon repeat offenses. Certain medical conditions may lead to the permanent revocation of one's driving privileges as well. There are many instances in which the privilege of driving can be revoked or suspended. Some states will revoke one's privilege to drive if they fail to maintain auto insurance on their vehicle.

Marriage in the much same way is a *privilege*. In the case of marriage, either party joined in said union can "revoke" that privilege of marriage for any reason…simply by filing for divorce or separation. In most states one has to apply for a license, issued by the government, in order to obtain the federally recognized *privilege* of marriage.

Before the SCOTUS stepped in a created a new "right" to marriage on June 26th, 2015, (Something which went far *beyond* the scope of the power of the Court; and which most certainly seems an unconstitutional ruling.), there existed a certain, set criteria that needed to be met in order to qualify for the privilege of marriage. This criteria included, but was not limited to, the following: Each party was required to be of a *different* sex, each party must have met the minimum age requirements, neither party was allowed to be currently married to another party, and the applicants couldn't be closely related to one another. All of these things applied because marriage is a privilege; with all of the expected rules, regulations, and restrictions that come with along with a privilege. By the very restrictions imposed upon the privilege of marriage, it can't truly be a right.

Conversely, no one can revoke one's right to freedom of speech. There's no limit on how much one can use it. There's no expiration date for the right. There's no one who can take it away from, or deny it to, a US citizen. It's simply ours from birth. It lasts until our death.

The same can be said for one's right to privacy. We're protected from government searches and seizure without due cause. We receive this right upon birth. There're no requirements to receive this right. The right to privacy can only be abridged in special circumstances, only for a limited time, and usually only when one has broken the law or is suspected of having broken the law.

Freedom of religion is also a right. No one can suspend or abridge an American's right to freedom of religion. One can't be forced to worship a particular God, nor prohibited from worshiping the God of their choice. (Although, the left would love to impugn and abridge both the right to freedom of speech and the right to freedom of religion in many cases.)

These are all common traits among the rights that we're granted by the Founders of this country, and by the Constitution they drafted: irrevocability, inheritance by birth, and no limitations or expiration. No special applications or paperwork required. No special conditions to be met. In other words, a right is nearly the polar opposite of what we think of when we contemplate a privilege.

■■

So, now we've established that marriage isn't actually a right, by both the definition thereof and the characteristic differences between a "right" and a "privilege".

Yet, the left continues to dishonestly invoke the term "civil rights" when promoting issues like gay "marriage". In recent days, they've taken to applying that same false label to, and endeavoring to defend, the "right" for men who dress and present themselves as women (and women who dress and present themselves as men) to have access to public restrooms and changing rooms of the opposite sex.

They've invented a spurious "right" to use the bathroom of their choice…depending upon whatever sex they wish to identify themselves as on any given day. They claim that there are multiple genders, instead of reality. There are two and only two genders.

Oh boy…or is it girl?

Where're we headed next?

Despite the wrong, and wholly unconstitutional SCOTUS ruling, that legalized gay "marriage", the fact remains that marriage is *not* actually a right. Despite the Supreme Court ruling on June 26th, 2015, marriage is and always has been a privilege. By its very definitions, secular, legal, and religious, marriage can't be "gay" either.

I'm confident that at some point in the near future, the Supreme Court ruling that legalized gay "marriage" will be revisited. Possibly that ruling will be vacated, or amended, and marriage will once again be restored as the *privilege* that it was meant to be. There's hope, however small, that marriage will be restored to the definition that it previously held for the last 3500+ years.

■■

Yet another way the left perverts the concept of "civil rights" is when it comes to race relations within the US. Yes, as a country we've had a checkered and very blemished past when it comes to *real* civil rights violations and race relations. Yes, sometimes *real* civil rights need to be defended, and must be defended vigorously. Sometimes we must fight against those who'd seek to violate the rights of others. But, things that are often heralded as "civil rights" today happen to be nothing more than government sanctioned racism or special treatment for one group of Americans over another.

The left's support of the policy of Affirmative Action is one such case of misidentified "civil rights" protections in modern society.

Why do we need artificial racial quotas in this day and age?

And if we're going to promote Affirmative Action, shouldn't it include protections for all races?

Or should we limit those protections to minorities only?

Are there really that many people out there in this day and age who won't hire qualified individuals solely based on their race?

Do we really need government sanctioned racial quotas in order to be "fair"?

The whole concept of applying racial quotas (which happens to be a form of racism in and of itself) to hiring, job promotion, and other aspects of employment is ridiculous. It leads to unfair hiring practices. It also bears mentioning that these policies actually *increase* racial tensions within our communities. I've witnessed the unjustness of Affirmative Action with my own eyes; not to mention the culture of racism and entitlement that these policies help create and foster.

I'll share a couple of personal anecdotal experiences with AA that I've witnessed or been a part of. About thirty years ago, someone in my family went to apply for a job with an auto body repair shop. This individual interviewed on the same day as a second candidate; both vying for the same job. The first candidate was white; the second candidate was black. My relative, the first candidate, was more experienced in the field and held a much more impressive resume than the other candidate. He simply was the better fit for this particular job.

However, the black candidate had done his research and homework well. At the time, the shop had no minority workers out of the ten people who were employed there. This is hardly surprising given that the city, and surrounding area in which the shop was located, had a racial demographic at the time that was around 95% Caucasian, 4% black, and 1% Latino or other. This other candidate openly told my relative the following, verbatim quote, while they waited outside the manager's office for the boss to begin their interviews:

"You aren't getting this job, because he doesn't have any black employees."

That's a direct quote as related by my family member *and* a separate witness who was present at the time of this conversation. Needless to say, my relative didn't quite know what to say in response to this.

The long story made short of this situation is this: because of government instituted racial quotas, the shop owner had no choice but to hire the underqualified, and largely inexperienced, candidate for the job. The shop owner didn't care that the man was black. His race had nothing to do with his preference to hire the other candidate. His only criteria for preferring the other candidate was that he had more qualifications and a better work record in the industry.

This is what *should* have mattered; the *only* thing that should've mattered, in making a hiring decision. In the end, the owner was confronted by the black candidate who told him that either he would hire him, or he'd would immediately file a complaint against him with the EEOC and the Labor Board. Scared of being fined, or worse, for not meeting artificial government racial quotas, the shop owner hired the candidate who was less qualified...against his better judgment and against the best interests of his business.

How does this make good sense to anyone?

My point in sharing this particular anecdote with you is this: I want you, the reader, to consider whether racial harmony was enhanced or hindered in this case? Contemplate the mindset that Affirmative Action led to in regard to the black applicant.

Do we really want to foster this smug sense of entitlement over a sense of achievement on merit?

Does the attitude of "I'm getting the job because of my race, and I need not worry about my qualifications" help or hinder a person in life?

Do you, the reader, think that Affirmative Action, and the mindset that comes with it, has helped or hindered many minorities throughout their lives?

I'd love to know what became of this man in the nearly thirty years since this event took place. Sadly, I doubt he's prospered in life...unless he underwent a radical retooling of his thought processes. Affirmative Action will only carry a person so far in life. Success, however, knows no color and no race. Success in life can't be legislated with artificial racial quotas. It can only be achieved through hard work, ambition, and a motivation to make a better life for oneself.

■■■

I experienced my own sad Affirmative Action horror stories when I was in my early twenties, employed as a restaurant manager. I ran a successful, high volume delivery and carryout pizza restaurant for one of the three major pizza chains. One day, while I was working a morning shift, I was confronted by a very angry and openly hostile black woman. She demanded to know why I hadn't hired her son, who she said had put in an application two months prior.

My response?

"Because I didn't need anyone back then, and I don't have any open positions right now."

That should've been the end of the conversation, right?

Most businesses don't hire someone unless they need someone to fill a position; and all of my positions were filled. My store had a very low employee turnover rate.

But, no, this lady *demanded* that I hire her son, even though I didn't have an open position at the time. She accused me of being a racist and a bigot...all without cause. All without anything to back that ludicrous claim up. She even accused me of *"throwing his application in the trash because he's black."* After I showed her the drawer filled with the applications from prospective employees, and she saw for herself that her son's application was still on file, she *still* wasn't satisfied. She continued to demand that her son be hired, even though I didn't have any open positions in my restaurant at the time.

Why?

Why would she make such ridiculous demands?

When we got down to the nuts and bolts of the argument, it came down to the fact that he was black...and *only* that he was black. She held this fact out as if it were a magical card that allowed the holder to instantly get hired.

That's what she actually said to me when I asked her why she felt that I *had* to hire her son...*"Because he's black!"* She stated this without the slightest hesitation, and without any thought as to the merits of this notion.

Now, being young and inexperienced in such things, I didn't get the Affirmative Action/racial quotas connection. This was a learning experience to be sure. She informed me that she'd watched the store the last few times when she came in to pick up her pizzas. She said that she didn't see any black people working there, so by law, I had to hire her son. Intimidated by her threatening demeanor and her squawking about "reports and lawsuits", I promised to interview her son the following week. Although I knew that I'd done nothing wrong, it was still an intimidating encounter to say the least.

After the encounter, I immediately called my Area Supervisor, who happened to be a black man himself. A man who'd worked his way up the corporate ladder through a successful career and stellar job performance. Lloyd had started out with the company some fifteen years prior, becoming a cook at a young age. Here was a man who hadn't had *anything* handed to him because of his race. Nor do I believe that he would've accepted any such thing. He had too much dignity and self-respect to allow anyone to hand him a job...or a title that he hadn't earned.

Lloyd's response to this situation was two part. He referred to this woman as an "AA-er" or an "Affirmative Actioner". He explained to me what that term meant. Then he explained something else that was equally, and possibly much more, important to the situation at hand.

Being very familiar with all of my employees, he knew something that I hadn't given thought to. He had me pull the weekly schedule that was posted on the wall at the front of the store. He waited patiently on the phone until I retrieved it and came back. He then had me read the names of all the employees on that schedule. Then he made a list.

"It sounds like out of twenty-three employees, you have three Arabs, three Hispanics, two Bulgarians or Russians, and one Asian. So, at least nine of your employees are minorities. Should she file a complaint, it'll go nowhere. It's obvious that race is *not* a factor in your hiring practices."

You see, he pointed out a very salient point: Affirmative Action isn't just for black Americans, it's meant to protect *all* minorities as a whole. Given that nearly forty percent of my employees were minorities, this woman's complaints were invalid. Null and void. In fact, I daresay that her own words and actions were truly racist. She was the one who made race an issue where it shouldn't have been one.

Still, one has to wonder what the Founding Fathers would have thought about government enforced racism and racial quotas?

After all, the *truest* definition of racism, is treating someone *differently* based solely on race. It doesn't matter whether that *different* treatment is harmful or beneficial to the person being treated differently. In other words, it's just as racist for a black employer to hire an applicant solely because he's black as it is for a white employer to fail to hire the same employee likewise solely because he's black. Both scenarios involve abject racism. Both scenarios involve race as a motivating factor in making hiring decisions.

The guarantee of getting a job that you're not qualified for, or when there's no open position, simply because of your race is *not* a civil right, despite what the left claims.

■■

When it comes to civil rights, doesn't it seem funny that the political party that claims to be the protector of all things under the civil rights banner is also the party who, historically, has always been one of the biggest abusers of civil rights?

If you were to research the sordid history of slavery, civil rights, and racism, you'd find that the Democrats were the slave owners, the founders of the KKK, and the party that tried to keep the Civil Rights Act from being passed. But, alas, all of that is material for another book.

So what part of institutionalized racism and fictional "civil rights", such as Affirmative Action, gay "marriage", and "transgendered bathroom rights" do you think that Jesus would approve of or side with?

What Would The DNC Do?:
Equal Opportunity

Equal opportunity for all…

*Sounds exactly like a concept that Jesus would just **have** to stand behind right?*

Yes, on the surface, it sounds great…but again, the left doesn't really mean "equal opportunity for all" when they use that misnomer. It's just another game of bait and switch, sleight of hand, and illusion with them. What they're really speaking of is *their* belief that everyone should be "equal" in material goods and wealth. They want a guarantee of an "equal outcome" in life.

That's *not* the same thing!

Equal opportunity does *not* ensure equal outcomes. What they're truly talking about is a utopian, pie-in-the-sky concept of everyone possessing the same material goods and wealth as everyone else; without variation or disparity. Common sense should dictate that this isn't a reasonable expectation in life. As the saying goes, "You get out of life what you put in to it."

Yes, Jesus would be all for "equal opportunity" for all people, in the most accurate sense of the phrase.

Who doesn't want equal opportunity for all?

Only a truly evil person would oppose such. Thus, it's important to understand the distinction between "equal opportunity for all people" and all people having an "equal outcome" in life. One is obtainable and sustainable, the other is not.

We're all created equal in the eyes of our God. That much is very clear. I don't think there are too many people in our twenty-first century world trying to dispute the idea that all people are equal in human value. That being said, all people will *never* achieve equal outcomes or be "equal" as far as talents, material goods, stations in life, and financial wealth.

It's simply not possible.

Why?

Because of human nature. Even in a fantasy world of a Bernie Sanders/Barack Obama/Elizabeth Warren utopian society, this wouldn't be sustainable. Let's fantasize for a moment and imagine that we can hit a reset button on society. Let's say we confiscate all personal wealth, while wiping out all personal debt. Corporations and companies become government entities, owned and operated by the federal government.

Now, let's say that we redistribute all wealth, handing every single American a $250,000 home, and a guaranteed income of fifty thousand dollars per person, per year. Everyone starts from this point forward in our utopian society with equal possessions, equal money, and equal incomes. Poverty, wealth, and debt are wiped out in one fell swoop. Homelessness solved. Hunger issues solved.

Sounds great huh?

Well, maybe if you're a liberal. Or unable, or unwilling, to see beyond the theory behind this move…unable or unwilling to follow reality to its logical conclusion. Often what sounds great in our heads isn't actually workable in the real world…and *this* is the problem with liberalism. Too many grand ideas that don't work in the real world and aren't even remotely connected to reality.

Why would this not work?

Simple: We'd still have human nature to contend with.

People are different. Some people tend to be wise, frugal, energetic, or inventive; while yet others are lazy, complacent, lethargic, and unwilling. Those differences from one person to the next will always ensure that equal outcomes are never possible.

For example if you gave two different people a $250,000 home, wiped out all their debt, and provided a guaranteed income of fifty thousand dollars per year, the end results will still differ wildly. Person X, may spend that money wisely, using only what is necessary to live, while investing the rest. He or she will take care of their home, maintaining it, and caring for it. The home will last and over the years, their investments and their home will grow in value. They might even take some of that money they're handed and start a business with it.

Meanwhile Person Y, wastes all of that money in a year with nothing left to show for it. They possibly spend more than the amount of their government stipend, thereby incurring debt. They might not take care of their home. It falls into disrepair and needs constant maintenance due to lack of upkeep. This person will continue to barely get by in life, despite having the same advantages and opportunities from the onset as Person X.

See the problem here?

Even though both parties were started on completely equal footing, with completely equal opportunities, human nature plays a deciding factor to ensure that the actual outcomes in this scenario are far from equal.

Equal opportunity has never, and can never, equate to equal outcomes.

■■

Throughout the time that Jesus walked the earth, inequality existed among citizens of the same cities, different cities, and different walks of life among the peoples therein. Jesus recognized those differences and not only accepted them, but commanded us to obey those who are in authority above us. Those at the top of the societal chain and those who are in power have always had more wealth and material goods than those below them.

Think about that for a moment.

What about a king, is he "equal" to his subjects?

In the eyes of God, yes, but in a worldly power structure, of course the king is above his subjects. As a result, a king always has more material wealth and possessions than his subjects.

Are you "equal" to your boss?

Again, in the eyes of God, yes, but in the eyes of the workplace structure? No. You're in a lesser position than your employer. Therefore, you get paid less and don't have as much power within the company.

What about in a court setting?

Are you then equal to the Judge?

No, and I wouldn't advise acting as such...if you value your freedom. The very order of society demands that some are in positions of power over others, otherwise chaos would reign supreme. *And, if we were all limited to having the exact same material goods, power, and wealth as everyone else, what would drive anyone to be better at whatever it is they endeavor to do?*

Why would anyone strive to achieve more than their neighbor if they weren't allowed to profit from their efforts?

If the liberals in politics had their way, everyone would possess the same wealth, both material and financial, and the same station in life as everyone else. No one would be allowed to possess more than their neighbor. While this sounds like a utopian society to some, it would not and could not stand for very long.

Why not?

Because if everyone has the exact same material goods and wealth as everyone else, and no one is allowed to prosper, what incentive would there be for anyone to excel...at anything?

Who'd waste their time, money, sweat, and tears on inventing new technologies and material goods if they weren't allowed to profit from their own efforts?

Why would anyone toil through years of higher education if that education couldn't be used in such a way to improve upon their own station and circumstances in life?

■■

Years ago I read a fictional book by an author named Terry Goodkind. This book, although a work of pure fiction, speaks to this notion of socialism in a very powerful way. The book was called *The Faith of The Fallen* and was an installment in the author's *Sword of Truth* series.

In the book, the main character is a hero. A benevolent ruler who becomes imprisoned by an evil emperor from a distant land. The conflict with the evil emperor arises from the fact that *he* doesn't realize that his policies are evil. He doesn't realize that his policies are little more than brutal tyranny thrust upon his people. He actually thinks that *he's* the good guy and that the hero (who is the kind ruler of a capitalistic free society) is the one who's promoting evil. The diabolical emperor puts his grand plan into action: He captures the hero and attempts to force him to see that *he's* the one who's right. He endeavors to show him how much better the emperor's way of life is by forcing him to live among the people, living exactly as they do.

In the course of the story, the hero accepts his fate as a captive, largely because he has no other recourse. Since he cannot escape his fate, he decides to make the best of his situation while captive. (Sounds a little like the story of Daniel in the Bible to me.) All around him the people who live under the oppressive rule of the evil emperor dwell in identical squalid apartments. They receive the same meager wages, they all wear the same frayed clothing, and they're forced into possessing the same dreary lack of initiative. In the emperor's society, the very act of expressing the desire to have anything more than one's neighbor is considered treason. It's a crime punishable by extreme torture or even death. Conditions in this country are dire. The people are suffering and downcast. In a scene reminiscent of the communist U.S.S.R., the people stand in long lines just to get the same stale and weevil laden bread as everyone else. The people are listless and devoid of any sense of purpose and drive.

Richard, the hero of the series, unknowingly begins a revolution by showing people that they *can* improve upon their daily lives, simply by taking care of the little that they *do* have. He shows them how their apartments, which have become run down due to neglect, can be repaired and made nicer. He shows them how to make small improvements to their daily lives, all while living within their meager means. He shows them that while they might have very little, they *can* take care of what little they do have. And, beyond that, they can help their neighbors and enrich themselves through love and compassion towards others, if not by any other means.

Little by little the people begin to see past the brainwashing they've known their entire lives. They begin to see that there's nothing wrong with trying to make a better life for yourself. That it's not a crime to want to be something more or to possess something more. In the end, a large-scale revolution happens and capitalism wins the day. The hero unwittingly leads a revolt where the people desire to be free and possess the right to use their skills, talents, and knowledge to create a better life for themselves and their families.

The reason that this book resonated with me is because it accurately describes what would happen in a liberal utopian society where all people are guaranteed equal outcomes with no real chance to make their lives better. This book is a vivid picture of what would happen should liberals such as Nancy Pelosi, Hillary Clinton, Bernie Sanders, Barack Obama, or Elizabeth Warren get their way on a grand, worldwide scale.

■■■

We can examine the not-so-distant past to get a glimpse of what happens when governments try to guarantee equal outcomes rather than equal opportunities. Take a look back through history to the original settlers of the United States. When we hear about the history of the USA, we always hear how the first settlers almost died out...only to be saved in the nick of time by help from the indigenous Native American Indians. While that's partially true, what most of the history books omit is the main reason that the first American settlers almost died out in the first place: socialism. Or what we now know as what passes as the modern day ideology of the Democratic Party. (28)

The original American settlers made a compact agreeing that each person would contribute their talents, their labor, and their skills to the common good of the colony. This concept was quoted as "from each according to his abilities, to each according to his needs." This essentially meant that each person was expected to produce as much as they possibly could for the common stock, and then take from the common stock only the bare necessities of what they and their families needed to get by. This "from each according to his ability, to each according to his need" was the earliest form of socialism in the US. It's currently cropping up again. This time on Facebook profiles and memes as the mantra and rallying cry of the Bernie Sanders crowd.

As you can imagine this idea, one that sounded good on paper, led to a huge disparity between the takers and the earners. The same disparity that we see in today's modern society.

(NOTE: Under Barack Obama's presidency we saw huge increases in Welfare and Food Stamps recipients, and partakers of other entitlements, while the labor participation rate dropped to forty year lows. In essence we had more people taking and less people making under Barack Obama. Under Trump the numbers of people on entitlement programs has dropped drastically, while the workforce is

gaining people and the labor participation rate is rapidly rising.) (29) (30) (31)

Back in early America, there were also those who worked harder than others and took very little. Then there were those who worked just hard enough to get by and took just about as much as they put in. Finally, there were those who conversely worked very little and took more out of the common stock than they contributed.

On the surface this ideology sounds like a great arrangement. At least in theory. Everyone was expected to put everything they had, they made, they grew, or they produced into the common stock.

But what happened when someone didn't produce their fair share, but still took from the common stock?

As you can imagine, it didn't take long for the nearly fatal flaws in this well-meaning blunder to set in. Famine, bitterness, envy, and strife quickly ensued. People became lazy and unproductive. Vegetables and crops began to rot on the vines, which led to famine and plague. The system fell apart within a few short years.

For example: A young, strong, unmarried male might be able to hunt enough meat and grow enough crops to supply thirty people in the colony with meat and vegetables. This would all go into the common stock warehouses. In return he'd be expected to only take enough of the common stock food and material goods for his own personal needs.

Conversely, an older man who's a father of five might only hunt enough meat and grow enough crops to supply six people with meat and vegetables. His family consists of seven people. So even though he doesn't produce enough to even take care of his own family, he's allowed to take enough out of the common stock to provide for his entire family. One can easily see how this arrangement would begin to cause festering resentment amongst those who produced more and took less.

In Plymouth, it was only when the Governor of the Colony abolished this early system of socialism that the colony finally flourished. Property rights were granted and this led to a revival. When these same settlers were given a plot of land and were told that they could keep, sell, barter, or trade all that they produced, suddenly the colony began to flourish.

Capitalism was born in America.

Other colonies such as Jamestown had similar systems of socialism in place from the start. In Jamestown, everyone was told that they were to receive an equal share of everything. That meant the seamstresses would provide clothing for all the settlers. They would in turn receive an equal share of the crops that the farmer grew. The builders would construct the houses, and then in turn receive an equal share of clothing and produce from the farmers and seamstresses.

But, what happened when someone in the chain fell ill and they could no longer be productive?

What happened when someone died and their place in the framework of society went unfilled?

Soon chaos ensued. People became resentful.

Why should the homebuilders work so hard to construct homes and structures for the family who was now producing little, or nothing at all, for the common good?

Why should the farmer provide free crops for the family that's no longer producing clothes, meat, or goods for the colony because of illness, injury, or even just plain laziness?

It's human nature to begin to see things this way.

It was only after the settlers rewrote their compact that they began to thrive. It was when the farmer became able to sell or trade his crops with others that he began to prosper. It was only after the seamstress was able to barter, trade, or sell her clothing to others for a fair price that she began to prosper. Once capitalism was introduced, the colony quickly began to thrive. Settlers now had an incentive to create new things, to work harder, to expand upon their knowledge, to push themselves harder and further, and to live a better life. Capitalism was the key that unlocked the door to America becoming the nation it is today.

When everyone receives the same rewards regardless of the effort they put forth, it takes away one's incentive to work harder than their neighbor.

If I am limited to making the exact same amount of money as you, or anyone else, regardless of my efforts, and not a single penny more, why would I spend my hard-earned money on a higher education?

If I can't make any more than the next person; if I can't have a nicer house, or buy a nicer car, why would I work harder than the next person? Inventors typically spend many years and thousands, even sometimes hundreds of thousands of dollars, of their personal money before they arrive at a finished and marketable product.

Would they invest their money, and considerable time, to conceive new things if there existed no opportunity to profit from their inventions?

■■■

While I think Jesus would definitely support equal opportunity for all, I don't get the sense that He's for everyone being made "equal" by the government. At least not in the material and financial sense as pushed by liberal politicians. There already exists the chance for "equal opportunity" for all in America. Equal outcomes are a different matter entirely. We aren't guaranteed equal outcomes...nor should we be.

Everyone, regardless of race, sex, color, religion, or national origin, has the chance to succeed in America. All anyone needs to do to succeed in life is possess the desire and drive to do so. In many cases the policies of the left help to defeat the very things that they claim to want for their constituents. Their "everyone made materially and financially equal" policy goals are no exception.

Oh, rest assured that equal opportunity still exists in America today, but the policies of the left often discourage the poor, especially poor minorities, from seeking those opportunities. Things like entitlement dependency, leads to the lack of desire to pursue those opportunities. People who become dependent upon entitlements often times don't seek better opportunities for the same reasons that almost destroyed Jamestown and Plymouth. *Why should one work hard for more when you have free housing, free food, and a little spending money that you didn't work for handed to you on a silver platter?*

What part of institutionalized laziness, and freeloading do you think that Jesus would stand behind?

What part of vote buying by the Democratic Party, using promises of material and financial equality, do you think He'd encourage?

(NOTE: I am all for entitlements helping those they were intended to help. However despite Democrat claims otherwise, these programs are so riddled with waste, fraud, and abuse that it's oftentimes those who don't need help, who receive the most while the real needy go wanting.)

Paul D. Little

What Would The DNC Do?:
Freedom of Speech

Freedom of speech...it's something that we all cherish, or rather something that as Americans we all *should* cherish. Those on left consistently promote themselves as the arbiters and protectors of free speech. Of course, as with most of the other things that they claim to champion, there's very little, if any truth to these claims. Again, it's time to clear away the clutter and cut through the bull, to get to the truth of the matter. It's time to expose that man behind the curtain so to speak.

The Founding Fathers intended for free speech to be just that. *Free.* Along with religious freedom, freedom of speech is a vital cornerstone of America's foundation. Free speech for one and for all. Even if we disagree vehemently with the ideas and opinions expressed by others, we must respect their right to voice those ideas and opinions. This was a very important tenet to the Founding Fathers in a time where speaking one's mind, at least politically, could result in their imprisonment for treason...or even their deaths.

One dared not speak out against the rulers of England once upon a time. The Founders sought to give more power to the people by ensuring that they couldn't be jailed, or worse, for expressing dissatisfaction with their political leadership. It's a good thing for many people too, given the things being said about our President today. Were this England, and the year was 1600, literally ninety percent of our media and most of the Democratic Party would be executed for treason.

Now fast forward to current day America. The left has become quite adept at using the original concept of freedom of speech in a way that the Founding Fathers never could've envisioned. Then, at the same time, they seek to disallow any speech they disagree with or find to be distasteful.

Do you believe that the Founding Fathers intended for the vilest of vile pornography to be included under the Freedom of Expression clause in the Constitution?

No, I can't see that, and neither can anyone else who's of sound mind. I don't believe for a second that this was the Founders intent with the 1st Amendment. Yet time and again the left has argued, in courts of law as well as courts of public opinion, that the most vile and reprehensible forms of pornography imaginable are allowed under the Constitution. During the Bush Administration, the Supreme Court actually ruled that simulated child pornography (wherein computer generated children are depicted in graphic and disgusting sexual acts with computer generated adults) was allowed as "freedom of expression" under the Constitution. (32)

I personally trust that the Founding Fathers would've hung someone from the nearest tree if they had advocated any such a thing in their presence. Especially had one told them their intent was to use the Founders own words to justify an atrocity such as this filth. In no way should such evil be allowed within our society, much less should it be protected under the guise of "Freedom of Expression".

We must also look at "hate speech", as the left likes to label certain ideas and communications they disagree with. *Do you disagree with homosexuality?* You might be guilty of "hate speech" in the eyes of the left.

Do you disagree with gay "marriage"?

You're sure to be labeled a "hate-monger".

Disagree with abortion?

That's right… you're engaging in "hate speech"…and you're "anti-woman" as well!

Want to say a prayer at a public event?

Nope. Can't allow that.

Mention Jesus at a public event?

You must be crazy to think that's acceptable!

In fact, wherever free speech is found, the left is usually there, waiting in the shadows to stamp it out...if what you're saying doesn't fit within the scope of their limited political beliefs. Calling people names like "homophobe" for simply opposing the homosexual agenda is nothing less than an open assault on free speech. If you oppose gay "marriage", or the way that pop culture is trying to shove the gay agenda and gay lifestyle down our throats, you get called "homophobic". That's nothing less than a blatant attempt to silence you. Sadly, this technique often works. People have been fired from their jobs for nothing more than because they've made comments on private social media accounts, or in private conversations, that were deemed "homophobic" by the left.

Their crime?

Exercising their right to free speech.

This behavior is hardly something that true champions of free speech would support.

Last year, a friend and I commented on an article that was posted in a Christian forum on Facebook. It didn't take long for the liberal, atheist, and homosexual internet trolls to step in and start calling anyone who didn't support the homosexual outlook that was presented in the article names like "bigots", "homophobes", and "haters". One especially rabid and vitriolic gay man threatened to take screenshots of my friend's comments (none of which were rude, offensive, vulgar, or otherwise distasteful) and try to use them to persuade his employer to fire him as a "hate-monger and homophobe". Conversely, I responded to this individual and floated the idea that maybe we should contact *his* employer and advise them that he was trying to infringe on the free speech rights of others by use of threats, foul language, and name-calling. To tell his employer that *he* was threatening to cause someone to lose their job based on their deeply held personal beliefs.

To his credit, this young man actually apologized for his actions; a truly rare trait among liberals today. This incident does illustrate the depths that the left will go to silence those who disagree with them.

What kind of world do we live in when someone threatens the very livelihood of someone else?

Especially for nothing more than a simple online disagreement on social policy issues?

Another question that begs to be asked: *Why are atheist liberals trolling Christian Facebook pages attempting to stamp out or chill the free speech of the Christians who post there anyway?*

I don't agree with atheists. Hence you won't find me entering into a den of atheists, on forums dedicated to atheists, attempting to rob them of their free speech…or attempting to shout them down. That's not something that someone who values free speech would do. Yet liberals, atheists, and homosexuals swamp Christian Facebook pages, often with as many as a dozen accounts each, attempting to do just that.

The whole concept of political correctness (a brainchild of the radical left) is to discourage political and social commentary that they disagree with by demonizing the people who speak against the ideals that they hold dear. By hurling words like "homophobe" at anyone who dares disagree with the homosexual agenda, in any manner, you discourage those people from speaking their minds.

Who wants to be labeled a "homophobe" or have their employment threatened by those who'd call you that?

Out of embarrassment and threat of social castigation, many people who'd otherwise express their opposing views, utilizing their right to free speech, are silenced by a very small but very *loud* minority of people. This is one of the reasons why public polling data on certain issues are so woefully skewed: people are simply afraid to let their real feelings be known. Many people would rather lie to a pollster rather than face the scorn of holding a viewpoint that they're made to feel they shouldn't hold.

We saw this with the 2016 Presidential Election. Pre-election polls were woefully skewed toward Hillary Clinton, largely because of the repetition in the media that anyone supporting Trump was a racist, a homophobe, a bigot, or even just plain stupid. Some polls in traditionally deeply red states showed double-digit advantages for Hillary just weeks before the election. Yet, when the actual election was held, and people had the anonymity of the ballot box to hide behind, Trump won those same states by double digit or near double digit margins.

■■

Do you think that abortion is wrong?

I would guess that many, I would even go as far as to say most, people who're reading this book probably disagree with abortion. However, many people are too scared to speak their beliefs on this issue out loud. They fear the name-calling and outrage that'll be directed at them from the left.

Ask yourself this, do you not have the same right to speak out against abortion as others do to speak in favor of abortion?

No one calls them awful names or directs hate toward them for expressing their beliefs. I think abortion is about as barbaric as any form of torture and murder that's ever been known to man. However, I don't target those expressing their belief in abortion as a "right". No matter how ridiculous their argument is, no matter how much I abhor and oppose abortion, I know that those who support it have the right to state what they believe in.

I'd give my very life today if it would abolish abortion for good, but by the same token, I do realize that those who advocate for it have the right to do so under Constitutional protection. I want to make that perfectly clear: I do *not* believe that there is a constitutional "right" to abortion, in fact, I believe abortion to be murder, but there exists constitutionally protected freedom of speech that provides the right to advocate for abortion should you choose to. That's one of the fundamental differences between the right and the left: while the left tries to stamp out speech they disagree with, the right tends to believe in free speech as intended by the Founding Fathers.

No matter how noxious that speech may be.

■■

As I sit here writing this book, enjoying my right to free speech, it's evidently become against the law in some countries in Europe to speak out against Islam and other hot button social issues. People have actually been jailed there for criticizing Islam or Mohammed. (33) Recently, two Christian street preachers were jailed in the UK for doing just that.

Their crimes?

Preaching that Jesus was the only way to Heaven! This is apparently "abuse" to those on the left. (34)

Could this happen here, in the US?

The answer is a resounding and frightening *"Yes"*, if liberal politicians have their way. We could one day soon see pastors and preachers, of all faiths, imprisoned for nothing more than preaching the truth about the immoralities and evils of things such as sexual sin, pornography, abortion, prostitution, drug abuse, and other sins.

All one needs to study to catch a glimpse of a forerunner of this coming time is to look at what just happened in Texas. Yes, I said Texas, one of the reddest, if not the reddest of the red states in this country. A bastion of social conservatism if there ever was one.

The Houston area is a solidly blue, left-wing liberal island, in a state that's otherwise a sea of red-state conservatism. In Houston, a far-left wing lesbian mayor, (who as I am finishing this work, I am not unhappy to report, lost in the last election), conducted a campaign of discrimination against those who oppose sin. The mayor and liberal city council passed an ordinance condemning anyone for speaking out against homosexuality. They passed a contentious "anti-discrimination ordinance". After this ordinance passed, they then proceeded to serve subpoenas to churches, preachers, and religious organizations demanding to know what, if any, mention the churches or organizations may have made in sermons or meetings about homosexuality in general or specifically any mention of this ordinance. They actually sought to find those who spoke against ordinance's passage guilty of "discrimination" for doing so. The implied threat is that churches no longer have the legal right or freedoms to speak out against homosexuality...or any legislation that concerns the gay community. This should frighten anyone, even if you happen to side with the mayor of Houston on said ordinance. (35)

Thankfully, as I am finishing the final proofread of this book, the attempt of the former Mayor of Houston to subpoena these churches and ministers was slapped down as unconstitutional.

Freedom of speech coming under attack from *any* side and any group, is a grave threat to our American way of life. Those who supported this egregious attempt at silencing Christians, should reconsider their position carefully. With the way the pendulum of politics sways from one extreme to the other, if this was upheld, it likely wouldn't be long before they found themselves under fire for speaking against Christians and Christianity. Thankfully a higher court stepped in and ruled that the mayor overstepped her bounds in trying to stamp out religious freedom and free speech. They found it unconstitutional for the government to demand sermons and talking points from pastors and preachers, simply because a politician doesn't like what they're saying.

Yes, the far left claims to *love* freedom of speech...provided that said speech agrees with *their* ideals. Speak against anything, or anyone, on the left or against any sacred cow that they hold dear, and they *will* try to shut you up as quickly as possible. They'll also try to make sure that if they can't shut you up with "political correctness" or unconstitutional harassment, that the act of exercising your right to free speech is as painful and costly as they can possibly make it for you.

What part of this kind of behavior do you think Jesus would defend?

■ ■

Author's Note:

Now that we've examined the real way that the Democratic Party and the left actually operate in direct opposition to the beliefs they *profess* to hold dear, let's look at how their true ideals and policies hold up against what we know Jesus stood and still stands for.

We'll call this next section *"What Would Jesus Do?"* As in the previous section *"What Would The DNC Do?"* we'll examine each of these six points on their individual merits. We'll try to put into perspective what Jesus, the real Jesus, would likely do based upon the evidence presented to us in the Bible.

Paul D. Little

What Would Jesus Do?:
Religious Freedom

Jesus was a true believer in the purest definition of religious freedom. In fact, you might even say He was the Founding Father of the very concept of religious freedom. Yes, He was and is the Son of God. Yes, He was and is the foundation of Christianity. Yes, He did say that the only way to get to Heaven is through Him.

But did He command anyone to worship Him, or believe in Him, against their will?

No.

No, He did not. Jesus has never and will never force Himself on anyone.

Not once.

There's not a single account in the Holy Bible wherein Jesus is found *demanding* that anyone change their religious beliefs through coercive means. Jesus simply gave people the Gospel. Then He let them decide what they wanted to believe. He didn't try to silence the voices of dissent by keeping them from speaking against Him. He didn't try to legislate His way into widespread public acceptance. He simply stated the truth of who He was, what salvation consisted of, and how to get born again. Then He allowed those who'd believe to come to Him of their own free will.

Just as they still do today, people who disagreed with His message tried anything and everything to stop the Gospel message from

147

being spread. Back then, they tried many times to kill or capture Jesus, and His disciples, in an effort to keep His message from spreading. Before his conversion, the Apostle Paul was complicit in the jailing and killing of preachers, believers, and new converts.

Today we see similar forces trying to legislate against His message. We see the opposition using the nefarious notion of "political correctness" to silence those who'd dare spread the Gospel. We see people today who aren't literally stoning people to death for being Christians as in the early days of Christianity...instead they attack their employment, their families, their livelihoods, and their reputations. All because a follower of Jesus is vocal about their Christian beliefs. They won't stone you to death; no, but if you own a business, they'll just sue you out of business and into bankruptcy if they can. They'll settle for getting you fired from your employer. They'll settle for disrupting your family and harassing you where you live.

What would Jesus do with regard to Religious Freedoms?

The exact opposite of what left-wing politicos do and the same thing that He always did.

He'd present the truth and allow people the freedom to choose which path they want to follow. That's what true freedom of any kind is: The freedom to choose what to believe, what to take part in, or what to follow. Freedom is about having choices. When those choices are removed, freedom dies.

Imagine a restaurant where only steak is served, yet the owner claims to have an abundance of menu choices. Being able to choose how your steak is cooked doesn't diminish the fact that you're still limited to only steak as a choice for dinner. That's what liberals want when it comes to religious freedom. They want you to believe that you have choices...but in the end, the only choice is steak. Of course they also want to limit how that steak is cooked too.

Think freedoms, religious and otherwise, for a moment.

How do we punish criminals?

That's right. We take away their freedom. We put them in jail. We restrict their movements. We limit their choices of food. We decide their daily schedules and routines. We decide what time they go to bed and what time they wake. Convicted criminals cease being able to make all but the most rudimentary choices for themselves.

When the left seeks to remove our religious freedoms, they actually seek to "imprison" us within our own country. Jesus wouldn't want any part of that.

■■

Can you imagine Jesus in modern-day America attempting to force a baker to bake a cake for a purpose that they disagreed with on deeply held religious grounds?

No?

I can't either.

Can you imagine Jesus trying to block you from speaking about your religion in public, even if it differed from His own Gospel?

No?

I can't see Him doing that either.

Can you see Jesus lobbying lawmakers, encouraging them to prevent the mention of other religions, prayers, or religious beliefs in public schools?

No?

Me neither.

All the while that Jesus was spreading His Gospel, He never tried to shut down those who dissented by forbidding them to speak out against Him. In fact, He encouraged this dissent as it gave Him more opportunities to present the truth. He never tried to destroy the temples or synagogues of those who followed a different religion. He never tried to forcibly shut down another religion or religious viewpoint. He never tried to remove the symbols or icons of other religions from public view. Yet the Democratic Party has tried to do all of this and more, under the spurious guise of "protecting" religious freedoms.

Jesus taught in the synagogues and preached in the temples, but He never once tried to forcibly change what the people who worshipped in those places believed. He allowed these people to hear Him. To ask questions. To decide what they wanted to believe. If they chose Him, He was happy to receive them; if they rejected Him, He moved on without protest and with little fanfare.

Trying to shut down any religious viewpoints that disagree with your own, isn't religious freedom. It is religious tyranny, and Jesus wouldn't have any part in that.

What Would Jesus Do?:
Helping The Poor

Now that we've broken the mirrors and cleared out the smoke to get to the bottom of what the left *really* means when they mention "helping the poor", let's take a look at how these things relate to the claims they make when they say "Jesus agrees with us on this issue". Let's take a look at what "helping the poor" looks like in reality. Then we'll explore what Jesus meant when He commanded us to look after the poor.

When Jesus said to "help to the poor", He meant the *real* poor, not the socioeconomic classification that the left applies to those they've deemed as "the poor". When Jesus said that we are to feed, shelter, comfort, and clothe the poor, He meant people in actual dire need. People whose very existence might depend on whether they get to eat on any given day. Or their existence depends on whether they have shelter on any given night. He wasn't speaking of the person who considers themselves "poor" because they're a little short on cash this week, or because they can't afford to get their nails done this month. Or the person who has to cancel their deluxe cable and internet package because they can no longer afford it.

Today, in America at least, 60% of Americans who fall under the government guidelines of "the poor" own a recently released smartphone, subscribe to an expensive cable or a deluxe satellite television package, and eat out in restaurants frequently. Most of these people own at least two large flat-screen televisions, enjoy air-conditioned homes, wear nice clothes, own washers and dryers, and own at least one decent car. Some even own their own homes outright, mortgage free. Most poor Americans have larger, and more adequately appointed, living spaces than most non-poor Europeans. (40)

That's hardly the same standard of "the poor" we see depicted in the days of Jesus. Lazarus was poor. Truly, heartbreakingly poor. He laid at the gates of the rich man, covered with oozing, open, infected, extremely painful sores; his only possessions the scant clothes on his back. He longed for nothing more than to be able to sooth his gnawing hunger with the scant crumbs that fell from the rich man's table.

That's what poor truly looks like.

Most of us, even many of the poor among us, can't fathom that kind of hunger. The kind of hunger that would cause us to consume crumbs of food from the floor, or from trash cans and dumpsters. Most of those considered "poor" in this country couldn't even begin to comprehend the kind of hunger that would make them resemble dogs, begging for a nibble from their master's table.

In America, the closest we come to the poor of Biblical times can be found in the backwoods of the Appalachian Mountains. People there often live in ramshackle shacks with dirt floors; subsisting on the barest means of all. No electricity. No running water. No indoor plumbing. No heating and air. No television. No healthcare plans. No Food Stamps. No welfare. No dental care. No vehicles in most cases. These are the faces of the truly poor in America; not those you see using Food Stamps in the grocery store while clutching their I-phone 10's while clothed in the latest fashions, while also driving a late model car.

The unvarnished truth is that a plurality of the Americans who're classified as "poor" today are quite capable of providing adequate food and shelter for themselves…if they only sincerely tried to do so. Many simply don't want to do without the modern conveniences they've grown accustomed to. Some find it easier to collect entitlements, rather than work…largely because it *is*.

The poor of Jesus's day were very, very poor indeed. They were what we in the south used to call "dirt poor". Most of the poor people in biblical times relied on the charity of others to get by from day to day. Many of these people had severe physical or mental afflictions that kept them from being able to work, or kept them from being able to make a sufficient living to sustain themselves or their families. *These* are the people that Jesus admonished us to take care of. The widows. The innocent children. The disabled. The truly helpless. Those with no other recourse than to rely on others for sustenance. The *real* poor. Not those who think entitlements are "income". Or those who'd rather stay on those programs than take an entry level job at a restaurant or retail shop.

Today, when the Democratic Party starts invoking the term "the poor", they often mean what I call "the willingly poor". These are frequently people who can support themselves, but choose not to for any number of reasons.

Why would the Democratic Party seek to support these people who could otherwise support themselves?

VOTES.

It all comes down to votes. In most cases the Democratic Party's own agenda helps to keep these people poor. Often times, these people are more than willing to stay that way.

Why?

Because it's just easier that way. The path of least resistance is preferable to some folks. Some have become so entrenched in the entitlement culture, that they can't imagine anything else.

So would Jesus support the "vote-buying" entitlement apparatus that our government has put in place today?

Programs that are riddled with waste, fraud, and abuse?

Programs that tend to increase poverty rather than combat it?

Programs that rob people of motivation and the desire to achieve?

It's hard to believe that by any stretch of the imagination that He would support any of this. Jesus seemed to be very much in favor of self-sufficiency.

Jesus was *not* advocating for a confiscatory government program set up to take from one group to give to another when He told us to help the poor. What Jesus advocated for was for us to willfully and cheerfully give from our *own pockets* to the poor; not the taking from one group of people only to give to another. He wanted you and me to do what we could to help the real poor around us...from our own pockets and with a cheerful heart. He didn't want us to leave it to Caesar to take care of the poor.

Why?

Because He knew Caesar couldn't be trusted to do so. Not only are most Democrats woefully inadequate in their own personal giving, when it comes to contributing to the poor, they're often dismissive and downright hostile toward groups that are aimed at doing just that. They think that only they know best how to spend money purportedly raised for the poor. In their eyes, you couldn't possibly use your *own* money as efficiently as they can use *your* money to help those in need.

The sheer arrogance of that sentiment is astounding.

When then President George W. Bush tried to get the government to fund a faith-based initiative aimed at feeding and clothing the poor, the left very nearly rioted. They objected shrilly and loudly, not only because they hate any inclusion of God in our government, but also because increased faith-based giving would decrease dependency on the government and governmental programs. Without governmental program dependent voters, the Democrat's political power in Washington is greatly diminished. Simply put, they need the poor to remain poor in order to hold on to political power.

Churches are the entities that do the *most* for the *real* poor in their respective communities. They provide not only food, money, shelter, and clothing for the poor; they also provide a level of emotional and spiritual support that one will never get from a government program or from a hostile, underpaid government worker. Good luck getting one of the employees at a local welfare or DFACS office to see you as anything more than just another case number to be dealt with.

The real poor.

The forgotten poor.

The poor who probably haven't voted in years, if ever. That's who we're supposed to be helping.

What are the churches seeking from these people in return?
Nothing.

What can a poor person do for a church, besides maybe sit in a pew?

Even then, churches don't require membership, or even Sunday worship service attendance, in order to help those in need. They do it because it's just the right thing to do. And, they do it more efficiently than any bloated government program that's rife with waste, fraud, and abuse. A government program will never come close to the efficiency of a well-run church at helping those in need.

The left throws out the false argument that it's a violation of the Constitution for a church to have help from the government in feeding, clothing, or helping to house the poor. Ironically, they don't see the greedy self-serving politicians only hoping for reelection as being a problem.

How can they be so blind?

Or are they being willfully obtuse?

If I believed in gambling, my bet would be on willfully obtuse.

There's absolutely no conflict with the Constitution in allowing churches, to help the less fortunate. Or with the government helping to facilitate that. None at all.

The left raises the issue in the fear that God might be mentioned in the presence of a poor, hungry, or cold person. Or that someone might mention Jesus in the midst of providing financial assistance, food, clothing, or shelter to a poor person. These are their major concerns.

And yet, they don't seem to care that a majority of the money collected by the government purportedly for the same purposes never actually makes it to the poor?

What kind of logic is that?

So, we can't mention God in the midst of helping the poor, but it doesn't faze them at all that much of the money the government collects for the "poor" is absorbed by waste, fraud, and abuse? Or that it never makes it to the coffers of the programs the money was collected for in the first place because it's subverted for pet projects instead?

■■

SIDE NOTE: I keep running across liberal atheists who advocate for taxing churches. At the same time, they also advocate for more and more government entitlement spending under the guise of helping the poor. I usually point out the fallacy of this position. Not only would such taxation negate the Establish Clause (argument for a different book), but it would also rob the real poor of millions of dollars per year in aid. In a nutshell, churches pay their employees, electric bills, mortgages, and other bills first. What's left is the discretionary budget that usually goes toward helping the poor. Thousands of dollars in new taxation, per church, would come directly from the funds those churches use to help the poor…and very little of that money, confiscated from the church coffers and earmarked for the poor, would ever make it to the truly needy once that confiscated money is in greedy government hands.

****

*So **this** is what Jesus would have us do?*

No, I don't think that Jesus would approve of the poor being used as political bargaining chips in a game of power. Not. At. All. Newsflash for you liberals out there: When Jesus said to take care of the poor, he meant *FROM YOUR OWN POCKETS*. Not from mine. Not from the faceless and unnamed "rich" that you so love to demonize…from *YOUR OWN POCKETS*. So when you liberals bring up Jesus in trying to make your case for explosive growth in entitlement spending, just remember, that's not what Jesus wanted at all.

If you're going to invoke Jesus's name in conjunction with the needy, you'd better be prepared to crack open your own wallet, or your own purse, because *that* is what Jesus commanded.

When's the last time you personally bought or prepared a meal for a truly hungry person?

What Would Jesus Do?:
Women's Rights

So now, let's examine how Jesus would likely view the Democrat Party's real stance on "women's rights", based upon what we know of Him from the Bible. We've already examined what the left truly means when they use this snazzy catch phrase, so let's compare that with what we *know* about Jesus and His teachings.

Do you really think that Jesus would classify abortion as a "right" belonging to women?

I can't see that.

In fact, I can emphatically tell you that He would *not*. Not. At. All. No way. No how. Not on your life! Anyone who thinks otherwise clearly doesn't know much about the real Jesus.

In the Bible, Jesus says in His own words that it would be better for a millstone to be hung around your neck and for you to be cast into the depths of the sea than for you harm a child.

Let's examine what the Bible says on this subject. Luke 17:2 says:

> *"It were better for him that a millstone were hanged about his neck, and he cast into the sea, than that he should offend one of these little ones."*

How can anyone see abortion as anything other than causing harm to a child?

157

Abortion is the very act of violently and cold-bloodedly murdering a child. Ending the life of what is most often an otherwise perfectly healthy unborn child. If we put aside the nonsense and look at the facts objectively, the truth is that most abortions have nothing to do with the mother's health. They have nothing to do with rape or incest. They have nothing to do with a problem with the baby itself. Most abortions are about electing to kill a healthy, problem-free child.

Would the same Jesus who made such a bold statement concerning harming children support murdering the innocent unborn?

In most cases, simply because a woman thinks that it's her "right" to do so?

I think not.

Would He really support murder on-demand, simply because a baby would make the mother's life less convenient?

Or because a baby brings with it tough financial demands and lifestyle changes?

I think not.

Now, let's make this point perfectly clear: People on the left who support abortion often try to differentiate between a child who's already born and an unborn child. They often refer to the unborn child as simply a "fetus" or a "clump of tissue" in an effort to lessen the psychological impact of calling it what it truly is…a baby. A living human being within another living human being. I can tell you emphatically, that there's no difference in the eyes of God between the born child and the unborn child. Both are special to Him and both are endowed by Him with living souls.

Although abortion advocates often refer to an unborn baby as a "clump of tissue" and nothing more, that's about as willfully obtuse or dishonest as a person can get. God is the giver of life. If a baby is formed in the womb, it *is* a gift from God. That child, that *life*, has a purpose and a soul, just like every other child you see walking down the street or playing on the playground. That unborn baby has a purpose, just the same as you and I have a God-given purpose.

The Bible also clearly states that God knows us in the womb before we are born. This means He had a plan when He created us and gave us life:

Jeremiah 1:5 "Before I formed you in the womb I knew you..."

I think this scripture makes it clear that no matter what the left claims about when "personhood" begins, according to God, you're a "person" at the moment of conception. There's really no other moment at which a baby becomes a "person", other than at conception. When God forms a child in the womb, that child becomes a living human being. They're not one bit different than you and I. There is no discernable physiological differences in a baby that's inside the womb, and a baby that was just born. While all of their limbs, organs, and tissues may not be fully formed as of yet, they're still as much alive as you and I. In fact, tragically, if you watched a procedure of an abortion via ultrasound, you'd see the baby shrink away from the instruments of death coming to end their life.

Furthermore, the Bible says that intentionally causing the death of another human *is* murder and thereby a sin. (With the exception to that being cases of capital punishment for heinous crimes, as duly administered by government.) It's very clear that Jesus would consider abortion murder; a grievous sin. I cannot see how anyone could expect Him to advocate for murder. Particularly the murder of the innocent unborn.

No, Jesus would tell a pregnant woman that she'd created life in her womb, most of the time by her own actions, and she's now responsible for that life. He'd expect for her, at a very minimum, to see the pregnancy through to its natural end. Killing the child would never be an option that He'd endorse. Causing one's body to reject the child is not a course of action He'd support either.

Those on the left side of this argument are quick to throw out spurious scenarios such as "What about in cases of rape?" and "What about in cases of incest?" What they don't tell you is that abortions performed for those two reasons are so miniscule, so infrequent, as to be nearly nonexistent.

How infrequent and minute are the instances of women seeking abortion for these reasons?

Abortions for reasons of rape and incest make up less than 1% of all total abortions.

That's right. Read that again.

The proponents of abortion who throw out the *"What about in cases of rape and incest?"* question are literally bringing up something that occurs in less than ten out of every one thousand cases of women seeking an abortion. Even the New York Times, which is an uber-liberal, pro-abortion publication, backs this 1% number up. (36)

So my first question to these folks would be: *Why does nine hundred and ninety other children have to die, so that ten children who're the result of rape or incest can be aborted?* That makes no sense at all. This argument makes as much sense as subjecting another nine hundred and ninety people to chemotherapy because ten people have terminal cancer. (I also daresay the number of abortions performed because of "rape and incest" are probably much lower than the less than 1% number that's widely accepted. I once knew a girl who lied about being raped to make her abortion more "palatable" to her family and friends. I wouldn't be surprised if that's not a common occurrence.)

So why even bring this red herring up?

My next question to those who proffer this superbly weak argument is this: *"Do you think that God makes mistakes?"*

If the answer is *"No, God doesn't make mistakes."*, then they've admitted that *all* life comes from God. Since God allowed the pregnancy to happen, and since God formed that baby in the womb, God has a plan for that baby's life according to HIS perfect will…even if that will does match up with our own. (To be perfectly clear, God doesn't make mistakes and I'm personally against abortion in *all* cases for that reason. A life is a life. And life should be cherished as such.)

It doesn't really matter how that particular life was conceived, does it?

Does the fact that a child was conceived in less than ideal circumstances mean the child has no value and doesn't deserve life?

I'd argue no.

Why kill the baby because the events surrounding its conception happened to be tragic, or even very painful, for the mother?

■■

Think about Mary, the mother of Jesus, for just a moment.

She never asked to be pregnant. She never desired to be pregnant, at least not while unmarried. Nor did she do anything by which to become pregnant. The very fact that she *was* pregnant, while betrothed and unmarried, could've been her death sentence according to Mosaic Law. Mary was only a young, innocent girl. One favored by God, one who made a glorious decision to be obedient to the Will of God. I imagine she was probably more than a little terrified by her situation all the same. She probably worried about the implications of the coming child more than once. Not only was she pregnant with a child that she did nothing to conceive, she was betrothed to a man that she'd have to explain this to. Not to mention the added weight of knowing that she was carrying the Son of God, the promised Messiah within her womb.

Don't you think that this miraculous pregnancy changed the course of her life forever?

Of course it did!

We should thank God daily that Mary was a good and faithful servant. That she carried the Son of God to term. That she didn't put herself first, as so many do today.

How many young mothers have killed their unborn children in modern times?

The number is in the tens of millions.

How many innocent lives have been snuffed out?

Usually for nothing more than the sake of convenience?

Ponder that sobering thought for a moment.

▪▪

For as long as I can remember, there's been a sign on the side of a very busy road just outside of Murphy, North Carolina. This simple homemade sign carries a deeply profound, yet profoundly simple, message. One that causes me to lose myself in deep thought every time I see it.

It's a very plain sign really. Not very colorful. It isn't a professionally made work. Not slick or glossy in the presentation of its message. Not glamourous in any sort of way. It's a drab wooden sign by all accounts. One that's obviously hand-painted by an amateur artist. However, the message that this unpretentious sign conveys is extremely deep and very far-reaching.

The subject matter of the sign?

A depiction of a conversation emanating between Earth and Heaven. The humble sign features the planet Earth and a cloud representing Heaven. There are captions coming from each object. The caption above the Earth says, *"God please send us someone to cure cancer and diabetes."*

This is a prayer that I can imagine has been prayed over and over again by those affected by these horrible, life-changing diseases. The caption coming down from the clouds says it all when God responds to the pleas from Earth, *"I did...but you aborted him."*

Let that settle into your thoughts for a moment.

Isn't that a very powerful and profound message on abortion?

*How can this thought **not** give one pause?*

It's one of the simplest, yet most effective, counterpoints to the pro-abortion argument that I've ever heard voiced, or read in print. Even if you don't believe in God, you have to at least consider the underlying implications of the weighty message written upon that sign.

Who knows how many bright minds we've snuffed out prematurely through abortion?

Who would those aborted babies have grown up to be?

*Was one of the millions of aborted babies, in the US alone, **the** very person who would've unlocked the cure for cancer?*

Or diabetes?

Or Down syndrome?

Or one of the many other crippling or life-altering diseases that affect mankind?

*Was one of the millions of children, who've been snuffed out by their mothers, **the** person who would've become the next Albert Einstein?*

Would one of these children have grown into the next great inventor who would've changed mankind for the better?

Have we doomed ourselves to enduring much more human suffering than necessary, because we've killed off some of the very people who God was going to use to make our lives better?

Think about the inventions that we all enjoy and take for granted today. Air conditioning, electrical lights, television, the internet, automobiles, electric heat, ovens, microwaves, radios, telephones, etc.

What if we had aborted those who were responsible for these inventions?

How much different would our lives be today without all of the advances in technology that've been made over the last one hundred years?

What if Thomas Edison, Benjamin Franklin, Henry Ford, Harriet Tubman, Frederick Douglass, George Washington, Steve Jobs,

Abraham Lincoln, Martin Luther King Jr., or any other key historical figures had been aborted rather than allowed to live?

How much different would our country and our world be right now?

There's no way under the sun that Jesus would side with the Democratic Party when it comes to abortion. No argument for a pro-abortion Jesus will ever hold water because the Holy Bible makes it clear where He stands on the matter.

■■

So what about that other "right" that Democrats hold so dear and claim to champion on behalf of helpless women everywhere?

You know, free birth control for women at the taxpayer's expense of course?

Or the "right" to force employers to provide abortive contraceptives, and abortive procedures, to their employees even if it's in direct opposition of their deeply religious beliefs?

Well, let's delve into this "right" from a viewpoint of Jesus.

The number one reason that women use birth control is to prevent unwanted pregnancies. Most often to avoid pregnancy from premarital or even extramarital sex. The bulk of the time, it's used by unmarried women wanting to prevent pregnancy. Since the Bible teaches us that having sex before marriage, or outside of our marriages, is a sin, it's hard to see how Jesus would side with giving women a tool to help them further facilitate the commission of that sin. It's even much harder to believe that He'd want others to be forced to pay for such things with their hard-earned tax dollars.

Especially against their will.

Here's a novel question for you: *Why can't these women exercise personal responsibility over their own bodies?*

Or else pay for their own birth control themselves?

After all, we hear the argument over and over from the left that it's all about women's rights over their own bodies. One the one hand they argue that what they do with their own bodies is no one's business but their own.

Bodily autonomy don't you know?

163

On the other hand, they demand that the *public* pay for *their* private decisions. *Why can't these women either control their own sinful lusts or simply provide **their own** birth control at **their own** expense?*

*Rather than burdening the taxpayer with what should be, by their own admission, **their** responsibility and **their** problem?*

They can't have it both ways.

They don't get to yell, *"It's my body, it's my business!"* and then scream, *"You have to pay for what I do with my body!"*

Life doesn't work that way.

Their business becomes *my* business when I have to start financing *their* business with *my* tax dollars. Like it or not. We all have a right in this country to know what our tax dollars are being spent on. We also have a right to voice dissent when we disagree with the usage of those dollars. That's one of the foundations of this great country.

How do they not see the hypocrisy in claiming that when it comes to abortion that it's no one else's business, because *"It's my body, my decision, my business"*…yet when it comes to providing birth control, they claim we have an *obligation* to pay for it?

Huh?

How can they say that *"What a woman does with her body is solely her business"* on the one hand and then on the other hand tell us that we *have* to be involved in her business by paying for her birth control…because of what she intends to do with her body?

Shouldn't the financing of the drugs that allow her to engage in "her business" also solely be, *"her* business"?

Why is it that paying for "her business" becomes my business?
Or your business?

Especially when we don't want any part of it.

When it comes to the small number of women who actually have a physical *necessity* to be on birth control, for reasons other than trying to prevent a pregnancy, I don't see a problem with helping to provide it for them financially. I've known a few women who've had to take birth control to prevent serious health issues, such as excessive bleeding and hemorrhaging. I'm more than happy to contribute to the healthcare of those who truly can't afford it. I have no issues with my tax dollars funding birth control that's used to help women who have legitimate medical issues such as severe, heavy bleeding during their cycles, or those who need it to help control hormonal imbalances that can have serious long-term health consequences.

I personally know of no Christians who have a problem with *this* aspect of birth control. I doubt that Jesus would either. *If*, and that's a big if, the reason for usage is medically related, versus being used as a tool for the enabling of irresponsible behavior.

As I write this book, a court case is still being fought as to whether the government (through the healthcare monstrosity that is most often called Obamacare) can force employers who have religious objections to provide coverage that includes abortion or abortive contraceptives. This should be a no-brainer. Anyone with any sense of right and wrong should be able to see that it's wrong for anyone to try to force someone else into taking part in abortion.

Especially through forcing them to pay for it over their deeply held religious objections.

What's wrong with people?

Jesus wouldn't support any of this mess.

■■

Those in favor of forcing employers to cover abortion and contraceptives make their argument for this unconstitutional coercion based on the spurious logic that these things are "healthcare" or "health measures". Things that are necessary for maintaining women's good health. Yet, in most cases, that's simply not true. These claims simply don't hold up to scrutiny.

Abortion is, by and large, almost exclusively an *elective* procedure. Very few abortions out of the total number of abortions performed in the US each year are for "medically necessary" reasons. In truth abortions performed each year in the US for "medically necessary reasons", meaning if the pregnancy continued the life of the mother would be in danger, is also less than 1%. (37)

In almost all cases, having an abortion actually does nothing to improve a woman's health. Abortions, or complications from abortive procedures, can in fact lead to death, depression, and severe anxiety in the women who've had them. Not to mention possibility of creating new reproductive health issues for those women. Many women who've had abortions find it difficult, if not impossible, to conceive when they want to have a child later in life. Suicide rates among women who've had an abortion are up to six times higher than that of women who've never had an abortion. (38)

Abortion certainly doesn't increase the health of the unborn child.

Isn't the goal of "healthcare" to improve someone's personal health?

Isn't "healthcare" generally viewed as medically necessary care, or preventative care, aimed at improving lives?

And yet, abortion is neither medically necessary, nor does it improve lives of the mothers in most cases. It certainly doesn't improve the life of the child being killed.

So why the misnomer of calling this procedure "healthcare"?

■■

Let me give you an example of the hypocrisy of the left on this issue. Studies have shown that people who pray and are actively involved in their churches tend to be happier and healthier than those who don't have any religious beliefs at all. Similar studies have shown that daily prayer and reading the Bible have beneficial health effects as well. (39)

Given this information, we could call it a "health measure" or "healthcare" to have forced prayer and forced Bible reading in the workplace...that is, if we're applying liberal "logic", right?

Wrong.

It'd be just as wrong to do this as it is to force employers to cover abortive procedures and abortive prescriptions for their employees. Freedom of religion and religious beliefs should trump the spurious claims of those who'd force others to violate their consciences. And this is true for both sides of the fence. Don't attempt to force me to participate or recognize your gay "marriage" and I won't attempt to force you to read the Bible and pray.

The point is this: The left would go absolutely *nuts* if Christians tried to use a government mandate to force their employers to hold mandatory prayer or Bible reading time. Or, if atheist employers were forced to fund the purchases of Bibles for their employees...and, rightly so.

But, conversely, these same people have no problem with forcing others to participate in abortion, contraception, or abortive medicines against their will.

Why is that?

Talk about hypocrisy!

When it comes to birth control being used to facilitate a promiscuous lifestyle, or abortive contraceptives used to end a pregnancy after conceiving, I can tell you definitively that Jesus would have no part of either of those sins. Don't try to tell us that Jesus wants us to fund your promiscuity. Don't try to tell us that Jesus wants us to pay for your abortion.

He would not and does not support either.

When it comes to abortion, there's no way under the sun that Jesus would ever encourage, support, or tolerate the taking of innocent life…regardless of the circumstances that begat that life.

■ ■

What Would Jesus Do?:
Civil Rights

Civil rights?

You must be asking yourself: *How can anyone claim that Jesus would be against civil rights?*

That's a good question. One that hinges upon what you believe a "civil right" truly is.

When it comes to civil rights we must remember that, as I outlined a few pages back in the *"What Would The DNC Do"* section on this topic, the left doesn't exactly mean what most others mean when they invoke the term "civil rights".

If we look at civil rights through the same prism the left does, we can see how Jesus would want no part of their agenda.

What about things like gay "marriage"?

Can't see Him supporting that, or considering it a civil right either. Jesus is the Living Word of God, the Word made Flesh, and the Word of God unequivocally says that homosexuality is an abomination. It's a sin of the worst kind. The Old Testament calls homosexuality a sin. An abomination that's worthy of death. In fact, at one time, that was the very penalty that God demanded for that particular sin. The New Testament also condemns it as sin in multiple passages.

*Moreover, since Jesus was free from sin, and did not and does not **ever** condone sin, how could He support something that's as inherently wrong and sinful as a gay "marriage"?*

Who Stole Jesus

It's hard to believe that an argument in favor of this, from a Christian point of view, even exists when God's stance on this is so clear in the Bible.
Jude 7:

> *"Even as Sodom and Gomorrah, and the cities about them in like manner, giving themselves over to fornication, and going after strange flesh, are set forth for an example, suffering the vengeance of eternal fire."*

Revelation 21:8

> *"But the fearful, and unbelieving, and **the abominable**, and murderers, and whoremongers, and sorcerers, and idolaters, and all liars, shall have their part in the lake which burneth with fire and brimstone: which is the second death."*

■■

Now, let's look at the institutionalized racism in America called Affirmative Action, through the context of what we know about Jesus. *Would Jesus support this concept? Would He say that it's right to give a person a job or other social/economic advantages based solely on race alone?* Try as I might, I can't see that He would. The Bible makes clear that God is not a respecter of persons. This means He's the *only* being to truly look at all of us with pure objectively…regardless of our race, social standing, financial standing, or any other outside criteria.

To understand this argument, we must come to the knowledge of what "racism" truly means. Racism is the act of treating one person, or one group of people, *differently* based solely upon their race. That's something that's often missed in discussions of race relations. Let me repeat it again because this is an extremely important point if we're to have an open and honest discussion on race: racism = *treating someone differently based solely upon their race.*

*Notice that I did **not** say that racism is solely treating someone worse based on race?*

Too often that's what we think of when we hear the word "racism". We think of old white men, in long, flowing white robes capped with ridiculous pointed hats, burning crosses blazing in the

170

background while they threaten or attack blacks and minorities. In truth, racism is so much more than that. It's not simply the hurling of slurs, random acts of violence, and intimidation based on skin color that constitutes racism.

No, it goes far beyond that. It's the treating of someone *differently* based solely on race, or skin color, which makes it truly racism. That difference in treatment could be comprised of treating someone better *or* treating someone worse based solely upon their race.

For example, if one treats a white customer better than they would treat a black customer, or other minority customer, in the same exact circumstances that *is* racism. It doesn't matter if the offending party didn't treat a person of a minority *badly* per se. It's still racism because they gave preferential treatment to another party based upon sharing their race. Pure and simple. Although no one was technically hurt in the hypothetical situation above, it's still an example of racism.

A modern day example of this type of racism might be a restaurant manager giving white customers a discount...while not extending that same courtesy and discount to customers of color. No one was wronged, in a strictly technical sense, but an unfair advantage was doled out based solely upon race.

Likewise when an establishment with a majority of black or minority employees treats a white customer or white employee worse than, or fails to provide the same courtesies that they'd afford a black customer or employee, this is also abject racism. It doesn't matter whether a difference in treatment is for the better or for the worse. If that difference in treatment of an individual is based upon skin color alone, then those actions are indeed racist.

Why does this distinction matter?

Take a deeper look at the policy of Affirmative Action. Being forced to hire someone of color based upon an artificial racial quota set by the government *is* racism. If you're a minority and you get preferential treatment in any way, that *is* racism. It may be government sanctioned racism, but it is racism nonetheless. If that same consideration isn't offered to all, it's an unfair advantage. If that advantage is based only upon race, it's racism.

No question about it.

We shouldn't be extending any special treatment to anyone based on skin color alone.

■■

I'll share another anecdote that'll help illustrate this issue. This happened about two years after the first incident mentioned earlier in this book. As stated before, I managed a pizza restaurant in the small town where I was raised. A town wherein the racial demographic at the time was overwhelmingly Caucasian. I'll never forget this second confrontation with a prospective employee and his father.

This time, my store had received an application from a black teenager few weeks prior. At the time, same as before, I didn't need any help. So, I followed protocol and I put the application in the file drawer with all of the other recent applications we'd received. All as per usual. These applications were kept on file for two years for possible consideration if a position were to come available.

A few weeks after the application was handed in, this same young man came in and inquired on it. I informed him that at the time we weren't hiring. We were fully staffed. He was informed that I'd keep his application on file for future reference. He said "Okay, thank you.", and left.

The following day, I get a visit from this young man's very angry father. He proceeds to tell me that I *have* to hire his son based upon racial quotas in Affirmative Action mandates. His exact words to me were: "You don't have enough blacks working here." I repeated to this man that I had no problem hiring his son, when and if I needed someone to fill a position in the future.

Again, he proceeded to tell me that I *had* to hire his son immediately and that failure to do so would be reported to the labor board and the EEOC.

After several minutes of dealing with this irate, belligerent, and frankly irrational man, I proceeded to give him a lesson in Affirmative Action. You see, he based his wrongheaded claim that we were not meeting the artificial, government imposed racial quotas only on the number of *black* employees who he saw working there at any given time.

The problem with his warped line of reasoning is that while it was true that we only had one *black* teenager employed with us at the time, we also had many other employees who fell into various minority groups. In fact, at the time of this unfortunate confrontation, my restaurant had about thirty employees. While most were white, we had a total of seven employees who were minorities. Not all minorities are black. (Keep in mind the surrounding area consisted of a population of about only 5-10% of people who fell into various "minority" groups.)

In addition to the black teenager we employed at the store, the rest of the staff was made up of varying ethnic and racial groups. One employee was from Mexico, one originated from Panama, one was an Iraqi immigrant, one hailed from Bangladesh, one came from India, and one employee was Pakistani.

If you're keeping count, that's a total of seven minority employees out of a total of thirty employees. A ratio of higher than 23% minority staffing. That's well above the racial quotas set forth in Affirmative Action mandates. In fact, those numbers are decisively conclusive evidence that the restaurant showed absolutely no racial bias in its hiring standards.

Given that the general population of the local surrounding area was a mix of 90-95% Caucasians, with 10% or less minorities, and the fact that my staff consisted of 23% minorities, my store boasted a much greater minority-to-non-minority mix than many other local stores and restaurants. Our minority mix was nearly two-and-a-half times greater than the minority mix of the general population in the surrounding areas.

Still, even when confronted with the overwhelming evidence that he was wrong, this man followed up on his threats. He filed a claim based entirely upon his desire for us to hire his son…solely based upon his race. His claim was denied and I never heard from him again.

So, I ask you, who displayed the real racism in this sad interaction?

*Was it the man who tried to use Affirmative Action to **force** someone to hire his son…**solely** because of his race?*

Even though he knew the employer didn't need any help at the time?

Or was it the man who declined to hire the teenager for no other reason than the fact that his restaurant was already fully staffed?

I can't see Jesus cheerleading for this sort of institutionalized racism, especially since these sorts of programs actually seem to cause much greater division than they do unity. One will never promote racial harmony while also promoting racial disparity. It just can't happen.

Racism is a sin. To make the case that Jesus would support sin is to make the case that Jesus is a sinner. That's not really an argument that most believers would want to make.

· ·

I can't believe I'm even having to address the latest "civil rights" red herring that the left has thrown out there: Transgendered bathroom "rights". I have a hard time believing this is even a real issue in modern-day America.

What's the world coming to when we have to engage in a fight over who pees where?

So now, we have politicians who're fighting for the "right" for men and women who have mental disorders to enter the bathrooms, the locker rooms, and the shower rooms of the opposite sex.

Why?

Because they "believe" that they are a member of that opposite sex.

Oh, boy.

What could go wrong there, right?

Beyond just the insanity of helping to further the delusions of those with a mental condition, other, more serious issues present themselves with this problem.

As a former teen boy, I can tell you that if you think claiming to be "transgendered" wouldn't cross a young man's mind if it meant he'd be afforded a chance to have access to the girl's locker rooms and restrooms, then you've never been a teen boy, have you? It's the practically the very stuff that a teen boy's hormone driven dreams are made of.

Remember back in the 1980's?

Several very popular (and very ungodly) R-rated movies were released that had entire plotlines that revolved around peeking into and sneaking views of the girl's locker rooms and shower rooms at school. It was a major theme in many of the movies at the time. Given the opportunities presented with this new "transgendered" craze, it *will* happen. Somewhere some straight, normal boys out there *will* enter the girl's restrooms and locker rooms under these false "transgendered" premises. Simply because they can.

Thanks to former President Obama, they now, by and large, have a free pass to do so.

So what would Jesus think about this new so-called civil right?

Again, let's consult the Bible. In Matthew 19:4 Jesus has this to say:

> *"And he answered and said unto them, Have ye not read, that he which made them at the beginning made them male and female,"*

Notice, He didn't say "male and female...and transgendered"?

He said "male and female". Period. Nothing more. Nothing less. There's no "third gender" mentioned in the Bible. He didn't mention a mixing of the two. He said you were created either male, or female. That seems a pretty concise and clear statement.

Furthermore, for even more clarification, let's look at Deuteronomy 22:5:

> *"[5] The woman shall not wear that which pertaineth unto a man, neither shall a man put on a woman's garment: for all that do so are abomination unto the LORD thy God."*

Well, that would seem to be pretty clear and concise now wouldn't it?

So, if it's an abomination unto God for a man to present himself as a woman, or for a woman to present herself as a man, then that means it's a grievous sin to do so. If it's a sin, that means Jesus can't support it, or else He makes Himself a sinner. *If Jesus becomes a sinner, what hope of salvation is there for us?*

If we believe that Jesus is the Living Word, and the Word states that for a man to dress and act as a woman, or for a woman to dress and act as a man, is wrong then it would only follow that Jesus would want no part of the transgenderism craze that's currently sweeping the land.

▪▪

Despite the wholly delusional claims on the left, institutionalized racism and extending fake "rights" to those who don't qualify for those supposed "rights" is hardly a position that we can see Jesus taking. Making up special "civil rights" in order to legitimize sin and legislate sin as "moral" and "normal" is not something Jesus would want any part of.

If something, anything, is classified as a sin and an abomination to God, you can bet that it's *not* something Jesus would be found supporting.

■■

What Would Jesus Do?:
Equal Opportunity

So what would Jesus say about the "equal opportunity" for all argument, given the way that the left frames it?

Would He support this notion based upon the merits of the arguments of the left?

No. He'd be dead set against what they really mean when they say "equal opportunity"…at least based on what we know about Jesus.

Why?

Because first, we have to remember that when the left mentions "equal opportunity" what they really mean is guaranteed "equal outcomes" for all. Those are two wholly different concepts. Concepts that in truth aren't related to one another at all. Because a man, or woman, is given the same *opportunities* as another, doesn't mean that the two individuals will reach equal *outcomes* in life…unless an outside force, like the government, creates an artificial equal outcome on their behalf. Even then, that equal outcome is simply not sustainable for very long. Given time, the concept of equal outcomes always collapses like a house of cards built upon a lopsided table.

So where does Jesus fit into this notion?

Jesus knew and accepted that while God created all men equal, all men are *not*, and will never be equal in material goods, intelligence, or societal structure. At least not in this mortal life. Jesus acknowledged the need for men to have worldly rulers; people in positions of authority above the rest of us. Jesus also admonished us to follow those in authority who are established by God above us. The exception to this command being if those rulers impose laws or mandates that go directly against God…much like the previous Barack Obama Presidential Administration did.

A world in which there are no leaders, no one above us to provide order, is a world of chaos.

God Himself established an order of authority in which Adam and Eve were subject to Him; with Eve also being subject to Adam. *Without a power structure, a design for who is the final authority, who would lead?*

Who would make the rules that keep law and order in society?

Who would enforce such rules?

Who would provide security and protection from those who would take all we have away from us?

Including taking away our very lives and freedom?

During the time that Jesus walked among us on this earth, He never once stated that each person should have the exact same material goods and wealth as every other person. There were poor people who Jesus encountered daily in His travels. There were also rich and middle class people that Jesus encountered daily. He never once told the crowd at large that they had to divide all they had equally amongst themselves. He never once said that it was sin to have more than your neighbor. He never once said we all must have the same exact possessions.

I've heard the people who claim that Jesus was a "socialist". That claim is one hundred percent false. It's a fiction. It's a farce. It's a lie.

While Jesus admonished us to care for the poor and to see to their basic needs such as food, clothes, water and shelter, He never said: *"Take half of everything you have and give it to this person over here so that they have the exact same as you."* You've never read in the Bible an account of Jesus demanding that the same houses, the same livestock, the same amount of money, or the same material goods be distributed equally to each man, woman, and child. Jesus never said that it was a sin to have *more* than your neighbor. It only becomes sin to have more than your neighbor when your neighbor is perishing, or in jeopardy of perishing, and you have the means to help them. It becomes sin when you fail to help someone else while you have the means to do so. It becomes sin when your wealth or your possessions become your idols.

Liberals often point to a story in the Bible that we're all familiar with as "proof" of Jesus's socialist leanings. But, as per usual, they neither understand what's being expressed, or why, when they read this story. Instead, like the fine little Google Theologians they are, they take it out of context and run with it.

Mark 10:17-25

> [17] And when he was gone forth into the way, there came one running, and kneeled to him, and asked him, Good Master, what shall I do that I may inherit eternal life?
> [18] And Jesus said unto him, Why callest thou me good? there is none good but one, that is, God.
> [19] Thou knowest the commandments, Do not commit adultery, Do not kill, Do not steal, Do not bear false witness, Defraud not, Honour thy father and mother.
> [20] And he answered and said unto him, Master, all these have I observed from my youth.
> [21] Then Jesus beholding him loved him, and said unto him, One thing thou lackest: go thy way, sell whatsoever thou hast, and give to the poor, and thou shalt have treasure in heaven: and come, take up the cross, and follow me.
> [22] And he was sad at that saying, and went away grieved: for he had great possessions.
> [23] And Jesus looked round about, and saith unto his disciples, How hardly shall they that have riches enter into the kingdom of God!
> [24] And the disciples were astonished at his words. But Jesus answereth again, and saith unto them, Children, how hard is it for them that trust in riches to enter into the kingdom of God!
> [25] It is easier for a camel to go through the eye of a needle, than for a rich man to enter into the kingdom of God.

This scripture isn't anywhere close to advocating for "socialism". Not even in the slightest. Nor is it a blanket condemnation of those who possess wealth. The Lord was not condemning *riches* per se. He was condemning *idolatry*. He illustrated how some of us will let things; possessions, money, stuff, even our favorite sins, keep us from salvation...if we put them before our relationship with God through our Lord Jesus Christ.

You see the sin of the man who's mentioned in this passage wasn't that of being rich. The sin that keep the man from Heaven was his idolatry. His money, his riches, and his possessions became his golden calves. He bowed before the very Lord Jesus Christ Himself, with a chance to partake of salvation and join Him in His travels. All he was asked to do was give up his idols and follow Jesus. Because this man's heart was so attached to his possessions and his wealth, he turned away, rather than follow Jesus. He could not turn from his idolatry.

And *that* is what Jesus wanted to show us. It was never truly about the riches themselves. It was about a condition of the heart. The reason its "easier for a camel to go through the eye of a needle than a rich man to enter the kingdom of God" isn't the money, or abundance of wealth, itself. It's the all-consuming love of that money and wealth. It's the idolatry. It's not a sin to be rich. It's a sin to allow riches to stand in the way of your relationship with the Lord Jesus Christ. Being rich becomes an issue when you choose riches over a relationship with God. This same admonition holds true for all sins, all idols, that we refuse to repent of. It doesn't have to be riches. It can be pornography. It can be premarital sex. It can be drugs. It can be alcohol. It can be anything that we refuse to turn from and choose over the Lord Jesus Christ.

This passage is in no way a condemnation against riches in general. Nor does it tell us that we *all* must sell everything we own and give it away. Likewise, Jesus never advocates for socialism. Not in this scripture, nor anywhere else. To claim otherwise is just Google Theology failing once again, and making fools of those who engage in it.

(NOTE: This passage also illustrates why the myth of the "gay Christian" remains a myth, forever and always. This example illustrates the issue with total, crystal clear clarity. Just as the rich man was asked to give up his riches and follow Jesus, a homosexual would be asked to give up their sexual sin and follow Jesus. When they refuse, they sadly make the same choice that this rich man did. They can't accept Jesus at the same time that they refuse to let go of their idols and sins.)

Make no mistake I'm not advocating for unchecked greed. However, when the left mentions "equal opportunity" what they really mean is the redistribution of wealth, via government intervention. I *do* believe that Jesus would have us *all* give to the poor. He'd have us all to help those around us who we're able to help. *He'd have us do this from our own pockets.* Sometimes, I'd say that we, as Christians and as a country as a whole, do a poor job of this.

The Bible goes as far as to state that there *will* be differences in our rewards in Heaven. In His own words, Jesus tells us that some Christians will be rewarded more generously than others. This destroys the "equal outcomes for all" aspect of Jesus that liberals attempt to apply to our Savior.

See Matthew 16:27:

> *"For the Son of man shall come in the glory of his Father with his angels; and then he shall reward every man according to his works."*

"Works" in this passage means the works that are done by the redeemed *after* salvation. The works that are done before salvation count for nothing in Heaven; and works alone cannot save the lost. Don't mistake what I'm telling you here. Works do *not* save. A Christian should have works that proclaim that he/she is a child of God, but no amount of works will ever get someone into Heaven by virtue of those works alone.

The point in sharing this verse is that Jesus Himself said there would be disparity in the rewards He gives us, according to our post-salvation works.

If Jesus is a socialist, there wouldn't be differing levels of rewards in Heaven, would there?

Jealousy is a sin and there will be no sin in Heaven, but there will be those there who receive more rewards than others.

So if Jesus believed in "equal outcomes" wouldn't Heaven also have those same equal outcomes?

Why would He have sought socialism here on earth, and not in Heaven as well?

He didn't…and He wouldn't. Jesus was no more a socialist than He was an English professor.

■■

What the left generally means by conjuring up the phrase "equal opportunity for all" is that each person must be magically granted the same amount of material goods and financial resources as everyone else. At least in their version of a socialist utopia. What they desire is actually an "equal outcome", not true "equal opportunity". That much we've already established. They also mean that we need to have the US Government confiscate wealth from one group of people in order to make another group of people "more equal" than they currently are. This again, the same as with our entitlement programs, is nothing more than a thinly veiled attempt at vote-buying. This has little to nothing to do with the true advancement or betterment of the poor.

True equal opportunity is possessing the freedom to attempt to use one's talent, intelligence, and resources to become as successful as possible. All with limited interference by the Federal Government. It's the removal of the artificial barriers that keep or hinder us from being successful. It's capitalism in its purest form. Guaranteed "equal outcomes" on the other hand is socialism at its worst. This approach has never been successful at doing anything other than harming all those who get trapped under the oppressive weight of it.

No, Jesus wouldn't get behind this concept at all. If Jesus had been a true supporter of equal outcomes, He could have turned everything around Him to gold. He could have guaranteed everyone the same material wealth as everyone else. He could have commanded the secular and religious leaders at the time to make all people equal. He could have become the ultimate socialist redistributor of wealth. He could've made Heaven a place of "equal outcomes" as well.

Yet, He didn't.

He didn't do any of those things.

The one person, the only person in this world who could have created an "equal outcome" for everyone in this life is Jesus; and yet He declined to do so both on Earth and in Heaven.

However with that said, Jesus did provide a way in which *all* men have a chance at one particular "equal outcome"…it's called salvation. By accepting Him and believing on His death on the cross for the remission of our sins, and by believing in His resurrection, by faith with a repentant heart, we can *all* have an "equal outcome". As far as obtaining eternal life that is.

Upon death paying us a visit, all men are truly equal in all things for the first time in our lives. Material wealth will have passed away and the only thing that will matter is whether we've accepted or rejected our chance to have an equal outcome in salvation.

Birth and death are truly the only times in a man or woman's life that we are guaranteed equal outcomes. We are all born with nothing and we all take nothing with us when we die. You don't get more equal than that.

Who Stole Jesus

What Would Jesus Do?:
Freedom of Speech

So, freedom of speech...who wouldn't be for it?
Only a dictator would oppose freedom of speech, right?
I mean, you can't fully respect and appreciate a right as profound as this one until someone tries to deny it to you. At the time that Jesus traveled and taught the Gospel throughout the land, He was hounded by those who sought to silence Him. After He ascended back to Heaven, His disciples were likewise hounded, imprisoned, and even killed...simply for spreading the Gospel. Jesus paid the ultimate price, as per God's plan, for speaking inconvenient truths.

I think if anyone can fully appreciate freedom of speech, it's Jesus. However, as we covered a few pages back, much of what the left considers to be covered by "freedom of speech", Jesus would take no part of. We've already covered how the Democratic Party tries to use political correctness and hate-speech accusations against those they disagree with on hot-button political and social topics. Nothing more needs to be said on this front.

As someone who's had His own free speech threatened in the past; someone who in fact died on the cross because of what He proclaimed with His mouth, (in accordance, of course with God's plan), Jesus wouldn't want any part of the actions of these people. He wouldn't support stifling the speech of those we disagree with.

185

Upon looking at some of the other things that the left considers, "free speech", it's clear that Jesus wouldn't want any parts of those things either. I just can't see Jesus supporting shutting down the speech of those who would stand against homosexuality, gay "marriage", abortion, transgenderism, or other controversial social issues...while at the same time supporting vile pornography, depraved forms of "performance art", the advocating of sex with children, and other demented ideas as "free speech". Only someone who doesn't know Jesus at all could bring themselves to believe such utter nonsensical garbage.

Jesus was perhaps the *founder* of the original Freedom of Speech movement. Despite knowing that those who were against Him would seek to kill Him; He still spoke His mind and encouraged His disciples to do the same. Jesus knew that only through free speech could a person be reasoned with. Only through open dialogue could a sinner be reached with the Gospel. He'd in no way stand for the squashing of free speech, even if He disagreed with what was being said.

∎∎∎

Okay, so I know that this chapter was very long.

It contains a lot within it to digest, and I may have tapped dance on some of my reader's toes. But, I think I've clearly made my case. The "left-wing political Jesus" is as much a myth as all of the other counterfeit Jesus's. He's as fake as the buried Jesus, the married Jesus, and all the rest. Pure and simple. He's a forgery, a fake, a poorly made and low quality, easy-to-spot, knock-off of the real deal.

Jesus wouldn't want to be associated with any of the garbage that comes out of the liberal left. Not under any circumstances. Certainly not with the most insane of all the things they support.

If liberals actually believed in some of the things they *claim* to believe in, I could see Jesus supporting *some* of their political platform...however their lip service to helping the poor and loving others is just that; lip service only.

Oh, you better believe that He still loves these liberals just as much as He loves everyone else. He still wants to, and still can, save their souls and grant them eternal life. And, just like anyone else He ever met and saved from spiritual death, He'd tell them to "go, and sin no more".

That means He would say "No!" to crushing people's religious liberties; "No!" to using entitlement spending to buy the votes of the poor while keeping them poor; "No!" to abortion and coerced taxpayer participation; "No!" to contrived "civil rights"; "No!" to gay "marriage"; "No!" to "equal outcomes"; "No!" to sin disguised as "free speech"; "No!" to transgenderism; "No!" to hate packaged as "love"; and "No!" to religious persecution.

That means liberals would have to abandon liberalism and repent of its evil to truly follow in Jesus's footsteps.

Sadly, most won't do that.

Their political beliefs have become their personal golden calves and their idolatry.

Chapter 5:
The "Salvation Through Baptism Jesus"

Whew! After such a long chapter, I decided to take it easy on the readers with a short, relatively painless chapter. That's my hope anyway.

With that said, some people will find the information within this chapter offensive to their deeply held religious beliefs that they've grown up with. Make no mistake about it: while I don't ever intentionally try to offend anyone; it's not my job as a preacher to make anyone comfortable in their delusions, their misinformation…or their sins. My job is to preach truth, even if that truth is uncomfortable to those receiving it. Doing anything less would be a betrayal to my calling, and a sin on my part.

Here in this chapter, we find another Jesus who is just as false as all the other counterfeits out there. This "Jesus" ranks among the very top of the false "Jesus" personas for being one of the most dangerous to believe in. Several denominations, including the Catholic denomination and many others that spin off of Catholicism, wrongly believe and preach that baptism actually *imparts* salvation. Specifically troubling is the belief that the ritual of infant baptism grants salvation.

The Bible however teaches the exact opposite, that baptism without prior salvation is basically nothing more than an empty ritual. One devoid of any real meaning. Baptism alone does *not* and *cannot* impart salvation. Nor does it make you a "Christian". Infant baptism is especially troubling as it leads others to believe that they received salvation as an infant, when in fact, they did *not*. There are millions of people walking around who've been baptized, mostly as children, yet they've never actually accepted Christ as their personal Savior.

They've never come to the realization that they're a lost sinner. They've never felt the shame and regret for their sins that only Holy Spirit conviction brings. They've never made a conscious choice to repent of their sins and turn to Jesus. These people are still just as lost in sin as if they'd never gotten baptized at all. In fact, in some cases, this false pretense of salvation through baptism, specifically through infant baptism, has lulled these people into a false sense of security. This false belief that they already have salvation only serves to make it harder to get these people to repent and come to Jesus later in their lives.

When baptism happens before salvation, nothing changes; with the exception that those getting baptized get a little wet. Running through a garden sprinkler would be just as effective as baptism without prior salvation; and it requires far less pomp and circumstance. I don't mean to demean anyone's faith or religious beliefs. It's merely Biblical truth and I've never shied away from a Biblical truth…even if it causes hurt feelings for some people. Shoot…on more than one occasion, Biblical truth has hurt my own feelings.

Millions of people have their babies baptized believing that this magically transforms the child into a Christian…and thereby offers them protection from Hell. Unfortunately, that's just not true. Not in the least. Baptizing a baby does nothing at all for the child; with the exception that it can later cause them to die unsaved as an adult; thereby guaranteeing them a place in hell.

Why?

Because they died believing they're covered by an empty ritual of a baptism that occurred when they were a small child. A child who couldn't even speak, much less comprehend personal salvation, to make a conscious choice to believe in the Lord Jesus Christ and His sacrifice on the cross.

I recently witnessed a very clear indication of the destructive nature of this sad deception while speaking to a person online, inside of a Christian Facebook forum. This man was defending and promoting ungodly behaviors and lifestyles, all while claiming to be a "Christian". So I gently prodded him, asking him some questions. I wondered how anyone could believe the things he does while calling themselves a follower of Christ. Below is the exact conversation as it took place that day. I had suspicions going in that what I would find was a false profession of faith and a deep misunderstanding of salvation. Unfortunately, I was correct.

We'll call this other man "Bob" in order to protect his true identity.

Me: *"Bob, you said you're a Christian?"*

Bob: *"Yes, I am."*

Me: *"May I ask you a question?"*

Bob: *"Sure."*

Me: *"How did you become a Christian?"*

Bob: *"What do you mean?"*

Me: *"I was just wondering. How does one become a Christian, according to your understanding?"*

Bob: *"What do you want to know?"*

Me: *"I just wanted to know, how did you become a Christian? How did you specifically come by that title?"*

Bob: *"The Bible says you have to believe. I believe."*

Me: *"Believe what? What do you believe that makes you a Christian?"*

Bob: *"I believe that Jesus is part of the Trinity."*

Me: *"Of course. But, even Satan believes that. In fact he knows it, without a doubt. He knows it much more surely than any human does. Does that make you Christian? What else do you believe?"*

Bob: *"That Jesus is God."*

Me: *"Okay, that's good. That's a start, but even Satan and all of his demons believe the same thing. They know it in fact. Is that what makes you a Christian?"*

Bob: *"What are you asking?"*

Me: *I just wanted to know what event, what thing, what circumstance led to you becoming a Christian? How did it happen? At some point, you weren't a Christian, then at some point you became one, what was that catalyst? What happened?"*

Bob: *"I was raised as a Christian and I was baptized."*

Me: *"Okay, let me ask you a question. At any point in your life, did you ever feel like you were a lost sinner? Did you ever come to the realization that you were separated from God because of your sins and that you were bound for hell if you died in that lost condition? Did you ever come to the realization that you needed Jesus to save you from your sins and the consequences thereof?"*

Bob: *"Absolutely not! God made me the way I am and he doesn't make mistakes. Why would I ever feel the way that you described?"*

Me: *"Well, I hate to tell you this Bob, but you're not a Christian. Only a person who believes not only in Jesus as God, but also comes to Jesus with a repentant heart and accepts Him as their personal Lord and Savior gets birthed into the family of God and gets to call themselves a Christian. You must not only believe that Jesus is who the Bible says He is, but that He died on the cross for the remission of your sins. That He rose again on the third day. You must realize that without Jesus, without the realization that you're lost in the first place, you can't receive salvation."*

Bob: *"That's fine. I guess I'm not a Christian by your standards. Just stay away from my civil rights…"*

Unfortunately, this man believed he was a Christian because his parents had him baptized as an infant. He thought being "raised Christian" somehow granted him salvation by transference. However, he rejected the need to come to Jesus in repentance and get born again. The conversation devolved from there into a debate on current social policy issues.

Sadly, these conversations are quite common among those who've been deceived by the "Salvation through Baptism Jesus" and other false means of claiming Christ. The reason that they can so easily take part in, and often promote evil ideas and sin, is because they really aren't saved at all. They've believed in a lie and have been sorely deceived because of it. Unfortunately, in addition to the damage these people do to their own lives, and their own souls, they also cause others to believe that repentance isn't necessary in a Christian's life.

When people see these others who call themselves "Christians" acting just like the people around them, people who're clearly lost (because usually, they themselves are still lost), it causes others to think one of two disturbing things: That all Christians are hypocrites, or that repentance is not a necessary part of Christian life.

Both of these are heinous misconceptions. Neither of these are messages that we want to send to others around us. And both of these things can push others farther and farther away from the Lord.

Sadly, much like "Bob", when confronted with the truth of their lost condition, many people just shrug their shoulders and walk away. You see, "Bob", the very real man from the very real conversation above, happens to be an unrepentant homosexual. One who supports abortion on demand, pornography, transgenderism, and many other ungodly social policy positions.

Instead of being willing to truly come to Jesus with a heart of repentance, he chooses his lifestyle and his sin over Jesus and true salvation. He admitted that he's never come to the knowledge and conviction of being a lost sinner. Without that personal knowledge, without conviction, without acknowledgement of our lost condition, and without repentance, we cannot be saved. "Bob" proudly admitted that he thinks he's okay without God. And that he values his sin above a true relationship with Jesus. He values his ability to engage in counterfeit "marriage" above eternal salvation. And, that my friends is truly a sad, nay heartbreaking, thing to behold.

It's been well over two years now since I had that haunting conversation with "Bob". Nothing with him has changed. He's still online proudly proclaiming himself to be a Christian; although he's still *not* born again. He's still promoting, defending, and encouraging all manner of sinful behavior. He's still unconcerned about the condition of his soul and where he'll spend eternity.

I pray for him and those like him nightly, as we all should. Help me keep "Bob" in our prayers.

■■

The Bible is very clear that there's only one way to obtain the free pardon of sin. Jesus Himself told us the way to obtain salvation. Did Jesus say "get baptized in order to be saved"?

I haven't found that anywhere in the Bible. The Bible does command for us to get baptized *after* or in conjunction with salvation. Baptism is an important part of the believer's life, but the Bible is *clear* that baptism must come only *after* salvation.

How sad would it be to live all of your life believing that the baptism ritual that was performed on you as a child, or even later on in life, granted you salvation…only to find out on judgment day that you've believed in a lie?

You might have lived a life of service to others, and lived the life of a very decent and moral person, only to be cast into Hell because you believed in an empty ritual. I think it'd be safe to assume that the seams of Hell are strained to near bursting with the souls of the people who thought they were saved…only to find out upon death that they've believed in a great deception.

Baptism alone does not save.

It never has and it never will.

Consider this example: The thief on the cross.

The one who openly acknowledged Jesus as Lord. He did not come down from that cross to get baptized, yet Jesus promised him that he'd join Him in Heaven that same day. If only baptism imparted salvation, this statement would've made Jesus a liar. The thief on the cross was never baptized. His salvation was wrought through his faith in Jesus alone.

Luke 23:39-43

> *[39] And one of the malefactors which were hanged railed on him, saying, If thou be Christ, save thyself and us. [40] But the other answering rebuked him, saying, Dost not thou fear God, seeing thou art in the same condemnation? [41] And we indeed justly; for we receive the due reward of our deeds: but this man hath done nothing amiss. [42] And he said unto Jesus, Lord, remember me when thou comest into thy kingdom. [43] **And Jesus said unto him, Verily I say unto thee, Today shalt thou be with me in paradise.***

Consider the story of Zacchaeus for a moment as well. We know that he received salvation. Jesus told us so in the Bible. Yet, we read that Zacchaeus believed, but we don't read anything about him getting baptized. He received salvation by grace through faith and his repentant heart, not through baptism. I'm sure he probably was baptized at some later time, possibly even the same day, but the point is that when we see that he's received salvation, we see it's through faith, not baptism.

Luke 19:5-10 says

> *[5] And when Jesus came to the place, he looked up, and saw him, and said unto him, Zacchaeus, make haste, and come down; for today I must abide at thy house. [6] And he made haste, and came down, and received him joyfully. [7] And when they saw it, they all murmured, saying, That he was gone to be guest with a man that is a sinner. [8] And Zacchaeus stood, and said unto the Lord; Behold, Lord, the half of my goods I give to the poor; and if I have taken any thing from any man by false accusation, I restore him fourfold. [9] **And Jesus said unto him, This day is salvation come to this house, forsomuch as he also is a son of Abraham. [10] For the Son of man is come to seek and to save that which was lost.***

When Jesus proclaims that salvation has come upon Zacchaeus, He didn't say, "After he's been baptized." Jesus indicated that salvation was already there. Present at that time. If Zacchaeus already possessed salvation prior to baptism, how could baptism itself impart salvation?

All we see mentioned in the passage above is the public profession of saving faith by Zacchaeus. His belief in the Lord Jesus Christ, and his change in attitude which exposes his repentant heart. This. This is a picture of salvation in its entirety. A person hears about Jesus. They encounter Jesus (in modern times through the preaching of God's Word). They sincerely believe in Jesus with a repentant heart. They obtain salvation by grace through faith. They change their outlook on life, and the way that they conduct their daily lives because of that repentant heart, and the Holy Spirit living inside it. Baptism should follow shortly after salvation as a sign of obedience to the Lord.

I've stated publically before that if sprinkling water on someone's forehead were all that was required to impart salvation, I'd be carrying a huge bucket of water with me at all times. People would be seen running from the crazy preacher man who chased them with large buckets of water, trying to baptize them! I can only imagine how many times I'd be arrested for "assaulting" people with copious amounts of water.

The salvation of my fellow man is *that* important to me, that if *I* were able to grant it, I would grant it freely and often. The thought of one soul languishing in Hell, is a terrible thought indeed. Fortunately, salvation cannot rest in the hands of, or through the actions of, any mortal man.

God knew what He was doing when He put salvation into the hands of the only person able to grant it with impartiality, and grant it in truth: The Lord Jesus Christ. God knew that if salvation were left in the hands of man, we'd mess it up. Much like we've messed up most of everything else that God's entrusted us with. If man were able to grant salvation with a simple sprinkling of water, or even full immersion water baptism, rest assured, we'd make a terrible mess of that too. Man would use this power for his own good, rather than for the glory of God. Man would be tempted to withhold salvation from his enemies, while gladly bestowing it upon his friends and loved ones. If baptism imparted salvation, mere men would be able to withhold salvation from anyone whom they considered "undesirable".

No, I for one am glad that the precious shed blood of The Lord Jesus Christ is the *only* way by which we can receive salvation. God so wisely kept salvation out of the hands of mortal man. I couldn't be happier about that. It exemplifies what a truly just and glorious creator we serve.

So what does Jesus and the Bible say about the subject of salvation?

Let's take a look at some of the verses below.

> **John 3:16** – *"For God so loved the world, that he gave his only begotten Son, that whosoever believeth in him should not perish, but have everlasting life."*

> **Romans 10:8-10** – *"But what saith it? The word is nigh thee, [even] in thy mouth, and in thy heart: that is, the word of faith, which we preach;* [9] *That if thou shalt confess with thy mouth the Lord Jesus, and shalt believe in thine heart that God hath raised him from the dead, thou shalt be saved.* [10] *For with the heart man believeth unto righteousness; and with the mouth confession is made unto salvation."*

> **Ephesians 2:8-9** – *"For by grace are ye saved through faith; and that not of yourselves: it is the gift of God:* [9] *Not of works, lest any man should boast.*

> **Acts 2:21** – *"And it shall come to pass, that whosoever shall call on the name of the Lord shall be saved."*

> **John 14:6** – *"Jesus saith unto him, I am the way, the truth, and the life: no man cometh unto the Father, but by me."*

Notice that the verse in Ephesians states that no works can save a person? Baptism *is* a work. It's something man can do. Saving faith is the opposite of a work. It's the ultimate act of submission. Of throwing oneself at the feet of the Lord and admitting there's nothing one can do to save themselves. It's a complete trust in the unseen, a complete belief solely in the Lord Jesus Christ and His saving power.

Notice that none of those verses mention baptism?

Please know that I say this with great love and grave concern for the souls of mankind: if you're reading this and you've been baptized, but you've never come to a place where you realized that you needed Jesus, that you were lost in sin without Jesus, and you've never prayed and asked for the forgiveness of your sins through sincere belief and faith in Jesus with a repentant heart, you're likely *not* a Christian. No matter what any parent, friend, preacher, or priest tells you, if you haven't made a conscious and willing choice to surrender to the Lord Jesus Christ by faith, and faith alone, you're *not* saved. You're *not* a Christian. Without a conscious submission and sincere faith, you're just as lost as the worst of all sinners. No amount of baptism, confessional booths, or blessings by a priest will ever change that.

That is, unless you repent and come to Jesus with an open heart. A heart that seeks the Savior with a willingness to change. A desire to walk away from a life of sin and become a child of God. That's a decision we must all make. One that is truly a matter of life and death.

So, are you trusting in baptism alone to save you?

Or are you trusting in the precious shed blood of the Lord Jesus Christ and His amazing grace through faith?

Chapter 6:
The "Good Man, But Only A Man, Jesus"

Here we find another of the most dangerous and deadly counterfeit Jesus characters. He's perhaps one of the most perilous of all to believe in. Or, at the very least, he's right up there, tied for first place with a few other counterfeits.

Why's that?

Because, while believing in many of the other false Jesus characterizations out there might cause you to look foolish; following this false Jesus can land you in directly in Hell. If Jesus was only a man, albeit a very good man and teacher as some claim, then we have no hope of salvation. None at all.

Surprisingly a large number of people who believe in this Jesus actually call themselves Christians. Yes, you read that correctly; a large part of the group of people who call themselves Christians actually reject Jesus as the Risen Savior. They also reject that Jesus is God the Son.

These people justify calling themselves "Christians" because they cherry-pick certain teachings of Jesus and claim that following those certain teachings about "love and kindness" is enough to call themselves Christian. I came upon this specific revelation one day while engaging in an online conversation with a completely deceived woman. Oh, she was pleasant enough, in the beginning. However, being kind, being pleasant, even being generous, doesn't actually allow someone to call themselves by the name of Christ.

Several years ago, while perusing an online article covering the controversy of using "X-Mas" over, and instead of, "Christmas", I encountered a lot of chatter from people claiming to be "proud members of the Christian left". That struck me as very odd. I hadn't known prior to this that there were so many clusters of people who embrace radical leftism and call themselves Christians at the same time. That seems to be pretty much one glaringly huge and obvious oxy-moron. The kind of thing that makes one actually shake their head in wonder.

These people, and their comments about Jesus and Christianity, utterly confounded me. I happen to know that Jesus wouldn't concur with a majority of the ideals that the left holds dear. This caused me to wonder what kind of justification anyone could have for referring to themselves as a "liberal Christian". I sent one of the less aggressive, and more seemingly reasonable online commenters a respectful, private email asking for clarification as to what being a member of the "Christian left" might entail. I was truly curious, but I have to say, I did suspect from the start what I later found out to be true.

The first response that I received was cordial enough. By the time that the conversation was over however, the tone of the lady I corresponded with had changed drastically. I was astonished that anyone could be so thoroughly, and completely, deceived. It served as a very powerful reminder of how effective Satan can be when it comes to his ability to deceive and misdirect the lost. The level and very depth of this woman's deception, along her wholehearted certainty that she's correct in her misconceptions, broke my heart completely. It was a deeply frustrating conversation to say the least. It showed me with startling clarity how deeply Satan can deceive people who're willing to allow him to gain a foothold. So much so that they deny the concrete truths of God...all while claiming to love and follow Jesus.

Below I have included the exact, word for word transcript of this exhaustive online conversation which took place through multiple email exchanges over several days. Bear with me and read through all of these comments. I believe there's an important lesson to be gleaned in these messages.

I've included this conversation in its entirety as part of this book to illustrate how Satan works to blind the minds of those who truly need Jesus the most. I apologize in advance for any grammatical, syntax, or spelling errors on my part. I've left the emails unedited and as they were originally sent nearly ten years ago, grammatical and spelling errors and all.

Beginning Conversation 12/09/2009:

"Hi Bekah and thanks for your input to the forum. I am not trying to be snarky or funny in any way, but I always wondered how it's even really possible to be a member of the "radical Christian left", as you called yourself? The reason I ask is that SO very much that the left stands for is the antithesis of Christ and his teachings.

What about homosexuality, abortion, and other far left issues? These are decidely un-Christian concepts. Is it that liberal Christians don't believe it necessary to "be in God's will"? I think there may be in some people's mind confusion as to what denotes a Christian. Anyone can be a Christian as long as they:

1. *Believe that Jesus is the Son of God*
2. *That He died on the cross for our sins*
3. *That He rose again on the 3rd day*
4. *That you must surrender your life to him*
5. *And that He is coming again.*
6. *And you must believe these things with a repentant heart: willing to turn from your sins.*

*Without these things a person is **not** a Christian. But even after getting saved, there is a mandate to live "in God's will" and to repent and turn away from sin. Voting for politicians who support abortion, gay marriage, and a myriad of other sinful things certainly is not God's will. I think the most disturbing thing to me as a Christian is those who pervert Christianity and preach a false Gospel. Among those people are those that dispute the Bible. Some claim that it was "written by men......" and not the inspired word of God, penned as inspired and dictated by God himself. We were warned of those persons in the Bible:*

**"Beware of false prophets, which come to you in sheep's clothing, but inwardly they are ravening wolves."
Matthew 7:15, KJV**

"For I know this, that after my departing shall grievous wolves enter in among you, not sparing the flock." Acts 20:29, KJV

Today there are many grievous wolves inside the flock. Ever heard of female ministers? This is an anti-Biblical thing. No such thing is allowed. Gay Deacons or Ministers? God help us. Some people are out there preaching that homosexuality is normal or okay....Well... not by the Bible. Today Satan has entered the church and has many "ministers" teaching false and dangerous things. These are "the wolves" mentioned several times in the Bible. After all what better way to take down a religion than to enter it from within, spread lies and deceit, and slowly infect the Word by perverting it? It's a master plan, I must say. And if you are one of those who only chooses to believe in a small portion of the Bible, why stop there? Why not throw the whole thing out? Why even believe in Jesus? I wish you the best in life and I hope you are truly saved. I wish no one to go to hell. Also, I know that I am likely to be called a "hatemonger" and other terms that those on the left like to state, but I have no hate in my heart and I have espoused no hate here, so please let's not go there. I am just worried about the perversion of my faith and seek understanding from those who claim to be Christian, but yet don't live it.

Thanks,
Paul

∎∎∎

(AUTHOR'S NOTE: This "Bekah" and I had already shared several brief online exchange inside of the same Christian discussion forum. I decided that a one-on-one approach might be easier for the free exchange of ideas in a more civilized form, without having to field all of the hateful interjections by other parties inside a public forum. A meaningful two-person conversation is often hard to hold within such forums because of the nonstop interruptions from third parties constantly chiming in.

In typing this message to "Bekah", my sincere goal was to truly try to understand what justification one could have for calling themselves "Christian", yet living in a direction, and supporting political and theological doctrines, that are seemingly the polar opposite of The Lord Jesus Christ and what He taught. It took only a short time to diagnose the real root of her problem: she didn't really know what being a "Christian" meant. She falsely claims Christ, without ever having truly received salvation. She seeks to claim Christ, while openly denying Christ at the same time. Talk about a confusing mess!

Her responses to me were very informative and I'll share them here for purposes of clarification and illustration.)

■■

First Response From "Bekah"

Paul,

The Christian Radical Left is about pacifism, socialist values, love your neighbor, etc. This, as far as I can see, is what Christ taught. The Christians I see are mostly concerned with hating their neighbor if s/he's different in any way. I don't understand how people who call themselves Christians can cut off welfare and illegal immigration, support capital punishment and war, oppose gay marriage, etc. and say they're about anything I would call love, tolerance, forgiveness and so on. That just doesn't sound like anything I would call love.

■■

(AUTHOR'S NOTE: I want you to take note of a few important points right away in regard to this communication. First, she starts off with the false premise that "Christians want to cut off welfare". That's simply another boldfaced lie of the left; one that they've been telling for quite some time. No one, neither private citizen nor politician; Christian or otherwise has *ever* "proposed cutting off welfare". Not anyone. Some Republican politicians have proposed cutting the *rate of growth* of entitlement programs and also rooting out and cutting out the waste, fraud, and abuse which these programs are riddled with. However, that's an argument for another book. It's also not even close to "cutting off welfare".

■■

Secondly, in regard to illegal immigration: illegal immigration causes a great many problems in society. Not least of which are higher crimes rates, increased human trafficking, and increased poverty. While I believe that Jesus would fully support legal, and in extremely rare cases illegal immigration, I can't see that'd He'd be encouraging of the type of mess we see today with those streaming over our borders and the havoc that ensues because of it. Again, a topic better addressed in a different book.

Third, "socialist values" are values that Jesus would absolutely want no part of. He had the chance to advocate for socialism and equal outcomes when He walked the earth, yet He didn't. Socialism, true socialism, actually calls for the denial of a God as part of its core belief system.

Fourth, I noticed right away that she didn't seem concerned with what Jesus or God called love, but rather what she herself deemed as appropriate "love"; meaning an "anything goes" approach to "love". In truth, this is the opposite of what the Bible qualifies as "love". That's very telling!

And fifth, "tolerance", as used in this connotation, to mean the open tolerance of sin, does not appear in the Bible. Not in any form or aspect. Not. Even. Once.

"Tolerance" of sin was never a true characteristic of Jesus.)

■■■

Bekah's first response continued:

Fortunately, I don't believe that's what Christ was talking about. I think I'm in God's will if I'm living the principles set forth in the Bible and taught by Christ (not as taught by the local church classes). Worship is cheap. Christ didn't say anything about homosexuality - Paul MIGHT have - depends on how you read it. If God made a person a homosexual, then that's how he has to be to live "in God's will."

■■■

(AUTHOR'S NOTE: Okay, I've got to address this one here and now. My original plan was to present these emails without commercial interruption, or with as few interruptions by me as possible. I'd planned on presenting the emails in their entirety and then addressing the fallacies in her arguments in one fell swoop. However, as I'm quickly finding out, it may be more effective to address each fallacy as we move along. This point is vitally important. The first part of her last talking point, "*Jesus never said...*" is a pervasive but entirely false argument; and a juvenile one at that. More on this will come later. The second part of her last talking point, "Paul MIGHT have- depends on how you read it", is an absolute, all-out, satanically inspired, blatant lie. There's no way that the writings of Paul could be read as anything but a wholesale condemnation of homosexuality.

For reference, look at Romans 1:26-27

> *26 For this cause God gave them up unto vile affections: for even their women did change the natural use into that which is against nature:*

> *27 And likewise also the men, leaving the natural use of the woman, burned in their lust one toward another; men with men working that which is unseemly, and receiving in themselves that recompence of their error which was meet.*

It is amazingly clear to most people who possess basic reading comprehension skills that homosexuality is indeed the subject at hand in this passage. This passage not only condemns homosexuality, but it clearly condemns male/male homosexuality as well as lesbianism. So, for her to endeavor to cast doubt upon whether Paul said anything about homosexuality, is either outright dishonesty or willful ignorance. These verses are just a few of many penned by Paul (as inspired by God) that reference homosexuality. None of which reference that sin in a positive light.

Her third point, "if God made a person a homosexual..." is also based on another entirely false premise. God *never* "made anyone a homosexual". It never happened. God doesn't make people homosexual and then condemn them because of the way that He made them. It's a lifestyle choice. There's never been any actual science that shows that anyone is born gay. In fact, many studies have proven just the opposite to be true.) (41) (42)

Bekah's first response continued:

Read the Bible and ONLY read the parts which CHRIST said - forget everything you've heard that the Christians say it means. Read it for yourself. You will be amazed. Christ is a messenger of God's love - that's it. God is God and Jesus was his messenger. Am I a Christian if I sincerely try to follow the precepts of Christ, but don't accept him as any kind of personal savior? God was Jesus' God, that's good enough for me - I don't get down and worship the messenger. I try to listen to and follow the directions in the message. Period. But I think you'll say I'm not really a Christian although I think I'm a pretty good one. The above is pretty close to what most Quakers and Unitarians believe. - Do Christians all have to believe exactly the same thing? Are Quakers Christian? Or does their socially active, pacifist tolerance eliminate them?
Bekah

■■■

(AUTHOR'S NOTE: Does reading this email make anyone else's head, as well as their hearts, ache? It makes both my head spin at the same time it makes my heart ache that she's been so utterly deceived. She advises me to read the Bible, and more specifically to read *only* the parts that Jesus spoke…yet she seems to have missed the passages where Jesus proclaimed that there's no other way to Heaven except through Him.
See John 14:6-

[6] Jesus saith unto him, I am the way, the truth, and the life: no man cometh unto the Father, but by me.

Then she goes even further, denying Christ while yet attempting to claim His name. She asks, in a tone of sarcasm, why I wouldn't consider her to be a "Christian".
Could the cognitive dissonance be any stronger?
Oh, boy…

Even all of these years later, my heart still aches just as much for her as when I first participated in this email exchange.

How can anyone be this entirely, completely, devastatingly spiritually blind?

My initial reaction as I read this material over again, for the purpose of writing this chapter, was "Wow, just wow!!" I couldn't believe what I was reading on my screen...for a second time. When I first received these emails, I remember vividly that my mouth was hanging wide open by this point. We're talking literal, jaw-dropping astonishment. The type of reaction usually only seen in Saturday morning cartoons.

To be frank, I half expected a "just kidding" email to follow on the tails of her first message. I honestly thought that maybe she was just trolling me; having a little fun. I waited in anticipation of the "just joshing you" moment that unfortunately never came.

The fact that she actually *believes* what she wrote is so very, utterly, terribly heartbreaking. It's extremely frustrating at the same time. I don't care if this sounds unmanly or not, I actually shed tears for this woman when I reread her responses for the third time.

I must've poured over these emails countless times, believing I had misunderstood or read something into them that wasn't there. I had a very difficult time believing that this was *not* a joke. This one relatively short email exchange contained so much that was incorrect regarding Christianity, Scripture, and the Lord Jesus Christ that it's nearly impossible to process it all in one sitting.

There has to be a hidden joke in there somewhere, right?

In fact, I initially read this message; then I must have reread it over and over again a dozen times or more. I waited for nearly two full days before responding to her. I think I gave it so much time before responding because I really couldn't believe that what I was reading were the thoughts of a rational person.

Could it be true that there're large groups of people out there who really believe this absurd stuff?

Sadly, I've found out in the years that've passed since this exchange that there are indeed millions of people who believe the same inaccurate and blatantly false things she espoused.

Once again we see that word "tolerance" rearing its ugly little head here; as in the ever-so-fictional "tolerant Jesus". We see a misinterpretation of the Biblical definition of "love"; as in her assertion that God's "love" is synonymous with "anything goes". She makes the fallacious argument that allowing social entitlement programs to grow unchecked, allowing them to become more and more costly, year after year, is somehow "love". That allowing these programs to remain fraught with waste, fraud, and abuse is "love". That enslaving people through entitlement programs in exchange for political votes is "love".

I tend to think that true love would entail trying to find a solution to the root causes of poverty. Rather than spending an ever-increasing amount on these programs that do nothing to eliminate poverty each and every year, perhaps we should attempt to alleviate the causes of the problem in the first place? There'll come a point where we can't fund these programs any longer, if the growth of these programs continue at their current rate. Allowing them to crash and burn, thereby harming those who *actually*, truly, need them isn't love. Solving the real causes of poverty would be real love. Attempting to alleviate poverty through better education, better job training, and better opportunities doesn't even seem to cross her mind. Allowing entitlement programs to continue to be abused is "love" in her eyes. Don't even get me started on how it's liberal policies and social outlooks that contribute more to poverty than any other factor. That's material for a different book.

She seems to think that allowing unchecked and unsustainable illegal immigration to continue is "love".

Love for who?

The already overburdened taxpayers who foot the sizable annual bill for illegal immigrants?

How is it "love" to further burden those who're struggling in America?

How's it "love" to reward those who would break the law and enter the US illegally, while those trying to immigrate to America through the proper channels endure long waits and hardships?

How's it love to continue to propagate a group of people living in the shadows, doomed to a life of poverty and welfare dependence because they can't speak the language and possess little to no marketable job skills?

How's it love to support modern day slavery by relegating an entire group of people to jobs in which, by and large, they have no choice but to work in roles serving others? Like gardeners, maids, and handymen.

How's it "love" to allow a minority group to be used as nothing more than disposable pawns in a devious political game?

A game that has the end goal of minting fifteen to twenty million new Democrat voters?

She indicated that she actually believes that standing against the perversion of marriage by allowing gay "marriage" is "un-Christian". (True marriage is outlined and defined in the book of Genesis and was reiterated by Jesus Himself.)

Huh?

I'd love to hear the justification of that one. Oh, wait. No. No, I wouldn't. I've heard all of the false arguments in support of gay "marriage" before; including by those who claim to be "Christian". Jesus wouldn't support such perversion at all.

Also of note is that "Bekah" seems to think the death penalty somehow goes against Christianity. She's wrong. It most certainly doesn't. The death penalty was used during the time of Jesus's ministry here on earth too. He spoke against it not even one time. Not once did He argue to end it. Without the death penalty, there'd be no salvation for us as believers. Jesus was put to death on the cross for the remission of our sins. Without His death and subsequent resurrection, we have no hope of salvation. Jesus Himself was subjected to the death penalty, although He committed no crimes and no sins to warrant that punishment. He did and said nothing to give us an indication that He was against the death penalty for those who commit heinous crimes.

The saddest part of this email exchange, of course, is the mind-boggling denial of Christ as her personal Savior. The vehement denial that Christ is the Son of God; actually God in the flesh. Her assertion that Jesus is nothing but a "messenger of God" means that she *isn't* a Christian...by her own admission. She's rejecting Christ, while claiming to embrace Him at the same time.

Interesting to note is the fact that this woman states that I should read the words of Christ and follow them. She chastises me not to believe what others say about what Christ said, but to follow only what He said in the Bible. Then in the same breath she denies that Christ is God, and denies that Christ is the way to Heaven. However, in His very own words He states that He's the *only* way to Heaven.

Did she miss some of the very words she just asked me to read?

Or is she reading a Bible that has words, and likely entire passages, missing from it?

You know, perhaps she should read those very same words that she encouraged me to read?

If she did, she'd find Christ proclaiming Himself as the only way to Heaven. She'd find Christ proclaiming that He was much more than just a "messenger".

After shaking my head, staring at my monitor in utter disbelief, and after much prayer about the situation with this woman, I felt obligated to respond to her.

Not for the sake of argument.

Not for the sake of being right.

Rather for the sake of her very soul, which is in mortal danger. She'd exhibited that she was lost and hell-bound and I felt a burning need to try to reach her.)

• •

(AUTHOR'S NOTE: My first response back to this lady's astoundingly incorrect and frankly absurd email follows.)

Hi Bekah,

In order to better explain things, I have taken your original text and answered it in blue text.

(AUTHOR'S NOTE: For the purposes of this book, since the blue type won't show up in a printed volume, I've converted my "blue text" answers to a different font for purposes of distinguishing her initial comments from my own responses. My responses to her appear in this font.)

YOU SAID: "The Christian Radical Left is about pacifism, socialist values, love your neighbor, etc."

The Christian "right" is all about pacifism too, but to a point. Sometimes wars are necessary and unavoidable, and one must protect one's country and family.

Socialist values:

Real socialist values are NOT compatible with ANY religious belief, much less Christianity. Socialism sounds good, till you see it in action. Remember the USSR? Over time people under socialism lose any hope and faith and drive to "become something more", no one tries to achieve more than anyone else, because they think "why should I try harder than the next guy when I am not allowed to have anything more than the next guy?" Terry Goodkind wrote a series of fantasy books. One of those in the series is "Faith of The Fallen". You really MUST read it. It deals with a socialist ruler and the havoc he creates while thinking he is the "good guy". It paints an accurate portrayal of Socialism at work.

Love your neighbor?

That is exactly what the Christian "Right" is about.....loving a neighbor however is different from "acceptance", ie. My former neighbor is an alcoholic who beats his wife. I love him and pray for him...do I accept this behavior? NO, I have spoken to him about it and he has threatened me...I also have a homosexual neighbor. I love and pray for him as well. We are friends....but, do I accept his lifestyle choice as legitimate and moral? No. Nothing changes the fact that it is **not** moral or legitimate and nothing changes the fact that I still care deeply for this person. "Love" and "Acceptance of Sin" are 2 different things. While we must Love each other, we are not supposed to "accept" sin as being okay.

YOU SAID: "The Christians I see are mostly concerned with hating their neighbor if s/he's different in any way."

Any Christian who "hates" **anyone** is not in the will of God. But, let's be clear here: Many on the left use the words like "hate" to describe not accepting someone's behavior as normal. Read what I said above. Is that hate? No. So the left tries to use "hate" as a lie and a weapon against those who disagree with them. It's a clever form of censorship. But unless a Christian is actively involved in a real "hate" group or purposely tries to hurt someone else, the "hate" argument is intellectually dishonest at best. Standing up for traditional marriage is not "hate". It's about protecting a Christian value.

YOU SAID: "I don't understand how people who call themselves Christians can cut off welfare and illegal immigration, support capital punishment and war, oppose gay marriage, etc."

"Welfare":

No Christian or Conservative group has EVER tried to cut off welfare. That's an age old Democratic lie that has been perpetrated by them and the media left. When a proposal to **"cut the rate of growth"** of **new welfare recipients** was proposed the left called it a **"cut"**. Once again this is a lie and completely intellectually dishonest. Here's an example of "cutting the rate of growth". Let's say at your job you make $10/hr. And let's say your boss gives you a 10% raise every year. Now this year, times are tough. The boss can only afford 5% as your raise this year. So your pay still went up by 5%. Did the boss cut your pay? No, your pay still increased. So if I said your boss "cut" your pay, that is in effect a lie, is it not? This is the same thing the left does. Now they also left out that the right had proposed to do this by using the other money from the budget to offer free vocational training programs to minorities and those on welfare, spending more money on education in poor minority and poor white communities, etc....Who could be against that? Shouldn't the goal be to give everyone the opportunity make a better life for themselves?

"Illegal immigration":

Most Christians are for LEGAL immigration. I think Jesus would be also. Illegal immigrants break the law and take a lot of money from the American people that they do not deserve. I dated an illegal immigrant for a short time. I spent more than half a year in that Community, I know what goes on. The **illegal** mothers "loan" the social security numbers of their children born here to a **legal** mother (usually one of their friends or sisters who married to become legal) and then they claim **thousands** of dollars in tax refunds (Earned Income Credit) for money they did not earn or pay taxes on! Any way you slice it, that is called **stealing!!** This is a huge and widespread problem in the illegal immigrant community. They also burden the hospitals by going in and getting treatments for minor illnesses that we would see a primary care doctor for. They lie about their identity and since no one can prove who they are, they don't have to pay a dime. The next time they get a cold they go to the hospital and get treated again under a different name and get treated again for free. I was very ill one day and we had to wait hours in the waiting room because the hospital where we were had 20-30 probable illegal immigrants getting seen for minor illnesses. Cold's, flu's, etc. While probably not one of them were paying a dime. They should have been at a primary care facility. They also rip off the American Government in the form of food stamps, etc. I watched 3 days ago as an illegal immigrant let her children mess up the front of a store while they were tearing things up, she never told them to stop. She was arguing with a cashier about using her food stamps for beer. The woman didn't know any English, so it was a long time before she understood. So, she finally buys $200 worth of food (all on the U.S. taxpayer) and then she pulls out a wad of cash (all $100 bills) and pays for the beer. There was at least $3000 there! She should never have been getting food stamps while carrying around that kind of cash. Saying that "illegal immigrants are all hard workers, etc" is partially true. About half are hardworking people, but even many of those use loopholes to rip the government off. Let's use another example. Let's say you come home to find me in your house. I broke in. You are mad at first, but I made you a nice dinner. I cut your grass, I washed your dishes and did your laundry. Okay fine. You decide I can stay for a while. One day, I take money from your purse, not once but over and over again. Then I invite all my friends to come over and do the same. I demand that even though English is your language, you must speak mine. I bring drugs into your house. I lie, steal and cheat, but your grass looks good and your laundry is done. I also bring in diseases that aren't common here. I pay no attention to your house rules and instead strive to create a "house within your house". All the while I am smiling and nodding at you. It's all okay, right? Now I start a gang in your house. What would you say? Should you do something? Or will you continue to let this ride?

"Capital Punishment":

Without capital punishment we would have no redemption. Jesus's death **was** capital punishment. The Bible clearly dictates that appointed Governments do have the right to punish, by death, heinous crimes.

"War":

War always has and always will be an unfortunate part of culture. Jesus spoke of upcoming wars, the Bible even shows where God took sides in wars. David and Goliath? There are many examples of this. The difference is righteous war and war for profit, etc. Righteous war is war defending people. Take the Jews for example. Who could blame anyone for wanting to stop Hitler? How about when 6 Arab countries attacked the Jews? Should Israel not have gone to war to protect itself? How about Muslim extremists bent on taking over and ruling the world while killing all who oppose Islam (this by the way IS what the Koran teaches: beheading non-believers and ambushing/killing Christians and Jews)? War is ugly, but sometimes necessary. History will bear out whether Iraq was necessary. Saddam's own generals say he moved chemical weapons to Syria and a few years ago some Syrian's were caught trying to explode a chemical bomb in Jordan. They stated the weapons came from Saddam's stockpile that was moved to Syria. Saddam is known to have designs on terrorism and a good book called "Saddam: King of Terror" exposes exactly what a terrorist threat this man was.

"Oppose Gay Marriage":

Even the term "gay marriage" amuses me. By definition there can be no such thing. Until it was made "politically correct" several years ago the Webster's dictionary *defined marriage as "The union of a man and woman under God". Now Webster's defines it as "the state of being united to a person of the opposite sex as husband or wife in a consensual and contractual relationship recognized by law". There is no such thing as "Gay Marriage". Now let's look at the Christian aspect of it...Christians MUST oppose gay marriage. Why? First homosexuality IS a sin. Sins are not to be celebrated or recognized as "normal". Second marriage is reserved for man and woman. Third, marriage is a deeply RELIGIOUS concept, that's why most are performed in CHURCHES. All manner of faiths throughout history have deemed marriage as a religious concept. By the government trying to force Christians and people of other faiths to accept "Gay" marriages, they are in DIRECT conflict with the First Amendment because the government is trying to force us to accept something that goes against our religious belief. Imagine if the Government tried to make a Muslim eat a ham sandwich. It's about the same concept.*

■■

(AUTHOR'S NOTE: I provided "Bekah" with the following scripture to back up my marriage arguments. It should also be noted that at the time this book was started that the SCOTUS had not ruled on marriage yet—a ruling that I sincerely believe was arrived at with faulty reasoning, not to mention unconstitutional footing. All those years ago, when these emails were exchanged, I could have never envisioned something like the heinous ruling the court handed down in 2015.)

Genesis 2:24 (KJV)
(24) Therefore shall a man leave his father and his mother, and shall cleave unto his wife: and they shall be one flesh.

I Corinthians 7:2-4 (KJV)
(2) Nevertheless, {to avoid} fornication, let every man have his own wife, and let every woman have her own husband. (3) Let the husband render unto the wife due benevolence: and likewise also the wife unto the husband. (4) The wife hath not power of her own body, but the husband: and likewise also the husband hath not power of his own body, but the wife.

Ephesians 5:22-33 (KJV)
(22) Wives, submit yourselves unto your own husbands, as unto the Lord. (23) For the husband is the head of the wife, even as Christ is the head of the church: and he is the saviour of the body. (24) Therefore as the church is subject unto Christ, so {let} the

wives {be} to their own husbands in every thing. (25) Husbands, love your wives, even as Christ also loved the church, and gave himself for it; (26) That he might sanctify and cleanse it with the washing of water by the word, (27) That he might present it to himself a glorious church, not having spot, or wrinkle, or any such thing; but that it should be holy and without blemish. (28) So ought men to love their wives as their own bodies. He that loveth his wife loveth himself. (29) For no man ever yet hated his own flesh; but nourisheth and cherisheth it, even as the Lord the church: (30) For we are members of his body, of his flesh, and of his bones. (31) For this cause shall a man leave his father and mother, and shall be joined unto his wife, and they two shall be one flesh. (32) This is a great mystery: but I speak concerning Christ and the church. (33) Nevertheless let every one of you in particular so love his wife even as himself; and the wife {see} that she reverence {her} husband.

■■

Continued 1ˢᵗ response to "Bekah":

Now there is also more to the argument. First, you simply cannot change a definition just because YOU want to. You cannot call a book a car, or a horse a dog, or a cat a computer. A book is a book, a horse is a horse, and a cat is a cat. The same as marriage is between a man and a woman. And lastly, we cannot keep mistaking marriage as a "right". There does not exist ANY "right" to marriage in the Constitution or our laws. Marriage is a privilege, much like driving, etc. It is not a right. A privilege. Rights are to all people at all times. Privileges have rules/conditions to be met. Like driving. In most states you must be 16 or older to drive. If you fail to meet that requirement, you can't drive. If you get drunk and drive or have too many accidents, the privilege can be taken away. A ten year old can't drive. Why? They don't meet the conditions for the privilege. Gays cannot marry. Why? They do not meet the definition of the privilege. Why are gay people not happy with civil unions? Most Christians don't have a problem with civil unions that offer the same privileges and protections as marriage. I will tell you why gays insist on calling it "marriage". The radical arm of the gay "rights" movement wants to hurt Christianity. By taking away the sacred marriage. I know this for a fact. I had a friend who attended a rally to hear what was going on years ago. Making it legal for gays to "marry" is like a slap in the face to Christians.

It's the same reason they stole the rainbow for their symbol. The rainbow is a deeply moving CHRISTIAN symbol. I will fight "gay marriage" till death. If it ever passes in my state I will use all my money and possessions to launch lawsuits under the argument of "Separation of Church & State". This is a big issue because in a state that allows these marriages, a Christian Bed and Breakfast retreat was sued because they did not allow a gay "married" couple to stay there. In the rules of the Bed & Breakfast it clearly defines that no unmarried couples can stay in the rooms and that un-Christian like behavior (swearing, drinking, etc) will result in your removal from the property. Since gay marriage and homosexuality is un-Christian like it was a proper grounds for not allowing them to stay. By siding with the gay couple the "very liberal" court allowed the government to "establish a religion" or religious belief because they expect the owner to "accept" gay marriage as proper and moral. This is not true at all.

YOU SAID *"And say they're about anything I would call love, tolerance, forgiveness and so on."*

Conservatives ARE all about love. Loving your neighbor is not the same as accepting everything they do. Did your parents ever discipline you? Does that mean they don't love you? Did they ever tell you that you were wrong? Does that mean they don't love you? I love EVERYONE. That doesn't mean I won't tell them when they are wrong. And telling someone they are wrong is not "judging" them either. The Bible commands Christians to, in a loving way, correct false teachings, and others who are committing sins.

Tolerance?

This is a crock of crap, a made up liberal concept and preached by hypocrites as well. Nowhere in the Bible are Christians commanded to be tolerant of immorality and sin. The liberals using this word as some of the most visceral and intolerant people in the world!

YOU SAID: "I think I'm in God's will if I'm living the principles set forth in the Bible and taught by Christ (not as taught by the local church classes). Worship is cheap."

You can only be in God's will if you are living the principles taught by Christ in the Bible as they appear **in the Bible**. Some churches do get it wrong. Many liberal "churches" today are teaching falsehoods and sometimes all out lies. Incorrect worship is cheap......Biblical Worship is priceless. You cannot be in God's will promoting homosexuality which is taught as a sin both by the New Testament, The Old Testament, Paul and Jesus. You cannot support the killing of unborn children if you are in God's will. Here's what the Bible says about unborn children:

"Thus saith the LORD that made thee, and formed thee from the womb, which will help thee; Fear not, O Jacob, my servant; and thou, Jesurun, whom I have chosen." Isaiah 44:2

There are many other scriptures that refer to God forming the child in the womb. If God formed the child in the womb and life begins at conception, how is abortion not murder? No you can't be in God's will by supporting left wing causes or politicians.

YOU SAID "Christ didn't say anything about homosexuality":

Really? First, this is a really, really, weak argument. Jesus didn't say not to kick my dog when I have a bad day, so should I? Jesus didn't say for men not to rape anyone, so should it be legal? Jesus didn't say don't beat your wife, so should I? Jesus didn't say not to burn my house down with my enemies inside, should I? Should I rob a bank because Jesus didn't say not to? See the point? No, Jesus may not have SPECIFICALLY mentioned homosexuality, but since many, many other places in the Bible calls it a sin, 2 cities were destroyed because of it, and Paul taught against it as well, it can pretty much be said that he meant homosexuality to be included when he preached about righteous behavior and against fornication and sinful behavior.

YOU SAID: "Paul MIGHT have"?

There's no might here, he DID! This from Romans Chapter 1:

*"Because that, when they knew God, they glorified him not as God, neither were thankful; but became vain in their imaginations, and their foolish heart was darkened. [22] **Professing themselves to be wise, they became fools,** (today's liberals?) [23] And changed the glory of the uncorruptible God into an image made like to corruptible man, and to birds, and fourfooted beasts, and creeping things. [24] Wherefore God also gave them up to uncleanness through the **lusts of their own hearts,** to **dishonour their own bodies between themselves:** [25] **Who changed the truth of God into a lie,** and **worshipped and served the creature more than the Creator** (Environmentalists who revere animals and the planet more than God who created them?), who is blessed for ever. Amen. [26] For this cause God gave them up unto vile affections: **for even their women did change the natural use into that which is against nature:** [27] And likewise also the men, leaving the natural use of the woman, burned in their lust one toward another; men with men working that which is unseemly, and receiving in themselves that recompence of their error which was meet.*

(These verses are a direct condemnation of Homosexuality)

[28] And even as they did not like to retain God in their knowledge (Like today's liberals trying to stamp out God from public life?), *God gave them over to a reprobate mind, to do those things which are not convenient;* (This means he gave up on them, because they would not change) *[29] Being filled with all unrighteousness, fornication, wickedness, covetousness, maliciousness; full of envy, murder, debate, deceit, malignity; whisperers,* *[30] Backbiters, haters of God, despiteful, proud, boasters, inventors of evil things, disobedient to parents,* *[31] Without understanding, covenantbreakers, without natural affection, implacable, unmerciful:* *[32] Who knowing the judgment of God, that they which commit such things are worthy of death* (I have seen some liberals misinterpret this and claim it means to kill homosexuals and they say that's what conservatives want, NOT TRUE, this passage means they are worthy of Spiritual Death and Hell), *not only do the same, but have pleasure in them that do them.*

See? Those passages sum it up. Homosexuality IS wrong. And Paul was a direct appointee of Christ and his words and teachings. No other man or woman has Christ appeared to after he ascended to Heaven. Paul would not have been allowed to teach these things if Jesus did not approve.

YOU SAID: "If God made a person a homosexual, then that's how he has to be to live "in God's will."

Here's the problem: God never made anyone a homosexual. This idea comes largely from a crazy move made by Clinton administration scientists. They claimed to be near finding a "homosexual gene". The cry went up premature and people took up the cry of "it's normal" or "you're born that way". Since then science has disproved the "homosexual gene" but people are still claiming "you're born that way". There is simply no proof at all of this. And to make things even funnier, the homosexual movement themselves deny the existence of a "gay" gene. If there was one found it would prove that homosexuality is a birth defect or a disease and therefore should be cured. So it's ironic that the false science that got people to accept homosexuality as "normal" would also prove it as a disease, but it's not normal and if it's a disease, the cause is unknown. **The point is that God would never make a person so that they had no choice but go against his word.** Although homosexuals can become Christian, they would have to give up their old lifestyle and I have seen it happen. When you become a Christian you "become a new creature, old things are passed away".

YOU SAID: *"Read the Bible and ONLY read the parts which CHRIST said - forget everything you've heard that the Christians say it means."*

I do read the Bible daily. I KNOW what it says. It says all that I have said it says above and more. You must read it in its entirety and read the "real" English version that has been around for 350+ years longer than any other, The King James Version.

YOU SAID: *"Read it for yourself."*

Oh I do, I love my Bible!

YOU SAID: *"You will be amazed."*

I am amazed! I am also amazed by what people don't know or try to leave out!

YOU SAID: *"Christ is a messenger of God's love - that's it."*

Wrong, wrong, wrong, wrong, wrong! Christ is God's son, a part of God himself. Yes, he is a messenger of God's love but he is also God in the flesh!

YOU SAID: *"God is God and Jesus was his messenger."*

Wrong, Wrong, Wrong, Wrong, Wrong.....God is God and Jesus is God. Jesus is the only son of God born of a woman and sent here as part of God in the flesh to be the sacrifice for mankind. Jesus was God's messenger, but also part of God himself. Jesus says so himself in the Bible. So do you believe Jesus or not?

YOU SAID: *"Am I a Christian if I sincerely try to follow the precepts of Christ, but don't accept him as any kind of personal savior?"*

No, Jesus himself in many passages proclaimed that He was the ONLY way to Heaven. Here's one:

John 14:6 "Jesus saith unto him, I am the way, the truth, and the life: no man cometh unto the Father, but by me."

*See? Jesus states that **NO ONE** gets to Heaven except through him! Here's another:*

John 10:9 "I am the gate (door); whoever enters through me will be saved. He will come in and go out, and find pasture.

YOU SAID: "God was Jesus' God, that's good enough for me - I don't get down and worship the messenger."

Jesus is God! Jesus is worthy of worship because without him, I and millions of others would be going to hell.

YOU SAID: "I try to listen to and follow the directions in the message. Period."

If you were truly listening to the Bible you will know that Jesus is God and the ONLY way to Heaven!

YOU SAID: "But I think you'll say I'm not really a Christian although I think I'm a pretty good one."

A pretty good person does not get into Heaven. Jesus said so himself. I am sorry to have to point this out but while you may try to live SOME of Jesus's teachings, you can't be a Christian unless you believe in him as your personal savior. That is the definition of "Christian". Look:

Romans 3:23 "For all have sinned, and come short of the glory of God."

Ephesians 2:8 "For by grace are ye saved through faith; and that not of yourselves: it is the gift of God: 9 Not of works, lest any man should boast."

I John 5:11 "And this is the record, that God hath given to us eternal life, and this life is in his Son. 12 He that hath the Son hath life; and he that hath not the Son of God hath not life. 13 These things have I written unto you that believe on the name of the Son of God; that ye may know that ye have eternal life, and that ye may believe on the name of the Son of God."

Romans 10:9 "That if thou shalt confess with thy mouth the Lord Jesus, and shalt believe in thine heart that God hath raised him from the dead, thou shalt be saved. 10 For with the heart man believeth unto righteousness; and with the mouth confession is *made unto salvation. 11 For the scripture saith, Whosoever believeth on him shall not be ashamed. 12 For there is no difference between the Jew and the Greek: for the same Lord over all is rich unto all that call upon him. 13 For whosoever shall call upon the name of the Lord shall be saved."*

Romans 3:23 "For all have sinned, and come short of the glory of God;"

YOU SAID: "The above is pretty close to what most Quakers and Unitarians believe. - Do Christians all have to believe exactly the same thing?"

All Christians must believe in Jesus as their personal savior, otherwise they are not Christian.
See Acts 11:26

"And when he had found him, he brought him unto Antioch. And it came to pass, that a whole year they assembled themselves with the church, and taught much people. And the disciples were called Christians first in Antioch."

See also:

Acts 26:28 "Then Agrippa said unto Paul, Almost thou persuadest me to be a **Christian"**

Persuaded? What does he mean by that? He meant he was ALMOST convinced to believe in Jesus as God's son and Holy sacrifice on the cross.....who needs to be persuaded to just be a good person if that's what Christianity consists of?

YOU SAID: Are Quakers Christian?

Yes, if they believed Jesus. That he was their Savior and Lord. That he died on the cross for their sins and rose again in 3 days to ascend to Heaven and return again one day for His church.

YOU SAID "Or does their socially active, pacifist tolerance eliminate them?"

It's okay to be socially active, but for the RIGHT causes (ie: homelessness, poverty, education, etc.) but not left-wing causes that are sinful or promote sin. Tolerance is a good thing as long as that doesn't mean giving up your morals and accepting homosexuality and other sinful acts as being okay. Love is a much better word. Love the sinner, hate the sin. Teach them the errors of their ways through love. That is not INTOLERANCE. Pacifism has its limits too. Christ taught that it is okay to protect home, the defenseless, and family. A better question is should we allow those bent on destroying anyone not of their religion to gain the means to do so? Did we create the bigger sin by letting Osama's ring of psychos kill thousands of Americans instead of killing him when we had a chance years ago?

Oh and by the way, my research on Quaker beliefs show that they too accepted Christ as personal Lord and Savior, The Son Of God, and his resurrection and impending return. It is only recent and can you believe, left-wing revisionists, that claim the Quakers believed otherwise. So yes, the Quakers were Christian.

Now I challenge. With an open mind read the scriptures....all of them. And the translation does matter. Ask yourself, if conservative Christians are so hateful and awful, why did I spend so much time in prayer and thought over this email? I don't know you. I will probably never meet you in this life. There is only one answer: Love. I can't stand for anyone to go to hell.

I know it may sound crazy but I would gladly give my life to keep one person from having to go to hell and face that kind of punishment. What can bring about that kind of Love? Only Jesus.

Bekah, if you think Christ and His teachings are awesome now, you know nothing yet! When a person gets saved and Christ lives in their heart, it's like nothing you can imagine. It's a joy unspeakable! It can cause you to love your enemies and forget all that's been done against you. It can make the toughest hearts tender.
I want to tell you about myself. In my teens I was a pretty rough character. I cursed like a sailor, drank like a fish, got in fights, and was generally "mean as a rattlesnake" as they say around here. I would get in a fight at the slightest provocation.
One day when I was 20, I visited a church. This was only because someone had invited me. I went to try and impress them and frankly to shock the church with my appearance. I

Paul D. Little

had a Mohawk, a black leather jacket, and a bad attitude. I kept going for a couple of weeks because I thought I was shocking the church just by being there in their midst.

One night something amazing happened. When the preacher was finished preaching he gave the traditional invitation. I went down to the front with tears streaming down my face and confessed that I needed to be saved. The pastor led me through the process and my life was forever changed.

Did I quit all the bad things instantly? No, it took time and a lot of prayer. But 15 years later I am a different man. I am a much more gentile person now. I give to the poor. I take wrapped presents to the children's hospital here on Christmas Eve. I visit the sick. I pray for those who need help. I am a loving husband and a gentle father. I help all those who need it whether they ask for help or not. I have had a drunk man curse me out and I only responded with love. I am completely faithful to my wife even though I've had the chance not to be. I don't curse, smoke, drink or do any drugs.......in fact just a year and a half ago I became a preacher myself.

What could do that to a man? Someone who was so full of hate and anger and emptiness? Only the love of a risen savior could change that kind of heart.

Bekah, I pray that with an open heart you would visit a church that teaches the Bible. The KJV version. The only English Bible that is over 350 years old. It does matter.

If you attend one of these for a day, a week or however long you wish and you feel a "tugging" at your heart when the invitation is given, don't resist it. That's Christ wanting in. Let him and your world will change like you could never imagine.

Even if you think you are happy with your world as it is. The difference is unimaginable!

I pray that you and I will meet in Heaven one day, but for that to happen, you have to accept Jesus's gift of salvation.

I thank you for your responses and I wish you only the best. I do love you.

If you would like any more information please feel free to ask. I am even willing to send you one of the best study Bibles there is, a Schofield KJV Study Bible, if you want it and will use it. These usually cost between $40 and $80. Call it a gift of love. And no we are not rich. We have only enough money to cover the bills most weeks but I would love to buy this for you if you so desire.

Thank you,
Grace and Peace Be Upon You,
In Christ's Holy Name,

Paul

■■

(AUTHOR'S NOTE: This was an exhaustingly long response to Bekah's initial response and I apologize for it. There was a lot of material to cover there. It took me over three days of prayer and writing to come up with the response that I gave her. I tried to be as thorough as possible, touching upon as many of the important issues that she brought up as possible. Sometimes you only get one chance to respond to lost sinners before they block you or shut you out.

Looking back on things, my responses are far, far from perfect. I know that. I also know that what I tried to share with her was done out of love. There was a lot to convey and as an imperfect servant, I tried my best at the time. I've matured much in my walk with Christ since that time and feel I could've done a much better job, looking back.

I also know that I had, and still have, a fierce concern for her very soul. I tried to be as in-depth as I knew how in answering each of the specific points that she brought up. In retrospect, I should've been even more thorough. I should've taken more time with each point and elaborated upon them in more detail. Especially in regard to those things concerning salvation.

Rereading these emails, I can see how some of my answers may have come across as arrogant or rude. Despite that, the intent was good and well-meaning. The basic content of the argument was spiritually and Biblically what she needed to hear. I've learned a lot about how to better present an argument in the nearly ten years since this conversation took place.

Unfortunately, as you'll see later on in this exchange, she continued to reject the truth. She desperately clung to her belief in the "Good Man Jesus". I hope she's still alive. I hope in the years since we corresponded that she's repented and been saved at some point. I might not ever know what became of her in this life. I might not even know what happened to her at all, unless she greets me one day in Heaven. What *is* sure is that if she dies believing as she does in these emails, she won't be there. I recently reached out to her again because I felt led to after rereading these messages.

She did not reply.

With that said, I now present to you her awkward attempt at rebutting my argument.)

■■■

"Bekah's" Second Response:

Paul,

It would be nice if the world were as you painted. I guess I just happen to know a whole bunch of "so-called" Christians who are not in the will of God. (That phrase makes me laugh - my ex-husband is/was a very religious man - he was convinced that his first marriage was not in the will of God.

■■■

(AUTHOR'S NOTE: This is typical of those under a false profession; they attempt to paint others as "lesser" or "so-called" Christians in an attempt to make themselves feel better about their own false claims of salvation. After all, as I said in the introduction of this book, if *her* Jesus and *my* Jesus disagree on nearly all points, one of us has to be following a counterfeit Jesus.

I have to mention the obvious here. She invokes her ex-husband as an example of what she calls a "very religious" person, yet the very fact that he was an obvious adulterer escaped her notice...how? She indicates that she was somehow taken in by him and his hypocrisy, yet by her own admission she knew going into their relationship that he was unrepentant about his adultery.

Dare we surmise that possibly his adultery was with her?

Dare we point out that it's not real surprising that he's now her ex-husband given that he was someone else's husband and then ex-husband before her?

Dare we point out that her marriage to this man makes her an adulteress as well?

And makes her just as guilty as he is of this sin? It makes me wonder how much of her hostility toward Biblical truth is coming from her disdain for her former "religious" spouse. It's possible, even probable, this "very religious man" did the same thing to her that he did to his previous spouse: cheated on and then left her.

In researching great volumes of material for this book, I encountered many of these types of people. What makes them even sadder is that most of the time those who call others "so-called Christians" are those who aren't Christian at all; although they wrongly believe themselves to be so.)

• •

Bekah's continued 2nd response:

> *I asked him what that made their three children - were they outside the "will of God" from birth and were they then automatically going to hell? The poor man didn't quite know how to answer. He loved his kids but as far as he was concerned, they'd been born outside the "will of God."*

• •

(AUTHOR'S NOTE: *I'm not even sure what argument she's trying to make here?*

I certainly never said anything like "if you're outside of the 'will of God' that you'll go to hell". Only rejection of Jesus can cause that predicament. It's the rejection of the Lord Jesus Christ that sends a person to hell. Nothing more. Nothing less.

It seems that her "deeply religious" ex-husband was probably just as profoundly deceived as she was. It's highly likely that while he may have been "deeply religious" that he wasn't a Christian either. Based on both her own comments, and the one that she shared that was allegedly from him, it seems that neither of the two understand God, Jesus, Christianity, or Scripture.

Being outside of "God's Will" is not what condemns someone to hell; rejecting Jesus as the only begotten Son of God and our Lord and risen Savior does that. Being outside of the Will of God won't cause a person to lose salvation if they're saved, but it *will* cause them to lose blessings. It *will* cause them to lose fellowship with the Lord, until such time as they repent and return to the Lord.

Certainly children aren't condemned to hell because of the circumstances of their births. I've never heard anything as patently ridiculous as this. And, if a child is born, that child's life is God's will, no matter the circumstances.)

■■

Continued 2ⁿᵈ response:

Curious why you don't distinguish between the "will of God" and the "perfect will of God" and the "permissible will of God."

■■

(AUTHOR'S NOTE: Again, I have no idea precisely what this person is attempting to convey here.

I've seen a version of this argument before. It goes something like this: God's "perfect will" is what He has planned and in store for us. Then the claim goes on to say that it's also God's "permissive will" that if we stray from the original path God would've had us to take, then He allows certain things to happen to us that weren't part of His original plan. Thus making it also His will, albeit his "permissive" will.

This line of thought seems to me to be not much more than an excuse to justify something like this: 'God's 'perfect will' was for me to marry my wife...but since I cheated on her, it must be God's 'permissive will' for me to be with my new lover, and file for divorce." In other words, this is little more than splitting hairs in order to justify sin.

As far as I know there's only one "will of God" and being that it is of God, if it's His will, it *is* perfect by default. We'd be better off simply seeking God's will every day through Bible reading and prayer. We'd all be better off by leaving the second guessing and splitting of hairs alone. If something we're doing involves sinning, it's not God's will for our lives! At all. Period.)

■■

Continued 2ⁿᵈ response:

I'm really not interested in your religion - I don't care how you try to gloss over the very real fact that Christian right tends to be the leading proponents of war, hatred of gays, racist ideologies and so on. I suggest you separate the healthy socialism of Norway from the Communism dictatorship of Stalin.

Are you aware of the Conservative movement to take the liberal bias out of the Bible? It's true - there's a new translation in the works.

http://conservapedia.com/Conservative_Bible_Project

It must have a few unglossable liberal aspects if the conservatives are changing it like this.

Bekah

∎∎

(AUTHOR'S NOTE: Wow. Even reading this again, all these years later as I write this book, it's still very hard. It still makes my heart ache for this poor, deceived woman. My head also aches with the astounding ignorance contained in this email.

Two quick things I'd like to point out in the latter part of her message:

#1: There happens to be no such thing as "healthy socialism". No country or peoples have ever *truly* thrived on socialism. It's not possible by the very nature of what true socialism entails. Socialism isn't healthy. Socialism destroys. It destroys wealth, it destroys lives, it destroys economies, and it destroys civilizations. While it may carry a shiny veneer of "success" for a short while, socialism almost always implodes from within given enough time.

#2: I think that she clearly missed the point of the link that she provided. She makes the assertion that the Bible must have "liberal biases" in it since there's a group trying to "remove liberal bias" from it. What she seems to have missed is what this group has given as their *reason* for their new "Bible project".

You see, since the early 1970's various groups have been republishing the Bible into "modern English" translations. The problem with this is, and always has been, that some of these outfits have very spurious reasons for doing so. Not the least of which is a strong profit motive. Many newer English translations of the Bible exist solely for the copyright thereof. If a company produces a new translation, they get a copyright and can therefore profit off that translation. Think about it…if you sell only a million copies of your "new English translation", and profit only a dollar for each copy you sell, you're still a millionaire. That's a pretty strong motive for producing a new "translation".

Other motives for retranslating the Bible can be even more nefarious. Take the most well-known and most commonly used of the newer translations of the English Bible, the NIV. Any serious researcher has to question the motivations of the publisher and copyright holder of the NIV Bible.

Why?

Well for starters, it's published by Zondervan.

Why does that matter?

Oh, no reason…except for the fact that Zondervan is owned by the parent company Harper Collins.

Why does this matter?

Because Harper Collins is the premiere publisher of some of the most vitriolic, Anti-American, Anti-Semitic, and Anti-Christian literature available in bookstores today. *How could a new Bible translation that is compiled, copyrighted, and published by one of the most ungodly publishing outfits in the world today, not fall under suspicion?* Not to mention that they actually *own* this version of the Bible. Yes, they are the copyright holders. Let that sink in.

One must also consider all of the verses and Scripture that the NIV, as well as other "modern English" translations, leave out and/or change the meaning of. It's quite appalling when you get deeper into the changes that were made and the effect that these changes can have on the meaning of certain Scriptural verses. But, alas, that's an argument I'll have to tackle in another book because there's so much material to cover there. Entirely too much for this project.

The point is that the argument this woman attempted to make is a completely false argument. She missed the fact that this group she cited was seeking to publish a new "modern English version of the Bible" without all of the liberalism that the other "modern English versions of the Bible" *added* to the original Bible in the first place. Things that weren't there before and shouldn't be there now. That's right. There's *no* liberalism in the Bible. Nothing in the KJV Bible even remotely resembles modern-day political liberalism. Nothing at all.

The compilers of this "new" Bible version *never* alleged that the *original* KJV Bible contained liberalism or even liberal ideas. Quite the opposite. In fact, they make the claim (and rightly so) that all of the other "modern English versions of the Bible" have injected artificial liberalism into the Word, in contrast to the original Scriptures. This new "Bible project" was an attempt to remove the "modern English" liberal bias that never existed prior to the 1970's.

Of course, I still prefer the KJV version. No removal of the added liberal bias is necessary when using this version of the Bible, because no liberal bias existed within it in the first place.

How do you argue with someone who doesn't even understand her own arguments?

How is it that she doesn't even understand the fact that the link she provided as backup for her argument goes against everything she's claiming?

Nevertheless, I still tried, even harder, to reach this woman through further communication.

■■

My Second Response To Bekah Follows:

Bekah,

I can't tell you how much your email saddens me on several fronts.

Yes, there are many "so-called" Christians, some on the right and <u>*most*</u> *of those on the left who claim to be "Christians" without accepting Christ. That's like being a Vegan who only eats meat, it defies logic! You can't be a Vegan who only eats meat and you can't be a Christian, who doesn't believe in Christ.*

The situation with your ex is a shame. Sounds like a very, very confused man. First if he was "in the will of God", he would know that divorce is only sanctioned in the case of infidelity according to the Bible...and then the man and woman are not to remarry unless and until their first spouse dies. So divorcing his first wife was "not in the will of God".

*Children cannot be born "outside the will of God" nor can they be accountable for the Gospel until they reach "the age of accountability", which is different for each child and begins when a child first has the ability to **know** and **understand** that they are actively committing sins (ie: lying, cheating, stealing, cursing, etc). All children who die before reaching this "age" and knowledge of sin absolutely go to Heaven.*

Like I said, he was a confused man. Religious does not equal Christian. Even any new Christian should have been able to supply the answer above to your question.

*As far as "the will of God" goes: There is only **1** will of God. Because it's God's will, it is PERFECT. There is no such thing as a "possible will of God", "maybe will of God", "could be will of God", etc.*

God's will is God's will and because it is the will of a perfect God, then God's will is perfect. Simple. Period.

It's a shame that you aren't interested in "my religion" as you have inaccurately labeled yourself as a member of it.

Your accusations of the "Christian Right" (which is like saying Christian Christian or Apple Apple) are totally false spin based on complete intolerance from the left

Christians do not like war, we simply realize that sometimes it is simply not avoidable. Sometimes you simply must fight. Same as Biblical times. God took sides in wars. Sometimes, unfortunately, Christians must do likewise.

*Hatred of Gays? That's complete and total bull-hockey. The left throws around words like "hate" to silence Christians. While there are a few nutty groups who preach hate, I know THOUSANDS of Christians and not one hates **anyone**. To be against an atrocity such as gay "marriage" is **not** hate. To reject homosexuality as normal is **not** hate.*

Using words like "hate" is a cheap way to try and silence debate on those issues. Plain and simple. It's a very dishonest way to try and bully those who dissent. Bogus argument. And the funny thing? Homosexuals by and large are some of the most hateful, arrogant, and nasty people towards Christians. Like the pot calling the kettle black.

So, telling the truth about homosexuality being a lifestyle choice, not accepting it as anything other than what it is, and preaching the truth as it is written in the Bible is not hate.

Hate is the left calling Christians who love homosexuals and pray for them hateful.

It's even sad, that during this email exchange the only "hatred" seems to come from you. Your response was more than a little terse. After all, I responded to you with only love and got your hate in return.

Racist????? What the heck? I have never, ever, ever heard anyone on the right, Christian or otherwise support any racist policies!

Affirmative Action and other leftist policies are the DEFINITION of racist. After all what is more racist than having race define who gets a job? Or a contract?

The definition of racism is treating someone of another race DIFFERENTLY than someone from your race based on the color of their skin. DIFFERENT means WORSE OR...BETTER. So if you are white and you treat a white person better simply because they are white, then you are a racist. The same thing applies though if you are black and you treat a black person better only because they are black. Racism is racism. Affirmative Action is government sanctioned racism.

Plain and simple, most racism these days comes from the left. The "poverty pimps" like Jesse Jackson and Al Sharpton have done their part to keep racism alive. It's funny when a complete clown like the false "reverend" Jackson calls Clarence Thomas a "house n-gger". No one gets upset. But maybe Jackson needs to understand what that term meant. A "house n-gger" was usually a slave who was treated much better, got to live in the master's house, got to eat better meals, sleep in a bed, etc. His main job was to keep dissent on the plantation down by telling the other slaves things like, "if you just behave, one day you can move into the master's house", and "you have it good here, the slaves down the road get beaten more", and so on and so forth. His job was to keep the other slaves complacent.

So that would make Jesse Jackson a modern day version of the same for the DNC wouldn't it? After all he tells minorities that "you can't make it without the Democrats". So yes there is a lot of racism to this day...mostly originating from Democrats.

Plain and simple there is no such thing as healthy socialism. Doesn't work/failed experiment. Sorry. You really need to read Faith of The Fallen. Besides that, America was never founded to be a socialist country. If that's what you desire, may I suggest you move to one?

Also, the government was never meant to take care of everyone from the cradle to the grave. Even the Bible teaches that if a man won't work for food, then neither should he eat! I guess with Obama in office you will get your wish on socialism.

*I laughed out loud for almost an hour on "taking liberalism out of the Bible". **Liberalism doesn't exist in the Bible!***
Did you know that the only accurate English version of the Bible older than 1970 is the King James Version? In the 70's, marijuana induced "Jesus Freaks" started creating new versions of the Bible to try to add liberalism in.

One of the oldest of the post 1970's Bibles is the NIV...funny the NIV is published by Zondervan...and Zondervan's parent company??? One of the most left-wing liberal anti-Christian, anti-American publishers in the world, Harper Collins! What a riot!

You see all of these "new" versions have become progressively more liberal with each new version. It's downright ridiculous! The NIV, NKJV, ECV, ECB, ASV, NASB, etc, etc, etc,

What comes next the ABC, 123, and OU812 Versions?

■■

(AUTHOR'S NOTE: Sadly since this email was first written in 2009, we've seen America take a huge shift toward socialism, just as I predicted back then. And just as predicted, it's not been a good thing either for our country, our freedoms, or our people. We have also seen several more new "translations" of the Bible in this time. No less than twenty new "Modern English versions" have been published since 2009.

Included in that, I kid you not, is the "Queen James Version"....no, seriously. They took my worst fears in 2009 and literally released a Bible that doesn't even attempt to hide it's mockery of God. It's literally an "LGBTQ-OU812 friendly" Bible. I guess that means that they've removed all the verses that condemn homosexuality. Although, I'd think they'd have to remove an even more substantial chunk of the Bible that deals with repentance and righteous living as well to make it truly "friendly" to these folk.

Thank the Lord, with the election of Donald Trump we have taken out the bridge to the socialist utopia that Barack Obama, Nancy Pelosi, Hillary Clinton, and Harry Reid were driving us toward. Now, America can begin to get back on the road to recovery. In fact, with the successful appointment of Brett Kavanaugh to replace Justice Anthony Kennedy, we've taken a great step towards that recovery.)

■■

My continued response to Bekah:

You see a "conservative" Bible has already existed for almost 400 years and more than 350 years before any liberalism was inserted. While I understand this group wanting to "get rid of Liberalism" in the Bible, all they have to do is pick up a copy of the only "real" English edition that exists.

I personally wouldn't want to be messing with God's word unless he appointed me to, like he did with King James in 1611. After all, you must be careful because God actually states in Revelation that anyone changing or corrupting his word would be destroyed in hell.

So I guess these concepts are liberal?

- *Homosexuality is a horrible sin*
- *Marriage is between man and woman*
- *Premarital sex is a sin*
- *God says "feed the poor" but also states that the poor must be willing to work AND help themselves.*
- *That foul language is wrong.*
- *That abortion is wrong.*
- *That divorce is wrong.*
- *That alcoholism is wrong.*
- *That drug use is wrong.*
- *That remarriage after divorce is wrong.*
- *That lying is wrong.*
- *That BIG government is bad.*
- *That justified capital punishment is okay.*
- *That men adorning themselves as women is wrong.*
- *That women dressing as men is wrong.*
- *That punishing a child "by the rod" or "spanking" as we now call it is the proper form of correcting a child.*
- *That **family** is supposed to help **family** and **neighbor** is supposed to help **neighbor**, and NOT rely on government handouts.*

- *Personal responsibility. You are responsible for your actions and your **inactions**.*

I could go on for hours......where's the liberalism? These are ALL IN THE BIBLE and they are all CONSERVATIVE beliefs. I can't think of one Liberal concept in the Bible.

And the funny thing is that although Liberals bill themselves as caring, loving, accepting, etc, etc, many of them are the most dishonest, hateful, spiteful, angry, Christophobic, greedy, lazy, and just downright mean people on the planet.

Another must read for you: Who Really Cares by Arthur C. Brooks. The author exposes just how much more CONSERVATIVES give to charity and how the actual percent of income given is a MOUNTAIN bigger on the conservative side. Across the entire range of the income spectrum.

So a leftwing nut like Rosie O'Donald might give to charity, but the percentage of her income that she gives is less than half of what my household gives and she makes about 1000 times more than me.

Funny huh? Us horrible Christians give so much more than all of Hollywood combined and yet we make nothing near what they do. So while Liberals have the media (90% off whom are liberals) fooled, we know the score.

So in closing. I hope one day you find true happiness. I hope one day you will become a Christian. I pray one day you will become a Christian.

But for that to happen you have to shut out your hate, open your heart, mind and soul.

Don't be afraid to let Christ have control. Only then will you be a Christian and truly happy.

*Keep in mind one day we will all have to answer to God for our actions here. And now that I have shared the **real** Christ Gospel with you, you are accountable for what you do with it.*

I just pray that come judgment day, I don't have to witness you (and others you have influenced by spreading false Gospels) being thrown into the lake of fire.

I still love and pray for you.

(AUTHOR'S NOTE: Okay, I maybe got a little more fired up in this latest response than I should have. I gave in more than I should have to the frustrating effect of the lies and the mischaracterizations that she kept throwing out there about "conservative Christians"…all while falsely proclaiming herself as a Christian.

Also, it bears pointing out, that at the same time I was responding to her privately, through personal emails, this woman was posting some nasty comments about me on the public forum where I initially encountered her. All because I dared to question what a "liberal Christian" was.

Needless to say, I could've handled things a little better, but with that said, *nothing* I said to her was untrue. Brace yourself for her coming responses. They get more and more terse, and much farther out into the weeds of the liberal, nonsensical, theological/ideological wilderness.)

■■

Bekah's third response:

Paul,

Got all this straight from the Bible, did you? (lol)
-It's blasphemous to worship the messenger.

■■

(AUTHOR'S NOTE: Here we go. When the truth starts getting more and more uncomfortable and their arguments begin to fall flat, liberals and atheists tend to ramp up the condescension, the arrogance, and the anger in their rhetoric. Let's face it, no one wants to be wrong. I've found more and more that telling a liberal that they're wrong is like entering into a den of ravenous lions with a raw steak in each hand. Or repeatedly kicking at a wasp's nest. With each argument you shoot down, they become more and more agitated. The more truth you drop on them, the angrier they get. It's not unusual for a simple confrontation with someone on the left to end in angry words, or even

Paul D. Little

foul language and personal attacks on their part. You can be sure that you won't walk away unscathed or unscarred when you argue with a liberal.

■■■

My third response to "Bekah":

Bekah,

__Everything__ I have said regarding Jesus comes __straight__ from the Bible!
I have never seen anything you've said in the Bible, but I have seen numerous times where Jesus himself states the only way to Heaven is through Him.
The apostles and disciples as well as all Biblical teachings herald Jesus as the Messiah and only way to Heaven.
Jesus is to be worshipped because __He is God__ and the __ONLY__ way to get to Heaven is through him.

Love and peace
Paul

■■

Bekah's fourth response:

Paul,

People who believe what Christ said and pray as he taught us to pray are not Christians? Okay fine. Only those who agree with your sect are Christians? (lol)

"you shall have no other gods before me" (Exodus 20.3, Deuteronomy 5.7, Exodus 34.14)

237

There is one god - his name is Abba.
Bekah

■■■

(AUTHOR'S NOTE: Again, you see the depth to which this woman is deceived and her confusion on Scripture. On the one hand she claims that she *believes* what Christ said, while in the next breath, she *denies* what Christ said about His own Divinity.

Why is it that she claims to believe and practice—in her own mind—what Jesus taught about love and kindness, while at the same time she's rejecting what He taught about Himself as being the only begotten Son of God?

How can she ignore what He said about being part of God Himself?

How can she claim to follow Jesus, when Jesus Himself said there's no way to Heaven other than through Him?

How can she reject what Jesus said about salvation and yet claim salvation at the same time?

One need look no further than the example of this poor woman to see how adept Satan is when it comes to deceiving humans. When I think about "Bekah", I can't help but think about Eve in the Garden. You see, it's not that this woman is *intentionally* evil. Quite the opposite. Much like Eve in the Garden, she's been *deceived*. Yet, she's just as guilty of sin as Eve was.

Being deceived by Satan is not an excuse for sin.

Why?

Because we have the Word of God. We have a way to *know* the truth, but we must seek the truth out in the Word of God. If Eve had heeded God's Word, she wouldn't have been deceived in the first place. Likewise if this "Bekah" would heed God's Word, she wouldn't be deceived like she is either.

Much like Eve was beguiled by Satan all those years ago into eating the fruit of the forbidden tree, this woman has been deceived by the prince of darkness too. All the while Eve ate the fruit, she was denying the consequences thereof. This woman is likewise rejecting Christ, all the while denying the consequences thereof. In both cases, Eve and this woman denied the Word of God and sought to follow their own selfish and foolish hearts. In both cases, the consequences of denying God's Word and seeking their own way are dire; as they are for *all* of us who do the same.

If this woman doesn't get saved at some point, she will be cast into the lake of fire, there to spend eternity dwelling upon her rebellion.

■■

My fourth response to "Bekah":

Bekah,

Do you really believe in what Christ said? Really? In full? Or just part of it?

If you really believe in what Christ said, you would believe that he is the only Son of God born of a woman, the Messiah and the key to Eternal Salvation.

Jesus saith unto him, "I am the way, the truth, and the life: no man cometh unto the Father, but by me."

Those *are* Jesus's words. These are too:

"I am the door. If anyone enters by Me, he will be saved, and will go in and find pasture ... I have come that they may have life, and that they may have it more abundantly."

"Jesus said to her, I am the resurrection and the life, he who believes in Me, though he may die, he shall live. And whoever lives and believes in Me shall never die."

"Then Jesus spoke to them again, saying, I am the light of the world. He who follows Me shall not walk in darkness, but have the light of life."

"And Jesus said to them, I am the bread of life. He who comes to Me shall never hunger and he who believes in Me shall never thirst."

"I am the living bread which came down from heaven. If anyone eats of this bread, he will live forever; and the bread that I shall give is My flesh, which I shall give for the life of the world."

Who Stole Jesus

"Therefore I said to you that you will die in your sins; for if you do not believe that I am He, you will die in your sins."

"And we have seen and testify that the Father has sent the Son as Savior of the world. Whoever confesses that Jesus is the Son of God, God abides in him, and he in God."

Seems pretty clear who Jesus taught that he was and how He laid out what to do in order to get to Heaven.

So do you believe in what Christ said? And if you don't believe in what Christ said how can you pray like Christ said? God only answers the prayers of the redeemed in Christ's blood.

No if you don't accept Christ, you are not Christian, plain and simple.

My sect? Sect? There's no such thing as a sect of Christianity. There is Christianity as taught by Jesus and non-Christianity as practiced by people like you. It's admirable that you follow SOME of Christ's teachings and misguidedly try to reconcile homosexuality with Christian life (although that's very wrongheaded), but you are not a Christian.

What you believe in can only be called a "cult", since MOST professing Christians believe the Bible on Christ.

See the definition below:

*A **Christian** (pronounced /ˈkrɪstʃən/) is a person who adheres to Christianity, an Abrahamic, monotheistic, religion based on the life and teachings of Jesus of Nazareth, who Christians believe was the Messiah (the Christ in Greek-derived terminology) prophesied in the Old Testament/Hebrew Bible, and the Son of God.*

***YOU SAID**: "you shall have no other gods before me (Exodus 20.3, Deuteronomy 5.7, Exodus 34.14)"*

Exactly. Jesus is GOD. There is no conflict there. Jesus stated so himself. And by the way while you are partially correct, God is called many names in the Bible itself, Yahweh for instance, the Alpha and The Omega, Jehovah, etc.

Jesus is God.

Funny, you can quote Scripture when it suites you, but you seem to ignore those that state homosexuality is an abomination, that Jesus is God and the only way to Heaven and all those other things you disagree with.

240

The Bible even states that Satan can even quote the scriptures to fit his purposes.

The real problem here is that Satan has infiltrated Christianity by having people spread the false Gospel that doesn't lead anywhere but to hell.

Christianity is the belief as Jesus the Savior. There is no way around that.

Much like a car cannot be a boat, or a house cannot be a duck, or a book cannot be an airplane, Christianity without Christ as Savior cannot be Christianity. You might as well be a Buddhist or some other religion that teaches goodness, without a living God. Christ is the only living and risen Savior.

Much like I cannot put a yarmulke on my head and take the Torah and discard 75% of it and say that I only believe 1/4 of it and call myself Jewish, you simply cannot be a Christian without accepting Christ.

THE BELIEF THAT CHRIST WAS SENT HERE BY GOD TO SERVE AS A SACRIFICE FOR OUR SINS AND THAT HE DIED AND WAS RESURRECTED AS A LIVING SAVIOR, THAT HE IS THE SON OF GOD AND PART OF GOD HIMSELF, AND THAT HE IS COMING AGAIN TO RECEIVE HIS FOLLOWERS IS THE DEFINITION OF CHRISTIAN.

*It's not my belief, my desire, my want, my "sect", it's the **truth!***

So if you believe that you can take a cardboard cutout of a car and convince yourself that it IS a real working car, then keep telling yourself you are a Christian. It's about the same. But calling oneself a Christian doesn't get you to Heaven.

Only Jesus can do that.

••

(AUTHOR'S NOTE: Again, I realize I let my passions run a little too loose in this response. By this time, her condescension and smarminess had gotten to me. The online attacks she was posting against me had rattled me more than a little. I'd have handled things a little differently today. Bear in mind this email exchange occurred nearly ten years ago. As we go further, her responses become even more hateful, as did her online campaign against me in an open forum.)

••

Who Stole Jesus

"Bekah's" fifth response:

Paul,

Do you consider the Quakers to be Christians? There are some who use the Bible and Jesus pretty literally - (although never legalistically) and there are others who seek guidance from Bible and Jesus, but use personal revelation as the real source of spiritual healing. Their views are very, very similar to mine - pacifist, tolerant, love oriented. I was a Quaker for a long time - I still am mostly, except there are no suitable (silent) meetings here (that I've found). Universalist Unitarians are pretty good, too.

Open your mind, look them up: http://www.uua.org/ (all religions are worth using in our mutual search for Truth) "Jesus [gives us] the strength to fight, the courage to love, and hearts that do not give up on anyone." http://orangecountyquakers.org/quakers/seekers/faq.htm

Robert Barclay, a founder, said that the Scriptures are only a declaration of the source and not the source itself. (Similar to don't worship the messenger.)

My sister is a lesbian and a nephew is gay and I love the heck out of them. My sister is retired from her career now but she's VOLUNTARILY working for peace and truth by helping some nuns restore their retreat. She and I believe that it's about loving your neighbor. After that she's looking at volunteer work for similar spiritually oriented situations. (Habitat for Humanity, etc). I'll be retiring in about a year and I look forward to volunteer work with a spiritually based group somewhere - (Quaker schools maybe).

Peace,
Bekah
There is one god - his name is Abba

● ●

(AUTHOR'S NOTE: *Okay, folks. Are you beginning to diagnose the problem here?* She's admitting that she's seeking to find a "religion"…and a *Jesus* that conforms to her worldview and her own image rather than conforming herself to Christ and *His* image. She

242

speaks of Universalist Unitarians as a great form of "Christian" ideology, yet, their beliefs aren't Christian at all.

This is a quote directly from the Universalist Unitarian website about their beliefs:

"Unitarian Universalism affirms and promotes seven Principles, grounded in the humanistic teachings of the world's religions. Our spirituality is unbounded, drawing from scripture and science, nature and philosophy, personal experience and ancient tradition as described in our six Sources." (43)

Pay attention to that folks. They admit that their teachings are "humanist"...not Christian. They also admit that they've cobbled together their beliefs from multiple "world religions", cherry-picking from each of these religions only the teachings that they wish to apply to themselves. Kind of like a "Piccadilly Café" of religiosity and theological dogma.

Furthermore, if you look at their stated "six sources" of beliefs, you see that they aren't founded on Christ at all. The only "source" that comes from the Bible is the fourth bullet point. Even then, they don't realize that in order to truly "love our neighbor as ourselves" we must first have Christ living in our hearts. Otherwise such love isn't possible because it's the Holy Spirit indwelling within us which allows us to truly become capable of such depths of love for others.

Here are their aforementioned "six sources", again taken directly from their website:

- Direct experience of that transcending mystery and wonder, affirmed in all cultures, which moves us to a renewal of the spirit and an openness to the forces which create and uphold life;
- Words and deeds of prophetic women and men which challenge us to confront powers and structures of evil with justice, compassion, and the transforming power of love;
- Wisdom from the world's religions which inspires us in our ethical and spiritual life;
- Jewish and Christian teachings which call us to respond to God's love by loving our neighbors as ourselves;

- Humanist teachings which counsel us to heed the guidance of reason and the results of science, and warn us against idolatries of the mind and spirit;
- Spiritual teachings of Earth-centered traditions which celebrate the sacred circle of life and instruct us to live in harmony with the rhythms of nature.

Utter. Theological. Garbage.

While some of their teachings sound nice, fuzzy, and warm, I can guarantee you that if this is all your spiritual life consists of, you'll never see a day of Heaven. This isn't a "new" religion, it's just a new take on the same old misguided, and satanically inspired, misconception that if "I'm a good person, God will let me into Heaven". I don't doubt that many of these followers, and even "Bekah" herself are "good people" by the standards of the world. However, the world doesn't get to decide who enters Heaven. God does…and if you don't meet *His* standard you won't ever enter therein.

Notice her emphasis on works?

Notice that she states that she's close to retirement and plans on focusing on charitable **works***?*

That's great. Charitable works and other good works are a good thing. Christians should have works that reflect their salvation. Works are an important part of a believer's life. However, the Bible is clear that works alone will *never* impart salvation. It's not possible.

We can't work our way into Heaven, no matter how hard we might try.)

■■■

My fifth response to "Bekah":

Bekah.

As I said before, if Quakers accept Jesus as their personal Lord and Savior, then yes they are Christians.

Based on my research and this taken from QUAKERINFO.COM, then yes they believed Jesus as God and Personal Lord and Savior, so yes, that would mean that they are in fact Christian.

From quakerinfo.com:

> ***1.*** *William Penn stoutly defended Quakers against the accusation that they deny Christ to be God. He called this charge "a most untrue and unreasonable censure," and, citing John 1:9 and 8:12, declared that the "great and characteristic principle" of the Quakers is, that Christ as the Divine Word enlightens everyone." Penn also defended Quakers against the accusation that they deny the human nature of Christ. "We never taught, said, or held so gross a thing," wrote Penn, who further affirmed the manhood of Christ Jesus--"of the seed of Abraham and David after the flesh and therefore truly and properly man, like us in all things, and once subject to all things for our sakes, sin only excepted." (The Key, sections VI and VII)*
> ***2.*** *The Bible authentically defines the person and work of Christ.* ***Robert Barclay*** *stated it plainly: "We believe that everything which is recorded in the holy scriptures concerning the birth, life, miracles, suffering, resurrection, and ascension of Christ actually happened."* ***(Apology***, *Proposition 5, xv, Freiday Edition p. 88. See also Proposition 3 on Scripture). To get a feel for how Barclay actually drew upon Scriptures as the "true and faithful record" one only has to scan the pages of his Catechism. An example:*
> > *"Q. Was Jesus Christ really crucified and raised again?*
> > *A. For I delivered unto you first of all, that which I also received, how that Christ died for our sins, according to the scriptures: and that he was buried, and that he rose again the third day, according to the scriptures. I Cor. 15. 3, 4." (Philadelphia, n.d., 16).*

*The Bible was **meant** to be taken literally, Bekah. It is God's Word. His whole Word, perfect in every way.*

I agree with you. Conservative Christianity is about love, pacifism within reason, and reaching out to others. This word "tolerance" is misused. You should not be tolerant of sin, but rather pray for the sinner and try to use the Word to bring them into God's circle.

*I am not seeking truth, I **know** the truth. Jesus Christ is God. Jesus Christ is the truth.*

This Robert Barclay is sadly mistaken about some things. This is evidenced by the Scriptures themselves: **"In the beginning was the Word, and the Word was with God, and the Word was God."**

This passage is alluding to Jesus being one and the same with Scripture and GOD!

"All Scripture is given by inspiration of God, and is profitable for doctrine, for reproof, for correction, for instruction in righteousness, that the man of God may be complete, thoroughly equipped for every good work." 2 Timothy 3:16-17

"And **the Word became flesh and dwelt among us***, and we beheld His glory, the glory as of the only begotten of the Father, full of grace and truth." John 1:14*

THE TRUTH IS THAT JESUS IS GOD. NO ONE GETS TO HEAVEN WITHOUT ACCEPTING HIM AS LORD AND SAVIOR, PLAIN AND SIMPLE.

No one has ever asked you not to love your sister or nephew. I have an alcoholic person in my family and I love him too.

You should **not** *however, support their lifestyle as valid, Godly, or acceptable in God's eyes. It's not. Neither is my family member's alcoholism.*

Both are **choices***, nothing else. Love them, pray for them, and witness to them, but tell them the* **TRUTH as God sees it***. They are sinning and they are LOST. Volunteering is good. I am not impressed with nuns, because there is a lot about Catholicism that is wrong, but helping someone is always good. Although you* <u>cannot</u> *get to Heaven by good works.*

If your sister is seeking truth and light, she needs to seek the <u>**REAL**</u> *Christ who is God. He will fill that void.*

The only true spiritual organizations are those who have their roots in the REAL Christ.

Christ is the fulfillment of the Word, He is the messiah, He is God.

Jesus was beaten, bruised, tortured, humiliated, and hung on a cross to die for your sins and mine. He rose again 3 days later and ascended to Heaven with a promise to return for us. And he did all this voluntarily because he is God!

He is God and he is coming again. Will you be with us when we go to Heaven?

Or, will Jesus say, "Bekah you have done some good things, however, you rejected me and I never knew you"?

Will you go to Heaven or Hell?

The Bible says that based on your current rejection of Christ, you will go to Hell.

I hope not Bekah. I have lain in bed, unable to sleep at night from worry over you. I pray honestly and fervently that you will accept Jesus and that I will see you one day in Heaven.

Please at least let me send you something and read it. Show some of that tolerance that you mentioned. It might just change your life forever in a good way.

Grace and Peace and Love

Paul,

PS. God has many names and Jesus is one of them!

• •

"Bekah's" sixth response:

Paul, you think Quakers hate gays? You think they believe the same thing you do? I don't think so - not from what you've said.

http://www.religioustolerance.org/hom_quak.htm

I guess if you say I'm not a Christian then I'm not a Christian - right? Okay fine - I still believe in what I believe Christ said - how he told us to live. I believe that the Lord's prayer is the most perfect prayer there ever was and I use it daily. I believe that God is still speaking to people through their hearts and consciences. I believe that there are more ways to God than through Jesus - I happen to have been chosen differently and I said yes to God.

I'm done with this conversation, Paul –
Peace,
Bekah

• •

(AUTHOR'S NOTE: *Isn't is sad how the conversation kept getting distorted?*

I don't think anywhere in this entire conversation I expressed any hatred toward anyone, gay or otherwise, but people who share this woman's viewpoint often misuse the term "hate". It's an odious attempt to try to silence those with differing opinions. I never once cited "hating homosexuals" as a prerequisite for Christianity. In fact, I was quite clear, I believe, that hating anyone is not Christian at all.

*Notice, by the way, how during this conversation it's **she** who ramps up the negativity, all while accusing me of being the person exhibiting hate?*

With each progressing email, as she loses more and more ground on her fallacious arguments, her rhetoric gets increasingly nastier in tone. In the gaps between responding to me each time, she engaged in posting nasty stuff about me in the online forum where we first engaged. Fueled on by her supporters, she continued to double down on her harsh rhetoric.

There's so much wrong with her arguments that I do believe I could write an entire book just based on her responses to my emails alone. Anyone with even a basic understanding of Christianity, Jesus, the Bible, and God can see the glaring holes in her statements and claims.

Notice at the end she claims that "there are more ways to God than through Jesus"?

Yet, she claims to follow Jesus's teachings, even though Jesus Himself said that He is the **only** way to God?

Then she boldly claims to have *"said yes to God"*!

How?

By rejecting Him?

Also of note is this line: *"I still believe in what I believe Christ said"*...Therein lies the root of her problem. Read that again. In truth, she does **not** believe in what Christ said...she believes in what <u>she believes Christ said</u>. She didn't say she believes in what Jesus actually said; only that she has faith in *her* belief and her personal interpretation thereof. She has faith in herself, that she's correctly interpreting what Jesus said, even though she's largely ignoring the *bulk* of what Jesus said. And, frankly it's hard to see how someone could purposefully

248

"misinterpret" much of what Jesus said which was strictly literal, and so straightforward that even elementary school children can understand it.

This is why she's so wrong. She's allowed *self* to get in the way of *truth*. That's always a dangerous error.)

■■■

My sixth response to "Bekah":

Bekah,

This will be my last email.
Please put the Kool-aid down!!! You keep mentioning this false notion that anyone, anywhere, said anything about hating gays!
Did you even read what I wrote? No one said anything about hating gays, except you. You simply are regurgitating that old and frankly stupid Liberal line about anyone who does not accept the lie of homosexuality being "normal" equals hate.
No one mentioned hate. I have over and over mentioned loving homosexuals while hating the SIN of homosexuality. Two very different things.
You are just either intellectually dishonest or you have no argument so you use the age old "hate" defense.
Quite pitiful actually.
True Quakers embrace the Bible. I am sure there are non-Believing Liberal offshoots, but LIBERALISM and the Holy Bible are completely and totally incompatible.
It's not whether I say you are a Christian or not. It's what you said.
You said you are not a Christian by your admission that you don't accept Jesus as your personal Lord and Savior.
How much more simple can I put this? The Bible says you are not a Christian unless you believe in the Lord Jesus Christ as your personal Lord and Savior. Simple as that.
Since you don't meet the requirements to be a Christian (the belief in Jesus as put forth in the Bible) then you can't be a Christian. I want to be a millionaire but I'm not. Why? Because to be a millionaire you must have at least a million dollars and I don't. See?
Just like you can't be a football player unless you play football or a police officer unless you are a police officer. You can't simple call

*yourself a police officer because you follow **some** laws. You must in fact **BE** a police officer to be a police officer.*

*The Lord's Prayer **is** the most perfect prayer, but God's **not** hearing your voice! Why? Because you have not repented, prayed to, and accepted Jesus and the free pardon of sin **first**.*

God does speak to hearts and minds. You know what he's saying? He's saying "Accept my Son Jesus Christ because He's the ONLY way to Heaven".

*I am so sorry you are LOST. I have provided example after example of Jesus in His own words asking you, pleading with you to accept him. I have provided example after example of **DIRECT** Bible quotes that state that Jesus is the **ONLY** way to Heaven, many coming from Jesus's own words.*

*Still you insist on throwing the "hate" word around and picking and choosing what **YOU** want to believe from the Bible instead of what is **IN** the Bible.*

*I am so sorry. I tried to throw you a lifeline. You have been fed a line of bull by puppets of Satan and now you are doomed to eternal death and hell if you don't find your way out by accepting Jesus. There is **NO** other way.*

I only hope that those who have convinced you to sell your soul for a lie burn a little hotter and face more anguish in their fire than you do in yours.

Again....Grace Peace and Love.

Paul

If you ever change your mind about obtaining salvation please let me know. Until then...

●●

(AUTHOR'S NOTE: Yes, I once again became more than a little impassioned in my above response. That much is clear. I admit, I was more than just a little rude in this response. I was more than a little frustrated at this point, both by her fundamental misunderstandings and deception regarding salvation, and her dishonesty in calling my disdain for the sin of homosexuality "hate". In between this email and the last, she'd also posted online that she was sure that I beat my wife and abused alcohol. Both of those are lies that couldn't be further from the truth. I deeply regret that nine years ago, I let my frustration come out as much as I did. I was a much younger Christian then. I shouldn't have let her angry rhetoric, name-calling, arrogance, and ignorance get to me. These days, I have better discernment to know these attacks for what they are: pushback because of Holy Ghost conviction. I'd handle this much differently today. Possibly by simply walking away, as at this point, I was pretty much casting my pearls before the swine.)

■■■

"Bekah's" seventh response:

Paul,

You want some intellectual honesty?
I'm an alcoholic - I sobered up almost 30 years ago (August 1980), slipped in December 1981 and have not had a drink or any kind of "substance" since. I did that in AA.
I prayed and prayed and that's where God sent me. In Step 3 I turned my life and my will over to God as I understood / understand him. I went to God - not Jesus.
I prayed to God - not Jesus. I still go to God, not Jesus. I will always go to God, not Jesus.
This is how I found sobriety, peace, love, and freedom. I'm not about to change horses.
You're quite wrong about liberal Christianity. It's about inclusion not exclusion - like Paul included gentiles.
Bekah

■■■

(AUTHOR'S NOTE: Again, this poor lady is confusing modern liberal political ideology with Christianity. By her own admission and her stated beliefs, or rather the lack thereof, she's not a Christian. She still doesn't get that without accepting Jesus, she's not truly "hearing" from God, even though she thinks she is. The Bible is very clear that God does not hear the prayers of those lost in sin. The only prayer He'll hear from a lost sinner is a pleading cry for mercy and forgiveness. Then, and only then, once they've submitted to Him, will

He answer their other prayers. Sometimes Satan can convince the lost that they're "hearing from God", when in fact, nothing could be further from the truth. If she were really hearing from God, what she would've heard is "Seek my Son."

Also worth mentioning is that she claimed "like Paul included the Gentiles". It wasn't Paul who included the Gentiles. It was the Lord Jesus Christ who did so after the Jews rejected Him. Paul didn't have the authority or power to preach anything other than what the Lord gave him to preach.)

∎∎

My seventh response to "Bekah":

Bekah,

I am truly happy for you regarding your sobriety.
*But without Jesus there is **NO** inclusion.*
Paul taught that because the Jews rejected Jesus and the gentiles accepted Jesus they obtained Salvation. And, he taught that because GOD wanted him to. God is the one who "included" the gentiles, not Paul himself.
*Accepting Jesus is not "changing horses" as Jesus **IS** God.*
Accepting Jesus means becoming a Christian and getting Salvation and going to Heaven.
*God may have gotten you through the hard times so that **we** could have this conversation and you could learn about accepting Jesus. Did you ever think about that? That this may be part of God's plan for you?*
The thing is, with your passion I really believe God could use you, if you accepted Jesus.
*Liberal Christianity would be better defined as Anti-Christianity since it is primarily contrary to what Christ taught, while claiming that it **is** what Christ taught.*
The Anti-Christ will be using much of the same rhetoric and much of the same deceit as the teachers of Liberal Christianity. The stage is being set for the coming of the Anti-Christ by Liberal Christianity.

*One thing for sure, Anti-Christianity and the people deceived by it **are** here.*

Paul

■■■

(AUTHOR'S NOTE: I truly hope that this woman went on to find true salvation in Jesus. What I said was truth. People like herself often have the most inspiring testimonies when they do, if they do, eventually get saved. Some of the most profound and powerful testimonies I've ever heard comes from those who were the most deeply lost in their sins, before Jesus found them and set them free. With her passion, she could possibly reach a lot of people for Christ. I pray God will reveal Himself to her and that she'll repent and allow herself to be used of God.)

■■■

"Bekah's" eighth response:

Paul,

I obviously connected to God (as I understand him) without Jesus. I'm not too concerned with heaven – I suspect that God is God over Jesus and that GOD's Grace - (HIS GRACE ALONE) will do whatever it needs to without my even believing in God. This is because GOD IS GOD. (See orthodox Lutheranism - By Grace Alone are we saved was Luther's primary principle.) Amazing Grace is an incredible song –

If Jesus is God (and I have a BIG problem with that one) why didn't we all die when he did on the cross? Did God die?

I believe God is using me now. I believe he has been using me for almost 30 years in helping other alkies to recover from a really bad disease. I think if I left God at this point and said that Jesus was God - omg - it would be traitorous blasphemy.

I say the Lord's Prayer (why would Jesus bother praying to God - and he prayed to God several times - if Jesus was God?)

And I also love these prayers:

Who Stole Jesus

Prayer of Saint Francis of Assisi

Lord, make me an instrument of your peace.
Where there is hatred, let me sow love;
where there is injury,pardon;
where there is doubt, faith;
where there is despair, hope;
where there is darkness, light;
and where there is sadness, joy.

****

O Divine Master, grant that I may not so much seek
to be consoled as to console;
to be understood as to understand;
to be loved as to love.
For it is in giving that we receive;
it is in pardoning that we are pardoned;
and it is in dying that we are born to eternal life. Amen

***

3rd Step Prayer of AA

God, I offer myself to Thee-
To build with me
and to do with me as Thou wilt.
Relieve me of the bondage of self,
that I may better do Thy will.
Take away my difficulties,
that victory over them may bear witness
to those I would help of Thy Power,
Thy Love, and Thy Way of life.
May I do Thy will always!

Paul D. Little

AA's 7th Step Prayer

My Creator, I am now willing that you should have all of me, good and bad. I pray that you now remove from me every single defect of character which stands in the way of my usefulness to You and my fellows. Grant me strength as, I go from here to do your bidding.

****

I go to God - the Big Guy - Abba, as Jesus called him - I find refuge, peace, and love. I found and have kept sobriety. If that's not enough for me I've got some problems.

I'll tell you what, Paul - when GOD tells me to go and worship Jesus - I probably will. (Somehow it seems highly unlikely that God would tell me to go worship Jesus). But Jesus telling me to worship Jesus doesn't quite cut it. I will listen to the message of Jesus as long as it's not about him telling me that the only way to God is through him.

Matthew 22:36-40 (New International Version)
36 "Teacher, which is the greatest commandment in the Law?" 37 Jesus replied: "Love the Lord your God with all your heart and with all your soul and with all your mind. 38 This is the first and greatest commandment. 39 And the second is like it: 'Love your neighbor as yourself.' 40 All the Law and the Prophets hang on these two commandments."

Imo, you have a lot of nerve questioning my religion and spirituality.

Bekah

■■

(AUTHOR NOTE: Okay, what you see here is something that's typical of when you delve deeper into the matter of salvation with those who aren't saved. Specifically those who claim salvation, yet don't possess it. Anger is their go-to response. She doesn't want to hear

255

about true salvation because that might mean she has to give up some of the sins that she enjoys.

Remember how this conversation began?

She admonished *me* to read the words of Jesus.

Now, she's admitting that she only considers the words of Jesus to be valid *if* those particular words fit her agenda and her personal belief system. If not, she's fine with picking and choosing what she wants to believe.

As for the prayers that she mentions in her latest message, I don't even get what relevance they have to this conversation?

There are many boilerplate prayers out there, some to "gods" I can't even begin to pronounce. Yet, as flowery and poetically pleasing as some prayers may be, if they aren't prayers to God, the only true God, then they might as well not be said at all.

The only prayer that we're given word for word in the Bible is the Lord's Prayer. None of the other prayers that she invoked appear in the Bible. When we pray, instead of the vain repetition of the manufactured prayers of long-dead sinners, we need to pray from our hearts. We should speak to God from what's inside us, not from the memorized, ritualistic prayers of the spiritually dead. The Lord's Prayer was given to us as an example of how we should pray. Prayer should be something that's intensely personal between us and God. We're speaking to our Father in Heaven. Right before Jesus referenced The Lord's Prayer, He warned against the sort of prayers that "Bekah" favors. (44)

You wouldn't call your mother, father, sister, brother, son, daughter, or other loved one on the phone with a pre-scripted, generic conversation would you?

Then why would we pray to our Heavenly Father with a pre-scripted, cookie-cutter, disingenuous prayer?—The Lord's Prayer is not meant to be included in this rhetorical question.)

■■■

"Bekah's" Ninth Response (note, this response followed immediately on the heels of her eighth response, with no response from me in between them):

Paul - you're wasting your time. I was raised a Lutheran. My parents and grandparents and great grandparents were devout Lutherans since the 1600s. Not only were/are they Lutheran but it's they were liberal Lutherans. Please do NOT write to me again - I will not read it I will not reply. Again - DO NOT POST ME AGAIN!

Bekah

∙∙

(AUTHOR'S NOTE: Okay. Perhaps I really should've stopped here, allowing her the final word. (Which also seems to be a common denominator with the lost, they always want to get in the final word.) In truth, I should've given up days prior to when I finally did. I did in fact walk away for a few days after this last round of messages. I really, really, wanted to walk away completely, sooner, but I remained deeply torn. I felt such loss over this woman. Just knowing that if she died soon, that she'd die lost, was a heavy burden on my soul. It was clear from her messages and online comments that she was likely in her mid-to-late sixties. With the average life expectancy for women in the US being eighty-five, I felt a sincere need to continue to try to reach her for Christ. To attempt to at least help plant a seed that maybe God would one day water.

Again, as a younger Christian, I should've done what I *would* do now. The Bible teaches us at some point we have to stop "casting our pearls before the swine", meaning at some point, it becomes a fruitless venture to continue on in discussion with an obstinate, and unrepentant lost sinner. I probably shouldn't have responded further, but instead should've continued to bring this woman before the Lord in prayer, and let Him do the rest.

She's been in my prayers since the first day I encountered her, and there she will remain until I either learn that she's passed on, or until I do so myself.

My eighth response to Bekah:

Bekah,

You may think you are "connected" with God, but His word disagrees:

"For all have sinned and come short of the glory of God."

God is Jesus. Jesus is God.
No one gets to Heaven without Jesus. It's a shame you are not concerned about Heaven.
*God **could** allow you to go there, but you rejected His son that He gave so that you could be washed of your sin and be redeemed:*

__John 3:16__ "For God so loved the world, that he gave his only begotten Son, that whosoever believeth in him should not perish, but have everlasting life."
KJV (the only accurate translation).

*Funny you should mention the Lutheran's, since they have things **COMPLETELY** wrong in most cases.*
*Amazing Grace **is** an incredible song. The author was a much hated slave trader and all around not very nice fellow. He wrote the song **after** accepting Jesus as Lord and Savior.*

"Amazing Grace how sweet the sound that __saved__ a wretch like me..."

*Note that word __saved__. **Saved** means saved by belief in the Lord Jesus Christ. Saved is the word uses to mean accepting The Lord Jesus Christ. I was saved in 1991. Saved means born again.*

*"I once was **lost** but now I'm found. Was **blind** but now I see..."*

*Note the word **lost**. **Lost** is the term to mean those who have not accepted Jesus and are going to hell. Also note the word **blind**. **Blind** refers to those who have not opened their eyes to the truth of Jesus. Spiritual blindness. The author was stating that he was blind to the truth but now he acknowledges Jesus as God's Son and his Savior.*

See what I mean?

Jesus is God. Have you never heard of the Holy Trinity?

God the Father, God the Son, and the Holy Ghost?

When God caused Mary to become pregnant with Jesus, he literally took part of himself and created the baby Jesus. Thus Jesus is God.

Second, when Jesus gave his life on the cross he literally died, and was resurrected in three days as prophesy proclaimed he would be.

Upon ascending to Heaven Jesus told the disciples that God would send "the great comforter" the Holy Spirit to come to earth to be with man.

So no God did not die on the cross. But a piece of himself, Jesus Christ did. And no Jesus is not dead. He is very much alive and coming again soon.

When He comes "every knee will bow and every tongue will confess that Jesus Christ is Lord".

On judgment day in Heaven, an account of your entire life will be read. The good and the bad. Every deed, every word. You will give an account of. When you have finished giving your account to God, you will face his judgment. The penalty of sin is death. Have you ever sinned? Ever lied? Anything? If so, you are guilty and the penalty is spiritual and everlasting death.

But, if you are redeemed by Jesus, ALL of your sins are removed, washed away and forgiven. Jesus will stand and claim you as His and you will enjoy everlasting life, with no pain, no heartache and no tears.....ever!

If Jesus proclaims "I never knew you", you will be cast into the lake of fire. Many a religious person resides there now. All those who reject Jesus reside there now.

You said God is using you.

*Someone is using you. But it's not God. Satan is using you to help spread **his** gospel. Look at this passage taken **DIRECTLY** from the Bible:*

2nd Corinthians 11: 3 But I fear, lest by any means, as the serpent beguiled Eve through his subtilty, so your minds should be corrupted from the simplicity that is in Christ. 4 For if he that cometh preacheth another Jesus, whom we have not preached, or if ye receive another spirit, which ye have not received, or another gospel, which ye have not accepted, ye might well bear with him. KJV

and

2nd Corinthians 11: 13 For such are false apostles, deceitful workers, transforming themselves into the apostles of Christ. 14 And no marvel; for Satan himself is transformed into an angel of light. 15 Therefore it is no great thing if his ministers also be transformed as the ministers of righteousness; whose end shall be according to their works. KJV

Take note that even Satan can do seemingly kind and benevolent works in order to confuse and corrupt would be Christians.
Isn't it funny that we are having a conversation about the false liberal "Christians" when the Bible warned us about them nearly 2000 years ago?

No one has asked you to "leave" God. Only to accept his Son as the sacrifice He intended Him to be. Traitorous? Hardly since God COMMANDS it.
It is in fact traitorous not to accept Christ. I can imagine God now saying "Bekah, I brought you through your alcoholism, your pain, and your sickness, only to have you reject my offer of eternal Salvation".
Those preaching "liberal Christianity" are Satan's ministers as mentioned in the Bible.
Regarding The Lord's Prayer: Why is it called The Lord's Prayer, if Jesus was not the Lord???? It was Jesus's prayer to God the Father, not God's prayer, hence it's called THE LORD'S PRAYER after the Lord Jesus Christ.

You said: Prayer of Saint Francis of Assisi:

I don't know this person. I do know that he's not in the Bible. Not sure the relevance here, but it is a nice prayer, although I hear just as nice prayers every Sunday and Wednesday by regular church goers.

It's funny. In all those other prayers asking for eternal life and freedom from bondage, that is exactly what the Bible teaches that Jesus was sent to deliver, if you accept him.

All it takes is a simple prayer, if spoken with a truly repentant heart, and true belief in who and what the Bible proclaims Jesus is:

> *"Lord please forgive me, a sinner. I know I have sinned and come short of the glory of God. Lord I believe that Jesus Christ is your Son and that he died on the cross for my sins and rose again as he said he would. I confess all to you now and ask your forgiveness. I ask Jesus to live in my heart and for the Eternal Life promised in your word. Amen."*

Simple as that this prayer or one like it, when asked with a believing heart changes live FOREVER!

I am glad you beat alcoholism, but you do have a BIG problem. That's going to Hell one day. Sure you can put that problem away for now, but what would happen if you died 5 minutes ago? You would be in torment already.

As I proved before God has many names used in the Bible and Jesus called him by more than one. The Bible also tells us that NO ONE will be able to utter the true name of God until we are in Heaven.

GOD DID TELL YOU TO WORSHIP JESUS. IT'S OVER AND OVER AGAIN IS HIS WORD, THE BIBLE.

It's funny, you as much as admitted that you pick and choose what teachings of Jesus you will follow, but you claim to follow him? After all more than half of what Jesus teaches is about Salvation and worshiping Him.

Let's compare some Scripture using your quoted verses first:

> **(Matthew 22:36-40 (New International Version)**
> *36- "Teacher, which is the greatest commandment in the Law?" 37 Jesus replied: "Love the Lord your God with all your heart and with all your soul and with all your mind. 38 This is the first and greatest commandment. 39 And the second is like it: 'Love*

your neighbor as yourself. 40 All the Law and the Prophets hang on these two commandments.")

(Same verse. (KJV version)

36- Master, *which is the great commandment in the law? 37 Jesus said unto him, Thou shalt love the Lord thy God with all thy heart, and with all thy soul, and with all thy mind. 38 This is the first and great commandment. 39 And the second is like unto it, Thou shalt love thy neighbour as thyself. 40 On these two commandments hang all the law and the prophets.*

Notice a difference? In the non-Liberal 400 year old translation the speaker recognized Jesus as MASTER AND LORD!
In the 1970's Liberalized version MASTER has been changed to incorrect "teacher" which changes the verse drastically.
We have no disagreement on this subject, except that Jesus is God. Recognizing Jesus as Lord and Savior does not conflict with these teachings at all.
Also it's funny you neglected to look at the beginning of the very same chapter you quoted:

1 And Jesus answered and spake unto them again by parables, and said, 2 The kingdom of heaven is like unto a certain king, which made a marriage for his son, 3 And sent forth his servants to call them that were bidden to the wedding: and they would not come. 4 Again, he sent forth other servants, saying, Tell them which are bidden, Behold, I have prepared my dinner: my oxen and my fatlings are killed, and all things are ready: come unto the marriage. 5 But they made light of it, and went their ways, one to his farm, another to his merchandise: 6 And the remnant took his servants, and entreated them spitefully, and slew them. 7 But when the king heard thereof, he was wroth: and he sent forth his armies, and destroyed those murderers, and burned up their city. 8 Then saith he to his servants, The wedding is ready, but they which *were bidden were not worthy. **9** Go ye therefore into the highways, and as many as ye shall find, bid to the marriage. **10** So those servants went out into the highways, and gathered together all as many as they found, both bad and good: and the wedding was furnished with guests. **KJV***

The wedding parable is the parable of Jesus. He was sent first to the Jews (the wedding guests), the wedding was Heaven. God was saying "come, accept Jesus and come to be in Heaven". The Jews instead balked. And balked, and balked. Not only did they balk, they were responsible for the death of Jesus (the servants). In his anger God condemns those who refuse to believe to hell (burned up their city). God then sent His Word out to "gather" the gentiles to Heaven. So whoever accepts Jesus (the wedding invitation) will go to Heaven. So Heaven will be filled by those who accept God's invitation to the wedding in the form of Jesus.

I suggest you read and reread those verses above.

And as I said before Christianity, real Christianity is ALL about love. That's why we pray for sinners, homosexuals, etc. It's about love.

Which would you call love?

If I knew you were hooked on drugs and I teamed up with your family to intervene, or if I just let you kill yourself with the drugs? Which is love?

Same thing with homosexuality and other sins. By not accepting the sins and lovingly pointing the way to truth, that is love. Allowing someone to die in their sin without trying to help is NOT love.

***YOU SAID:** "Imo, you have a lot of nerve questioning my religion and spirituality."*

Do you remember how this thread started?

Well, Bekah, IMO, it takes a lot of nerve to mock and degrade my religion and my Savior by falsely claiming to be Christian and spreading false teachings and all out lies and misquoting scripture thereby helping to lead many people to hell.

The Bible so accurately warned of false teachers, false doctrine and those deceived by them. This was predicted over 2000 years ago.

I hope one day you will be able to sing Amazing Grace and KNOW what the author knew when he wrote it. One day maybe you can say "Amazing Grace how sweet the sound that saved a wretch like me. I once was lost but now I'm found, was blind but now I see".

I was a lost wretch at one time, but not anymore.

I likewise, much like you, fought and fought against the truth until one day God revealed it so clearly I had no choice but to accept Jesus.

I have tried to sow the seeds of God's word. I can only hope that one day God waters it and it takes root in you.

As I said before I will rejoice like no other should you get saved.

I will cry tears of joy for you, if that day comes. As it is, my spirit cries tears for you now.

Remember "religion" and works don't get you to Heaven. Only Jesus, and his precious shed blood can do that.

Peace and Love,
Paul

■■■

(AUTHOR'S NOTE: I really tried to throw it all out there at this point in a last ditch attempt to truly help this woman.

As the old saying goes, "You can lead a horse to water, but you can't make him drink." I tried to lead her to the living water that is the Lord Jesus Christ; sadly she refused to drink thereof.

I am saddened to this day by the thought of her dying lost in her sins. What a terrible price to pay for the sins of this life. I tried to reach out to her again recently to no avail.

My one regret as I reread through my responses to "Bekah" is that I let myself show too much emotion. That my words were tinged with too much "self" in my responses. I can't undo that now. But I have learned from it since then.)

■■■

"Bekah's" tenth response:

DO NOT POST ME AGAIN!

Bekah

■■■

That, unfortunately, was the end of our conversation.

I granted her wish and refrained from responding to her again. I knew at this point that there was nothing more I could say that would reach her hardened heart.

Sad, isn't it?

During the course of this discussion this woman used probably ever justification known to man to keep from accepting the Lord Jesus Christ. She was determined, fiercely so, to hold onto her false theology and her sins.

She misquoted Scripture.

She said she believed in Jesus's teachings…only to deny His most important words and teachings.

She denied the deity of Christ.

She denied that she needs to be saved.

She hinted that she believes that everyone goes to Heaven by God's Grace alone, without Jesus, without repentance, without anything else necessary. Kind of an "auto-salvation" plan, which begs the question, if God were just going to "auto-save" everyone, why did Jesus need to sacrifice Himself on the cross in the first place?

Why would God cause Jesus to be born, and allow Him to suffer and die on the cross if His shed blood wasn't necessary to get us into Heaven?

That seems rather sadistic to me. Definitely not the kind of God I'd want to worship.

She's accepted the false doctrines, the false prayers, and the posturing of man over the Word of God. She's deemed herself as a good and "godly" person. She's boasted of her works and her good deeds. She's deemed herself worthy of Heaven by her works alone.

She even touts *Amazing Grace* as her one of her favorite songs, yet she fails to recognize the entirely profound message of that simple song. She fails to see that it's about a man accepting Jesus Christ as his personal savior, receiving salvation, and receiving the blessings thereof.

Talk about deceived!

She doesn't even recognize that the very words of this song she claims to adore are crying out for her to accept Jesus into her heart!

This woman who seems, from what I can tell, to be possibly a quite decent person by the standards of man, is going to burn in an everlasting torment. Not because she was the worst person in the world. Not because she's inherently evil or awful; I believe she might be as nice as many Christians are. Not because she's done really horrible things by human standards alone. Not because she's necessarily committed awful or unforgiveable crimes.

No, the reason that she'll meet her eternal doom and damnation is because she refuses to believe the simple *truth* of who Jesus is. She refuses to accept the free pardon of sin offered by Grace through Faith in the Lord Jesus Christ.

When I think about "Bekah", I can't help but be reminded of the Biblical parable of Lazarus and the rich man that Jesus gave. When the rich man dies, he goes to eternal torment in Hell. As he's writhing in pain and anguish, suffering an unquenchable thirst, he looks up and sees Lazarus being comforted by Abraham. The rich man then asks for Abraham to send Lazarus to cool his tongue with a single drop of water. Abraham responds by telling the rich man that there's a great gulf fixed between the two places and that no one may pass in either direction. The rich man then beseeches Abraham to send Lazarus back from the dead to speak with his relatives; to try to keep them from sharing in his fate. Abraham declines because, just like himself, the rich man's family has already rejected the prophets of God. They likely wouldn't believe the testimony of a resurrected Lazarus either.

What a sad and horrible place for someone to be. I think one of the most torturous parts of Hell must be to be forever looking upward, seeing your neighbors and loved ones sharing in the glorious Kingdom of God and the bountiful beauty and riches thereof…only to know you'll never experience that joy. The pain of seeing your loved ones in Heaven, but knowing you'll never be part of their lives again. Part of the torture of Hell is the pain of knowing and seeing that your loved ones are walking with Jesus; while you're eternally separated from His presence. Part of the agony of an existence in Hell is that you no longer have any access to God. Your life will consist of nothing but darkness, misery, and pain.

I can't imagine how sad that existence might be. Aside from the physical pain, the emotional and spiritual pain would be immense. Think about the worst state of depression you've ever suffered. Or the worst time of your life. Now, imagine that darkness and depression increased a thousand-fold, with excruciating physical pain thrown on top of that.

Not a situation I'd want to end up in.

Nor would I wish that upon anyone else.

■■■

So many people are confused and deceived by this false "Just a Good Man Jesus" who Bekah believes in. *On one hand, it seems like a good thing to believe in, right?*

I mean, trying to follow Jesus's teachings on how to treat our fellow man *is* a noble goal. You can't really go wrong following any of the teachings of Jesus. The issue with that approach is this: You can't just follow Jesus's teachings on helping the poor and loving your fellow man. That won't get you to Heaven.

If you're truly going to call yourself a Christian, moreover if you want to receive salvation, you must follow *all* of the teachings of Christ, including those which are most important. Those wherein He tells us that He's the *only* way to Heaven and that no man comes to the Father except by and through Him.

So many people call themselves Christian today, but they haven't met the one all-important requirement for actually becoming a true Christian: the repentance of sin and acceptance Jesus Christ as the risen Savior.

If that one all-important ingredient is missing, or if Jesus was just a "good man" to you, I can promise you this: you may be a good person yourself, but you're going to miss out on going to Heaven.

Chapter 7:
"Long-Haired Jesus"

This is one the fake Jesus that a lot of people, including many of the truly redeemed in Christ, will have a problem letting go of. The "Long-Haired Jesus" is everywhere you look. I see His face in memes, profile pictures, or posts nearly every time I log into Facebook. It seems like there's always someone posting, or sharing, a meme or an article that features this man. He's literally nearly everywhere you go.

Now, while this false Jesus persona isn't personally dangerous per se, that doesn't change the fact that He's still an imposter. Not all of the counterfeit Jesus characters are inherently dangerous for one to believe in; this one is relatively benign in comparison to some of the others. Still, if we want to know more about the true Jesus of the Bible, this is one imposter we must examine as well.

I bet all of us have been inside of a church or two at some point that's featured at least one painting of the glowing, radiantly handsome, bronze-skinned man with long, flowing locks. This man who's supposed to be a representation of the real Jesus. I just attended an event at a Bible believing, Bible preaching church last week…and I was deeply disappointed to see that it had such a rendering of "Jesus" inside its walls.

So, what's the problem with this graven image you might ask?

Well, it's pretty simple really…It's not a Biblically accurate portrayal of our Lord and Savior. In fact, this representation of Jesus clearly goes against the image of Jesus that we're given in the Bible. I'll go so far as to call the "long-haired Jesus" anti-Biblical in fact. A graven image is exactly what this image is.

Now, I know, I know. No one alive today has seen Jesus in person and we don't have any photographs or reliable portraits that were painted *at the time* when He walked among us to go by. I've got that. Understood.

So, how then do we have any clue as to what the real Jesus might have looked like?

Easy.

We can turn to the same place we should always turn *first* when we have a question about any subject like this: the Holy Word of God: The Bible.

Okay, so let's break this argument down.

Where does it say anything about Jesus's hair in the Bible you ask?

Well, nowhere exactly. That is, if you're looking for a *direct* statement. Something to the effect of, "Jesus didn't have long hair." Or, "Jesus wore his hair short and close-cropped". You won't find that in the Bible; but, what you *will* find is Scripture that allows us to make an educated inference into what His appearance might have been like.

For example, let's take a look at 1st Corinthians 11:14 which states:

> *"Doth not even nature itself teach you, that, if a man have long hair, it is a shame unto him?"*

That should be pretty clear for everyone. But still, when shown this Bible verse, many people still balk at giving up their preconceived notion of Jesus with long, flowing hair. So, now we need to further examine this passage, and specifically a key word in it: *shame.*

We have to ask ourselves this question:

What's the root cause of shame?

Shame, not to be confused with *embarrassment* (which can be caused by non-sinful situations), is almost always caused by one thing and one thing only: sin. Given that shame comes only from sin, you could easily, and *correctly*, read the above passage as God saying that it's a *sin* for a man to have long hair.

Let's look at a practical example of the differences in the word *shame* versus the word *embarrassment*.

Let's say you're walking through a crowded hallway. You trip and fall down because someone left something lying on the floor. You'll probably end up very *embarrassed* by your public fall. Especially if there are people you know who witnessed your mishap. But you won't be *ashamed* of falling...because you did nothing wrong. You did nothing to be ashamed of. Accidents happen.

However, let's say you're walking down that same crowded hallway, except this time you're drunk and stumbling. You trip, stumble, and fall down. You try to get up, only to fall again. You'll likely be very embarrassed. You'll likely also be very ashamed as well. The following day, you end up issuing apologies to those who witnessed your falling down drunken behavior.

Why the difference?

Because in the first scenario, your fall had nothing to do with your own actions. In the second scenario, your sin of getting drunk was what led to your fall; therefore the sin of drunkenness leads to shame. While falling in a crowded hallway will be embarrassing to anyone for a few moments; the shame of having a crowd seeing you fall down in a drunken stupor will last much longer.

See the difference in the two scenarios?

Where sin is present, shame is usually present also.

Now, we all know that Jesus was the only person to ever walk in the flesh who was completely free from sin. Jesus did not sin. Not. Even. Once. Neither in thought, nor in deed, did He commit sin. That's something that no one else, living or dead, can lay claim to.

The root cause of shame, and the fact that Jesus never sinned, is a very important distinction to this argument. *Why?* Because, if long hair on a man causes the man shame (most likely because it's a sin), and we know that our Savior never sinned, we should be able to infer that He would *not* have had long hair. He wouldn't have done something that would have brought shame upon Himself.

Almost always when I discuss this issue with a believer or group of believers, I'll get questions like *"Well, what about Samson?"* or *"What about the Nazarites?"* These are valid questions. I'll be glad to provide the answers here for you...to the best of my ability.

Let's look at Nazarites first.

A Nazarite was a devout Jewish man who took a *voluntary* vow unto the Lord. This vow was customarily limited to a very specific length of time that the person undertaking the vow chose for themselves (usually thirty days or longer). During the time period covered by their vow, a Nazarite would adhere to the following very strict rules:

- They must abstain from wine, wine vinegar, grapes, raisins, intoxicating liquors, vinegar made from such substances, and eating or drinking any substance that contains any trace of grapes.
- They must refrain from cutting the hair on one's head; allowing the locks of the head's hair to grow unabated.
- They must make sure not to become ritually impure by contact with corpses or graves, even those of family members.

After following these requirements for the designated interval of time (which would be specified in the individual's vow), the Nazarite would immerse in a mikveh (a bath used for ritual immersion in water) and make three offerings: a lamb as a burnt offering (*olah*), an ewe as a sin-offering (*hatat*), and a ram as a peace offering (*shelamim*), in addition to a basket of unleavened bread, grain offerings and drink offerings, which accompanied the peace offering. They would shave their heads in the outer courtyard of the Temple (the Jerusalem Temple) and then place this hair on the same fire as the peace offering. (45) (46)

As you can see, there were very specific rules surrounding the Nazarites and their strict customs. If you know your Bible at all, you know that Jesus broke the first and third rules for a Jew under a Nazarite vow for sure. In the Bible we see that Jesus resurrected more than one person from the dead. Doing so would have been a direct conflict…had He been a Nazarite. He would have broken the Nazarite vow by doing so…and breaking a vow to God *is* a sin. He would've become a sinner and He would've thereby been unable to become a suitable sacrifice for the remission of the sins of man.

We also see that He turned the water into wine at the wedding. (Albeit, *not* alcoholic wine as we know it today.) This also would have been forbidden for a Nazarite. Contact with grapes would have resulted in a sin committed; the breaking of a vow to God.

We also see that by the Nazarite customs, there was a *beginning* and an *end* point to allowing one's hair to grow. People weren't walking around Jerusalem looking like hippies with long hair, day in and day out, year after year. Once their vow began, the Nazarite stopped the regular practice of cutting their hair. Once their vow was over, they would cut their hair short again, as was the custom of the Jewish people. Even if He had been a Nazarite (and He wasn't), Jesus wouldn't have been walking around with long hair for years on end. Certainly not for the three years of His active ministry and travels.

There's also much confusion between a *Nazarite* and a *Nazarene*. Jesus was a *Nazarene,* as in a Jew from the town of Nazareth. There's a big difference in these two words, and people often get these two distinct words and their meanings mixed up. A Nazarene is someone native to, or residing in, the city of Nazareth. A Nazarite is a Jewish man under a self-imposed vow to God. While you *could* have a person who happened to be both a Nazarene and a Nazarite at the same time, Jesus wasn't one of those for the reasons described above.

We're at a point in this discussion where a little history comes into play. Jesus was a Nazarene, born to parents who were citizens of Nazareth. We know that historically, the men among the people in this region wore their hair cut short, almost in the close cropped style of a Roman soldier. So, in addition to the fact that it would've been a sin for Jesus to have had long hair, it would've also been very out of place within the community where He lived and grew up.

No let's examine one more thing regarding this matter. I provided the Scripture, 1 Corinthians 11:14 which states that if a man has long hair it's a shame unto himself. Still, when presented with this Scripture, I've had people try to make the spurious argument that this passage was only directed toward a *specific group* of believers in Corinth. That line of thinking can lead us to dangerous, and unstable ground, if we allow it. If we start dissecting the Word of God into what we think applies *only* to a select group of people at a select time; picking and choosing what we think applies to us, we stand in danger of God's wrath coming down hard upon us through our error.

The Bible teaches us that *all* Scripture is important and given to us for a reason, see 2 Timothy 3:16:

"All scripture is given by inspiration of God, and is profitable for doctrine, for reproof, for correction, for instruction in righteousness:"

What this says to me is that everything in the Bible was given to us by God for good reason…He wanted us to know these things. They were given so that we'd have better understanding of God. So that we'd know how He expects us to act; so that we'd know right from wrong. Nothing in the Bible was included without cause. Nothing in the Bible was included by accident. God probably included the Scripture regarding long hair because He wanted us to *know* that His Son didn't have long hair.

Furthermore, for those who wish to argue or belabor this point, God had the author of this text include this follow-up Scripture. It serves to drive the point fully home.

See 1 Corinthians 11:16:

"But if any man seem to be contentious, we have no such custom, neither the churches of God."

This should settle the argument.

In a nutshell, the author (inspired by God to do so) makes it clear "If any man wants to argue the point, there's no such custom of men having long hair among the disciples. Neither is there any custom of men having long hair among the churches of God."

So where did this idea that Jesus had long hair come from?

I've addressed this elsewhere in this book, but basically, the idea of Jesus having long hair comes from artists. Artists who centuries ago first portrayed Jesus in their *own* images and likenesses in their paintings and sculptures. Da Vinci and other early artists were actually *opponents* of the church on many fronts. Da Vinci himself was known to have hated the church on many levels.

Throughout time, long-haired men have been an iconic symbol of rebellion. These artists, either through the desire to portray Jesus and the disciples in a rebellious light, or through the vanity of portraying Jesus and His followers in their own images, did so with intent. Their renderings were never meant to be accurate to reality.

Later in America, rebellious men with long hair, often referred to as "hippies", became part of our cultural landscape. It was during this time that the long-haired Jesus imagery gained more popularity than ever before.

■■■

Now, while this chapter is about Jesus and how He did *not* have long hair, I would be remiss if I didn't point out that the strikingly handsome, Caucasian face that often completes the long-haired Jesus imagery is not accurate either.

Why?

Why can't we cling to the images we have in our heads of a long, flowing haired, strikingly handsome Savior?

Because it's not accurate. Beyond that, it's also a graven image. I don't think we as believers need to be creating *any* images of Jesus, because frankly, no one alive has seen Him. No one alive will see Him until He returns again, or until they pass from this life to the next.

We don't worship an image.

We don't pray to a statue or a painting. At least we shouldn't. Those things won't do anything for us, nor does it help to have a false image of our Savior in our heads while we pray. We pray to a living Savior. One that no one has seen with their own eyes for at least the last nearly two-thousand years.

Let's look at Isaiah 53:2:

> *"For he shall grow up before him as a tender plant, and as a root out of a dry ground: **he hath no form nor comeliness; and when we shall see him, there is no beauty that we should desire him.**"*

Pay special attention to the last part of that Scripture, bolded for emphasis. "Comeliness" is a seldom used word in America these days, but it simply means "pleasing in appearance" or "attractiveness". So, we see that Jesus was *not* a beautiful man.

We have the end part of this sentence that drives the point home and reveals the purpose of Jesus lacking in comeliness. Jesus was not fashioned by God to be an attractive man.

Why?

So that His appearance wouldn't be a distraction to His Gospel message. God wanted the main focus to be on the message, not the messenger.

Could you imagine what would've happened if the strikingly beautiful man that we see depicted today was what Jesus really looked like?

He'd have had a much larger following, probably much, much larger than He truly had, but not for the right reasons. He would've been worshipped and adored…not for the reasons for which He came, but as more of a "rock-star". All because of His appearance and great beauty. That's a distraction that would've taken away from His purpose; and that's something that God wouldn't have allowed to happen.

What purpose would it serve if Jesus's appearance had become a stumbling block to the very people who needed Him the most?

■■■

God knows what He's doing.

He knew that in order for the sacrifice of Jesus to be perfect, that Jesus had to likewise be perfect. He needed to be the spotless Lamb of God. Unlike man, Jesus did not have the sin nature that resides in us all. Because of that, and because God's Word tells us that a man with long hair is shameful, and therefore sinful, we know that Jesus did *not* have long hair…no matter how many times we've seen Him depicted that way.

Chapter 8:
"The Grace Abounds Jesus"

Oh, brother…

Here we go again!

Ever wanted to smack your head up against the wall after talking with someone?

Well, if you ever get a chance to talk to someone who subscribes to the "grace abounds" false doctrine, and the false Jesus that goes along with this heresy, you'll know exactly what I mean. It's not that it's like talking to a brick wall. It's that it's like talking to a brick wall that's drunk and high on crack cocaine…and it talks back to you. It's like trying to argue with someone who only knows one response, "My salvation is secure", without ever truly grasping what that term means; much less what salvation is truly comprised of.

I've had several conversations with some "grace abounds" acolytes and I can tell you that, while I don't drink or do drugs, after a little while I've found myself wishing for some kind of sedative just to make the crazy go away. Talking to these "believers" is literally that bad! I can easily see how someone could be driven insane by the circular arguments and illogical reasoning offered up.

So what's this doctrine about?

What is this false belief system made up of?

Who's this false Jesus that these people worship?

Well, the "hyper-grace", "freedom" or "grace abounds" theoretical doctrine goes something like this: Jesus died on the cross for the sins of the whole world. Every sin. All sins. Each and every sin committed from the Garden of Eden to the final day when God wipes out His enemies and removes the curse forever.

Now, I know what you're thinking.

You're thinking *"Well, what's wrong with that?"*, because so far, they're right on target. Jesus *did* pay the price on the cross for all sins from the beginning of time until that day when our adversary will be defeated and cast into oblivion. That glorious day when there'll be no more sin.

It's in the second part of this belief system where the trouble is found. The rest of this apostasy goes like this: "Because Jesus paid the price on the cross, and because I'm saved and covered by grace, I now have the freedom to sin all I want."

I've also heard this heresy referred to as the "freedom doctrine" or "hyper-grace". It's a form of apostasy that's growing in popularity; especially among minority groups and millennials.

And why shouldn't it be increasing in popularity?

This belief system is attractive, and rapidly gaining ground, because it requires nothing on our parts. No sacrifices. No repentance. No turning away from our sins. No giving up things that we know that God doesn't approve of. It's "easy believe-ism" at its very finest. Even a fool can see the attraction of a belief system that offers all the comforts of salvation with none of the trappings of repentance and traditional Christianity.

The acolytes of this perversion of the Word make the claim that when Jesus said He "fulfilled the law" that this means that the law was abolished, or removed, for believers. That the need to *follow* the law went away too. That The Ten Commandments no longer matter for us.

That's simply not true.

Not even in the slightest.

This belief showcases a fundamental misunderstanding of what it means for the law to be "fulfilled". When something is "fulfilled" that doesn't mean that it no longer exists. It means that it's now a completed work. A finished deal. A project or goal seen through to fruition.

You see, when Jesus died on the cross, He fulfilled the law, in that we no longer have to perform the mandatory sacrifices for, or pay the dire consequences, up to and including death, that went along with breaking those laws of God. Fulfilling the law means that we no longer have to perform sacrificial rituals for atonement. It means that Jesus's precious shed blood fulfilled the requirement for a sacrifice for the remissions of our sins. It also means that certain sins that once required immediate physical death now no longer bear that requirement. That's the entire point of the story of the adulterous woman in John 8: Under the law, she was supposed to die for her sins. Jesus came to fulfill that law in the place of the sinner. This means she no longer had to face immediate *physical* death for her sins. He also, upon her acknowledgement of who He was, saved her from facing spiritual death for her sins. It doesn't mean that Jesus wants her to now continue to sin all she wants. Just because He fulfilled the law, that doesn't mean she's given a free pass to continue to commit adultery at will. Quite the opposite. In fact, we'd do well to remember Jesus's parting words to her, "Go and sin no more."

Jesus's fulfillment of the law means that we don't have to pay the price that is due of each of us when we die. We all have a sin debt. We all owe this debt that can't be paid. The only payment allowed for this sin was our eternal spiritual death, prior to Jesus's sacrifice. Jesus's fulfillment of the law made it possible for our sin debt to be paid for by His blood, substituted for our eternal torment. That was the fulfillment of the law; the payment of the penalty for our transgressions.

Oh, boy!

It's very dangerous ground one treads on if they subscribe to this "Grace Abounds", "Hyper-Grace", or "Freedom Doctrine" belief system. This is akin to just asking, nay begging, for God to strike them down. Not too smart. Not smart at all.

Why?

Well it should be common sense, but since someone reading this book might actually subscribe to these beliefs, I'll expound upon it. It's my duty as a preacher to speak against this sort of thing.

Jesus made it clear when He spoke to sinners and saved alike, that *repentance* is the key to salvation and a necessary part of the spiritual life of a Christian. To the sinner, He asked for their belief in Him…with a repentant heart. To the saved He asked that we become a new creature, wherein old things have passed away, and all things become new. (Read as: our old way of doing things and our old sin-filled lives are to be left behind.) New life. New desires. A new heart that is repentant of sin and ready to serve Him. Nowhere in any of His teachings can you find where He's encouraged anyone to continue on in their sins. Nowhere in the Bible can you find where He, or His disciples, encouraged the continuance of sin or the lack of repentance.

Paul preached passionately against this very same false doctrine. Even back in the early days of Christianity, some were mistaking what it meant to have the law "fulfilled" for us. They were guilty of the same error in thinking; this falsehood that the free pardon of sin, wrought by grace and the shed blood of Jesus Christ, equated to a free pass to sin at will.

Take a look at what Paul said about this in Romans 6:1-6:

6 What shall we say then? Shall we continue in sin, that grace may abound? ² God forbid. How shall we, that are dead to sin, live any longer therein? ³ Know ye not, that so many of us as were baptized into Jesus Christ were baptized into his death? ⁴ Therefore we are buried with him by baptism into death: that like as Christ was raised up from the dead by the glory of the Father, even so we also should walk in newness of life. ⁵ For if we have been planted together in the likeness of his death, we shall be also in the likeness of his resurrection: ⁶ Knowing this, that our old man is crucified with him, that the body of sin might be destroyed, that henceforth we should not serve sin.

Isn't it abundantly clear what Paul was trying to convey?

He actually said "God forbid" in reference to the "grace abounds" doctrine. He clearly expresses how once we obtain salvation, we are to crucify our flesh along with Christ. Just as Christ rose anew, we are supposed to arise in our rebirth in Christ as new creatures. Creatures seeking to no longer serve sin, but to turn away from it. To purposefully choose to serve God instead of serving self.

Jesus Himself said that if we love Him, we'll keep His Father's commandments. Think about that. If you truly love Jesus, you won't continue to sin on purpose. You won't remain the same as you were before you were saved.

Additionally, all throughout the Bible, we see that we're called to repent of our sins and to live righteously. There's no Biblical basis by which we can live a life of sin after salvation. Especially not with the expectation of being right with God. We can't have a strong relationship with God while maintaining a strong relationship with sin. It doesn't work that way.

I hate to break this to anyone who's bought into this doctrine, but if you can live by the "grace abounds" doctrine, whereby you can sin at will, and feel no deep remorse, guilt, or shame for those sins, you may very well need to examine your spiritual condition. If one truly has the Holy Spirit indwelling (which is a necessity to possess salvation) then you'll feel a deep, troubling guilt when you sin. You'll immediately feel the effects of that sin upon your soul. You'll immediately, or at least pretty quickly, have a desire to get right with God. A desire to have your fellowship with God restored in full.

■■

Now, while it would be technically possible to live under the "grace abounds" doctrine while actually possessing salvation (As stated before, it would be very, very hard to do so.), it wouldn't make sense to live that way. There're people who aren't really subscribing to "grace abounds" as much as they are what we'd call in the south "backslidden".

The difference between a "grace abounds" acolyte and a backslidden Christian is that the backslidden person *knows* they're backslidden and not living right. A follower of this false "grace abounds" doctrine actually *believes* they're on okay terms with God. That's a huge distinction. In many cases a backslidden person eventually makes their way back to the Lord. They're like the prodigal son when it comes to salvation.

Since you cannot lose salvation once you have it, a backslidden person may miss out on God's blessings, but they're still saved. They're still a child of God. Just like the Prodigal Son was still a child of his earthly father. However, a person under the "grace abounds" doctrine is likely not saved in the first place. The difference is the Holy Spirit indwelling. Whether they admit it or not, the backslidden Christian *feels* the Holy Spirit calling them back to the Father. A person who's never been saved never belonged to the Father in the first place. They won't experience the same thing.

Let's assume for a moment that person X is saved, but falls for this false doctrine. What harm could that do, you ask, if they can't lose their salvation?

Easy. This apostasy can harm all aspects of their lives in truth. In reality it makes a world of difference in their daily lives.

The Bible is quite clear that God does not hear or answer prayers, even the prayers of the redeemed…if a person remains unrepentant in their sins. When we're outside of the will of God and we're sinning without regard, He won't hear and answer our prayers. That is unless and until we pray a sincere prayer of repentance, confess our sins, and ask Him for forgiveness and mercy. "Get it under the blood", as southern preachers are known to say. When we stray from God and purposefully do that which we know is wrong, we must ask for forgiveness to be restored to full fellowship with Him.

While it *is* possible to live like a lost sinner while possessing salvation, that carries with it something else in common with a lost sinner. When we live like a lost sinner, we lose God from our daily lives. We've effectively shown Him the door and asked Him to leave, at least temporarily. He'll no longer bless our lives or hear and answer our prayers.

What a sad way for a child of God to live!

I can't imagine not having God's in my life. I don't want to imagine where I would be without His blessings in my life. I can't imagine where I would be if not for His faithful answers to my prayers.

Why would anyone want to strip that from their lives?

Here are a few passages that speak to this matter:

> *"**Now we know that God heareth not sinners:** but if any man be a worshipper of God, and doeth his will, him he heareth."* (John 9:31)

> *"And this is the confidence that we have in him, that, **if we ask any thing according to his will, he heareth us:** And if we know that he hear us, whatsoever we ask, we know that we have the petitions that we desired of him."* (1 John 5: 14-15)

> *"**If I regard iniquity in my heart, the Lord will not hear me:**"* (Psalm 66:18)

> *"But your iniquities have separated between you and your God, and your sins have hid his face from you, **that he will not hear.**"* (Isaiah 59:2)

*"Thus saith the LORD unto this people, Thus have they loved to wander, they have not refrained their feet, therefore the LORD doth not accept them; he will now remember their iniquity, and visit their sins. Then said the LORD unto me, Pray not for this people for their good. **When they fast, I will not hear their cry;** and when they offer burnt offering and an oblation, I will not accept them: but I will consume them by the sword, and by the famine, and by the pestilence."* (Jeremiah 14:10-12)

*"**Then shall they call upon me, but I will not answer; they shall seek me early, but they shall not find me:** [29] For that they hated knowledge, and did not choose the fear of the LORD: [30] They would none of my counsel: they despised all my reproof. [31] Therefore shall they eat of the fruit of their own way, and be filled with their own devices. [32] For the turning away of the simple shall slay them, and the prosperity of fools shall destroy them. [33] But whoso hearkeneth unto me shall dwell safely, and shall be quiet from fear of evil."* (Proverbs 1.28-33)

There's a lot more that the Bible says on this subject, but I think you can see the picture. God will only hear and answer prayers for mercy and forgiveness when it comes to the lost, or even the redeemed; when the redeemed are unrepentant in their sins.

If a person harbors darkness in their heart, how can they expect Jesus, the light of Heaven to exist there as well?

If a person is saved, they must be in proper fellowship with God in order to fully receive His blessings and have their daily prayers heard. Don't expect God to bless you with that new job, that new house, that healing, that emotional peace, that Godly spouse, or that other urgent need in your life, if at the same time you're living like a lost sinner.

It's not going to happen.

While we're on this subject, I also have to throw this out there: You'd better be sure *where* your blessings are coming from.

What does that mean?

Aren't all the things we consider "blessings" gifts from God?

No!

Not all things that some might call "blessings" are from God. Just like God blesses His children who love Him and who follow His will, Satan will also bless his children, or those doing his will, as well.

Think about that for a second.

Haven't we all known someone, an individual, a couple, maybe even an entire family, and thought, *"How the heck are they getting blessed, when they're living like the devil himself?"*

Now you know.

Satan blesses those who seek darkness the same way that God blesses those who seek the light. The difference is that Satan's "blessings" are often fleeting…and often leave us in a worse place than before; while the blessings of God will never leave a bitter taste in your mouth.

I recently had an interaction with a friend who claims to be saved, someone who clearly misunderstands Scripture and what God expects of the redeemed. The backstory is that this person was involved in a relationship that included living in sin…all while claiming Christ. She proclaimed that she loved the Lord, even while living in open rebellion against Him.

Her boyfriend, someone I've known for a very long time, was somewhat torn on the future of their relationship. He'd stated that he was seeking clarity from God on several matters. Included among the concerns that he sought clarity for was clarity on his relationship with this woman, and where God wanted their relationship to go.

Now, knowing what I knew about the situation, I kept quiet for a long while. I don't typically interfere or inject myself into the lives of others. Especially if my opinion or advice as a preacher hasn't been asked for. I tend to try to mind my own business.

But in this situation, it *was* asked for. This young lady asked my wife to have me speak to her boyfriend regarding his confusion and his desire for clarity on their relationship. I think she wanted me to reaffirm that they were doing "the right thing" so as to settle his doubts and fears. Basically, I believe he was under conviction for how they were living and *that* is what troubled his soul. Briefly, the conversation with him went something like this:

Note: Remember the person I was speaking to professes to be saved.

Me: *"If you're seeking clarity from God in your life, you need to make sure you've confessed and repented of any recurring sins in your life. Stop committing that sin. That way God will hear and will answer your prayers. Also make sure to read the Bible daily. Listen with an open heart for God's response. Make sure that you're attending a Bible believing and Bible preaching church. That's how one hears from God and gets clarity in their lives."*

Him: *"I'm doing those things. I'm just confused on some things and I'm looking for answers from God."*

Me: *"Okay. Again, make sure you're not committing* **any** *unrepentant sins over and over. Don't do things that you know you shouldn't. You can't sin at will while at the same time asking God for His blessings or His help. It doesn't work that way. You won't receive the answers you're looking for otherwise."*

The conversation went on for a long while, about two hours, but this was the basic gist of the Biblical advice I dispensed. He wanted "clarity" from God on the direction of his relationship and his life. I advised him that in order for that clarity to be obtained, he needed to stop sinning, confess, and repent of those sins.

Now, I didn't mention it to him specifically, but I knew that there were inappropriate aspects of this relationship. I also knew that God wouldn't be blessing that relationship, or answering pleas for clarity, while the couple remained embroiled in sin. In fact, in order to get the clarity he so desired, all this person would have needed to have done is open up the Bible. It's all spelled out there pretty clearly and concisely, in plain English.

Sadly, instead of taking this Biblical advice to heart, this friend turned on me. Largely due to the influence of his lover. Instead of seeing the truth for what it was, he allowed the enemy to deceive him. He allowed her to convince him that my counsel constituted a personal "attack" on him.

His reaction seems a lot like that of a lost person who's under conviction, doesn't it?

Additionally, his girlfriend, the person who initially asked me to speak with him, also turned on my wife too. She began attacking us both. She took offense at *"being called out for our sins"* as she put it when she relayed her outrage to my wife. Now, here's the meat and potatoes of this story, if you will. The main entrée. The salient point: Later on, in text messages to my wife, this misguided young lady actually said: *"Well, God doesn't seem to have a problem with what we're doing since He's blessing us so abundantly."*

Woah, Nelly!

Hold the horses!

Did she really just claim that in spite of living exactly how God said you're not supposed to live, that her sinful way of life resulted in God "blessing them abundantly"?

I had to read that text over and over again. I couldn't believe that two people who claimed to be saved, couldn't see the incredibly shaky and precarious theological ground they were standing on. One might as well shake their fist at the sky and bellow, *"God I dare you to do something about this!"*

Let's be clear about the background of this couple: The young lady in this anecdote was still married to her previous husband, although she'd filed for divorce on grounds of abuse and abandonment six months prior. She was carrying the child of her soon-to-be ex-husband. She also happened to be sleeping with her new lover...while still officially married to her first husband. This couple was basically cohabitating, although they weren't officially "shacking up" at this point. (Although they were in fact living together shortly before the wedding took place.) They couldn't even see past their own sexual passions to realize that the reason the young man was having those misgivings in the first place was that the Holy Spirit was grieving him about what they were doing. The Holy Spirit was attempting to convict him because of the sins they were engaged in. It's unconscionable that they actually believed that they were receiving *"God's blessings"* while openly fornicating and committing the sin of adultery.

If God blesses us all the same, in spite of our unrighteousness and rebellion, then what's the point of living righteously?

If He doesn't remove His hand of blessings when we sin at will, and without remorse, then what's all that talk about repentance about in the Bible?

Unfortunately, it sounds to me like this couple fell pretty hard for the false "grace abounds" doctrine.

Not surprisingly, the relationship has since fallen apart. Divorce has been filed, abuse has been alleged, and lives have been ruined. The marriage didn't even last six months. It's been clearly revealed to all that God wasn't blessing this relationship after all; and sadly, more lives than just the couple involved have been harmed by their sin.

■■■

In summing up, the "grace abounds", "hyper grace", or "freedom doctrine" are all versions of the same terrible lie from Satan. One that causes severe harm in the form of sewing confusion among the lost, as well as the redeemed. It causes deep spiritual harm in the form of missed blessings and unanswered prayers for the redeemed.

When it comes to the lost, imagine their confusion. On one hand, they hear people telling them to repent and turn to Jesus in order to receive salvation. On the other, they see supposed Christians living as ungodly, and sometimes more so, than the lost people they're supposed to be witnessing to.

How can the lost around us see us as anything less than hypocrites, if we do all of the same things that they do, commit the same sins that they do, or God forbid, do even worse things than they do?

How can we have a testimony and a witness for Jesus if our garments are just as sin-stained and soiled as those we would seek to lead to the Lord?

If someone witnesses us cursing, drunken, lying, stealing, cheating, engaged in adultery, fornicating, and railing, how does that show them that we're any different than they are? How is this shining a light for Jesus? We're <u>supposed</u> to be different. We are supposed to stand out, apart from the crowd. The Bible says we are to be a peculiar people.

I liken the "Christians" who continue living like they're lost sinners, and what their lifestyle looks like to the lost, this way: Imagine someone telling you that you really, really must eat at this amazing steakhouse. They say the food is to die for. No better food can be had on the face of the Earth they say. It's life-changing they say. But, then you notice something very odd. This person never eats the food there. They refuse to even take the smallest nibble. But yet, they still proclaim that this steakhouse is beyond compare. If you're like me, skepticism would set in and I wouldn't eat the food. Because words don't matter as much as actions do. And if they proclaim the food is delicious, but yet they won't eat it, to my mind, there's something wrong with the food.

This is the way it looks to lost sinners when we proclaim to be "Christians", yet we live in a way that says otherwise. They say, *"Man, that guy is worse than I am. If that's what a Christian is, why do I need Jesus? No, thanks."*

I'll be brutally honest with you, we as Christians are often more powerful than the devil at driving the lost further and further away from Christ, by the way we live. Something that we should all examine within our own lives.

Rest assured that this false "grace abounds", "hyper grace", or "freedom gospel", whatever label you give it, is one of Satan's most powerful weapons in the battle for people's eternal souls.

● ●

While we can never blame our sins on others, and ultimately we're responsible for our own actions, I'd like to share another instance with you of how our lives can cause others to stumble.

After I got saved, I attended church religiously (pun intended). I was there every Sunday morning, every Sunday night, every Wednesday night, and for most special events and services. One of the other young adults in the church was someone I really, really looked up to and deeply admired. He was always giving these glowing testimonies about what God had done for him and where God had brought him from. He was a very inspirational speaker. Someone everyone looked up to a great deal. Someone I thought was an awe-inspiring role model of what a good Christian should be. He was also the straw the broke the camel's back, and the person who afforded me the excuse to no longer attend church for many years. For a time, I lost my faith because of this guy.

For the sake of this book, we'll call this person "Greg". I literally did not step foot back inside a church for about five years after a single chance encounter with Greg.

So what happened?

What so utterly disenchanted me with Christians and church folk that I didn't want to attend my church any longer?

I saw the ugly side of Greg's life.

I saw his sin on full display.

I saw his duplicity.

The Hyde to his Jekyll if you will.

You see Greg, was a follower of the "grace abounds" doctrine, although I didn't even know what that was at the time. I thought he was a Christian. In my infant Christianity, I thought that all Christians were mostly the same. I had no clue about such false and dangerous doctrines. After all, this guy talked such a good talk…so long as he was in front of others and inside the church.

Here's what happened:

I managed a pizza restaurant that was located in the same outdoor shopping mall and just around the corner from the gym where I worked out. One day after leaving work, I met my brother at the gym. Following our workout, he wanted to play a game of pool at the little game-room next door to the gym. So, we went in, played a few games of pool, and started to leave. As we got ready to depart, in walks Greg.

Immediately, to my shock, I perceived that he was drunk or otherwise under the influence of some substance. His words were slurred, his eyes bloodshot, he staggered when he walked. A goofy, slightly confused grin was permanently plastered on his flushed face. He recognized me, greeted me with a slurred "Oh, hi'ya buddy!"…and then shocked me to the core with his next question:

"You wanna go smoke some pot?"

Needless to say, this left me utterly speechless.

(To know how profound me being stunned into utter speechlessness is, you'd have to ask my wife. She's always telling me I talk too much and that I don't know when to can it.)

Not only did I *not* smoke pot, but the boldness of such a question, asked by a fellow Christian and a fellow church member, floored me.

I quickly responded with a "No, thanks."

He then persisted, *"Why not? Several people at our church smoke. Are you a goody-goody?"*

Again I was floored. I'd always known that doing drugs wasn't a good thing. It certainly didn't seem acceptable for a church member to be engaged in smoking pot.

Especially out of bounds was to be roaming around in public, making a fool of oneself, whether he was drunk or high. Or both.

It seems in Greg, I'd found one of the hypocrites that atheists and nonbelievers are so quick to point to. Or, looking back on it all these years later, I'd possibly found a "grace abounds" disciple rather than an all-out hypocrite. Someone intent on sinning because he denies the need for Christians to live righteously.

Greg became my personal stumbling block.

He became my excuse not to return to church for many, many years. Even when I did eventually return to church, it took a long time for me to be able to trust that the people I saw praising God and giving such lovely testimonies each week were actually who they said they were. I was robbed of my previously trusting nature, and it took me a long time to regain that.

Don't be someone else's Greg!

While not attending church because of someone else's actions or deeds isn't a valid excuse, it *does* happen. Don't allow yourself to become the excuse someone else uses not to attend church.

■■

These false doctrines are not harmless.

They're not victimless.

They're not okay.

If we live by them, we shouldn't be surprised when God one day pulls us aside when we stand before Him and shows us those that we've missed the chance to lead to Christ; because we failed at living for Christ ourselves. If you're living like a lost sinner, and you feel no remorse, no shame, no guilt, no need to get right with God, I'd implore you to really examine your own heart and spiritual condition today.

You might just find that you're still a lost sinner.

Chapter 9:
"The Now You Have Me, Now You Don't Jesus"

Okay here's another ridiculous caricature of Jesus. While He's not dangerous per se, he is spiritually exhausting…and an imposter all the same.

I most recently came across this imposter while debating an atheist online, although I've discovered that he's a fixture in several prominent "Christian" denominations. This atheist's premise that he argued to me was that Christians live *"wasted and sad lives"* because we *"live our lives constantly trying to be good enough to get into Heaven."* Of course, anyone who knows Scripture knows this statement to be profoundly untrue.

Now, to be fair, I have to point out that it's not just random atheists who hold this incorrect view of salvation. There are actually those who profess to belong to Jesus who also believe in this false Jesus persona. It's hardly surprising that an atheist would get things wrong when it comes to salvation, I mean come on…they're atheists. As such, they're not expected to know the truth. If they did, they wouldn't be atheists.

At issue is that it's inconceivable that anyone who's read and studied the Bible could believe this apostasy, much less that entire denominations can believe this theological garbage.

Jesus Himself stated that once a person has been saved that *"no man can pluck them from my hand."* This means that you can't lose your salvation based on works, or even the lack thereof. Ephesians 2:8-9 makes it even clearer that salvation is a matter of faith, not of works. Any salvation that was based on being "good enough" would be a very tough thing.

Why?

Because we can never be good enough to deserve Heaven, or the sacrifice that Jesus made for us. There's no way to obtain righteousness through our own works and even if we could, we wouldn't be able to sustain our own righteousness long enough to get to Heaven.

I thank God daily, that it's His Grace, which is obtained through faith, which grants me title and deed in Heaven. I know I can never be worthy of Heaven outside of the finished work of Christ on the cross. If you're one of those who believes in work-based salvation, let's reason together for a moment. I'll show you exactly why God knows better than to leave a man's salvation in his own hands, through his own works.

And that's what those denominations that push the idea that you can lose salvation are really saying. They're saying that your salvation is left in *your* hands, rather than being held securely by *Jesus. If our own deeds can cause us to lose salvation, what security do we have?*

If you believe in the "Now you have me, now you don't Jesus", you must live in abject terror…because if Jesus can slip from our grasps at the slightest infraction, then what happens to those who die unexpectedly?

■■

Let's assume you believe in works based salvation…aka the *"Now you have me, now you don't Jesus."*

Imagine that you're trying your best to work your way towards Heaven. You're actively involved in feeding the hungry, housing the homeless, caring for the sick, and giving to the poor. That's great. That's as it should be. *All* of the redeemed should strive toward meeting these goals.

But, in the context of those who believe in "working their way to Heaven" or "maintaining their salvation", what happens when you hit a snag?

What happens when you slip and fall?

It all just goes away?
Do we lose it all, for a small mistake?
Bear with me a moment here as we break this down.
So you've done all the good works listed above.
You're a regular Mother Theresa, a Saint among Saints, a man or woman after God's own heart.
You've made it through an entire day, free from sin.
Then, you stub your toe getting into bed at night after an exhausting day of feeding, housing, clothing, and caring for the poor. Before you can stop it, a curse word escapes from your lips!
Gasp!
You've not said one of those words since you got saved, but there it is, it just pops out!
Oh, no!
Now, you've sinned!
You've just lost all that you worked so hard for during the day!
That one little invective has cost you your very soul!
An entire exhausting day of good works has gone out the window…according to this belief system that is.
See how ridiculous this sounds?
Your own righteousness failed you in a moment of weakness. As it always has and as it always will.
If you were trusting in yourself to "maintain your salvation", you just lost it with one small utterance.
Or, let's say you're a man and you dedicate all of your time to helping those in need.
You're doing the Lord's work each and every day. Maybe you're retired or independently wealthy. You're helping everyone you meet, caring for everyone you encounter. You're a regular Mini-me of Jesus in thought, deed, and action. All day, throughout the day. Every day. 24/7.
After a long day of devoting yourself, your money, your goods, and your time to others, you sit down, turn on the local news…and BAM! You're blindsided by a Victoria Secret ad that comes on the screen during a commercial break. You spend just a few moments too long watching those scantily clad women parading around in their overpriced, skimpy lingerie…
Well, you tried.

You did your best.

You attempted to do all that Jesus commanded of you, yet your own righteousness has just failed you…yet again. You just committed adultery in your heart with those scantily-clad women and now, all that you've worked for, all that you did during the day to help the poor and needy of this world is suddenly null and void. That one sin has stained your record and wiped out all of the righteousness you'd built up over the course of the day. Now you'll have to start earning your way to Heaven all over again in the morning. You failed again to maintain your own salvation. As you did the day before, and the day before that, and the day before that.

Now of course, these situations are both tongue-in-cheek examples that I set up to prove how quickly a person could lose their salvation…if salvation was measured on their works, instead of on faith and the grace that faith in the Lord imparts.

Outside of grace, our own attempts at maintaining our salvation will always fail. I am glad that Jesus won't let any man pluck us from his hands…including ourselves.

(I have to throw this in here: I don't condone using bad language, or lusting after lingerie models. I have to clarify this lest someone think otherwise. These were simply quick, easy to understand examples of a very real problem with this absurd doctrine.)

● ●

In these scenarios, the atheist I previously spoke of would've been correct. This *would* make for a mind-numbingly exhausting, unfulfilling, and sad existence.

Can you imagine working so hard to serve the Lord, only to lose it all every time you sinned?

Even the tiniest bit?

I can't. I can't imagine chasing a salvation that would always elude you by the end of the day.

Thank the good Lord above that's not how it is. We don't have to chase after our salvation like a rabid dog chasing a car.

● ●

As I've said before, there are entire denominations that believe in the "Now you have me, now you don't Jesus."

I have to reiterate, the purpose of this book isn't to denigrate anyone's personal beliefs or to tear down any one denomination. Nor is the goal to promote any one denomination over the others. The purpose of this tome is to share the real Jesus with folks. That's why I'm not calling out the denominations by name that follow this doctrine here.

I always wondered as a child, when watching television shows or movies that dealt with a character's death, why a priest or minister would rush to a dying man's side. I never really understood what good that would do for someone. In the movies or television shows the priest would perform some kind of ritual just before the person died…to the great relief of everyone else in the room.

Later, it was explained to me that some denominations think that a person has to have one last cleansing, one last forgiving of sins, performed by a priest, before they slip out into the afterlife. As a child this concept terrified me.

I mean, what if you died all alone, lost, deep in the middle of the woods?

What if a bear mauled you and there was no priest around to perform those rituals?

Would you then go to hell?

What happens if your luck is such?

What if you crash your car on a dark backroad and no one finds you before you slip from this world?

Does God condemn you to hell because you weren't fortunate enough to have a priest or preacher on hand?

That line of thinking is enough to drive a man crazy. You can imagine how much more it would scare a ten year-old child.

I have to point out that, not only is the concept of "last rites" unbiblical and just plain wrong, there's also no priest or preacher alive today who actually has the power to absolve you of your sins. No man can forgive you of your sins, regardless of his title or his piety. Only Jesus, and His shed blood, can do that. We no longer live in a day where a priest, a preacher, or a rabbi, can remove and forgive our sins.

It's not possible.

I'm so glad that we don't have to worry about last rites or losing salvation once we've obtained it. I'm incredibly thankful that the Jesus of the Bible is not a "now you have me, now you don't Jesus."

Salvation is eternal…we can't lose it.

There's nothing you can do to lose salvation, *if* you truly have it in the first place. God didn't intend for us to have to "measure up" to His standards after we received salvation. *He knew we could never do so.* However, that free gift of eternal salvation does come with the requirement and expectation that we attempt to live righteously. Just because we can't lose our salvation, that doesn't mean we have free license to sin.

As Paul said, "God forbid."

Chapter 10:
"The Gay-Affirming Jesus"

So, again, I can't even believe that I am having to address this false Jesus persona. In order to believe in this fake Jesus, you basically have to ignore most of the rest of the Bible, God's teachings on marriage, Jesus's teachings on marriage and sexual sin, and what the Bible says about homosexuality in multiple passages.

So what's this all this fuss about?

There's disturbing claims by the left surfacing that Jesus "affirmed" a homosexual relationship in the Bible; thereby meaning that homosexuality must not be a sin. I can tell you emphatically that this is a lie. Not just a lie, but a lie that is satanic in origin. In the last few years this lie has gained in popularity, and is spreading among the ungodly and wicked as a way of excusing their sin. There are many apostate churches and denominations that have adopted this lie as well.

As if this isn't bad enough, there's a companion claim to this lie that boldly proclaims that "Jesus said people are born gay." This is a boldfaced, Satan inspired lie as well. Jesus neither "affirmed a homosexual relationship" nor said "people were 'born gay'." It's deeply disturbing that people would even dare to slander our Lord and Savior this way. I can only imagine that Hell will be all the more torturous for those laying these claims at the feet of The Lord Jesus Christ.

Let's examine these spurious claims, starting with the "affirmation of a gay couple." The left uses the following Scripture to argue their tenuous position: Matthew 8:5-13

"5 And when Jesus was entered into Capernaum, there came unto him a centurion, beseeching him, 6 And saying, Lord, my servant lieth at home sick of the palsy, grievously tormented. 7 And Jesus saith unto him, I will come and heal him. 8 The centurion answered and said, Lord, I am not worthy that thou shouldest come under my roof: but speak the word only, and my servant shall be healed. 9 For I am a man under authority, having soldiers under me: and I say to this man, Go, and he goeth; and to another, Come, and he cometh; and to my servant, Do this, and he doeth it. 10 When Jesus heard it, he marvelled, and said to them that followed, Verily I say unto you, I have not found so great faith, no, not in Israel. 11 And I say unto you, That many shall come from the east and west, and shall sit down with Abraham, and Isaac, and Jacob, in the kingdom of heaven. 12 But the children of the kingdom shall be cast out into outer darkness: there shall be weeping and gnashing of teeth. 13 And Jesus said unto the centurion, Go thy way; and as thou hast believed, so be it done unto thee. And his servant was healed in the selfsame hour."

Liberals, atheists, homosexuals, and apostate "Christians" argue that because the word "pais" was used in the original Greek text, that this passage supposedly shows that Jesus healed the lover of a gay man. Then they surmise that because He didn't tell this soldier to "Go, and sin no more.", as He did with the adulterous woman in John 8, that this means He not only "affirmed" a gay relationship, but that He didn't see it as sin either.

Now, let's examine this claim in detail: First off, we have to go *really, really* far out into the weeds, and I mean -deeply lost with no hope of ever finding your way back- far into the weeds, to come up with the fantastically rare usage of the Greek word "pais" to mean "male sex slave". It's there, but it's very, very uncommon to say the least. Even in Jesus's day, the usage of the word "pais" to mean a male sex slave was archaic and almost never used.

In fact, the Greek word "pais" is used many times throughout the New Testament, with the most widely used and accepted definition of "pais" being "a child; son or daughter; an infant". It's also used in the Bible to mean children, slave, infant, or special attending servants (like a King's manservant). All of these meanings are more common than the very rare definition that the left chooses in making their fallacious argument. The definition they attempt to apply is the least common usage of the word; making it very implausible that it'd be used in this context. Strong's Concordance shows the word "pais" used twenty-six times in the Bible; including twice in the book of Acts to describe Jesus Himself. (47)

Now, here's where the rubber meets the road and it begins to gets very interesting; and I'd say frustrating for those who seek to use this passage to excuse their sin. You see, while the Greek word "pais" can very rarely (almost never) be used to mean a male lover--actually, always used in reference to a male sex slave rather than a consensual lover--, it can *never*, not ever, be used to describe an *adult* male lover or *adult* male sex slave. It always would refer to a child, as "pais" has no usage, in any of its definitions, that means an adult. Read that again. "Pais" can *never* mean an adult, whether we're speaking of a child, a servant, or a male sex slave. A "pais" would always denote that it's a child that's being spoken of.

Thus, this would mean that if we remove the correctly applied definition of "pais" in this passage, which is servant, and apply the seldom used definition of "a male sex slave" to the account of the Roman Centurion, it wouldn't be the account of a "gay man and his lover" at all. It'd be the account of a pedophile rapist and his male child victim that was being described. So, what these people are really arguing is *not* that Jesus "affirmed a gay relationship", but that He affirmed a pedophile rapist/victim relationship. I don't think Jesus would have any part of that!

What *does* make sense is that the KJV Bible is entirely correct when it calls this person who the Roman Centurion is seeking help for a "pais", using the second most common meaning of the word which is "servant". A Centurion in the Roman Army is a military officer who's in command of at least one group of one hundred men (sometimes even more than one group of a hundred). A person of this rank would necessarily have many "servants" to help him in his duties.

Can you imagine the logistics of having to be responsible for one hundred, up to one thousand, soldiers in a day and age where you'd have none of the modern conveniences that we enjoy now? That would be very hard to do without a *lot* of help. That's where these servants came in.

Often times, these servants were highly trusted individuals who became like part of the Centurion's family. Most of the time, these servants were orphaned children who were taken in by the army and trained as attendants, living around and with those they served, until they were of age and could fight in the army themselves. Then, they would go into the army, much of the time as officers, as they were already highly trained and competent soldiers.

These servants were often the children of fallen soldiers themselves. The Roman army did not waste able-bodied men who could fight in battle as simple servants. So, they wouldn't use adult males in these positions. Often, these servants would serve the Centurion from the time they were just a small child. These beloved servants would become like the Centurion's own children. It would make sense that this Roman Centurion would seek help for a trusted attendant (servant) who was a mere child. Especially a child who was like part of his own family.

In modern day terms...think Batman.

No seriously. Think Batman. In the Batman television shows, cartoons, and movies, Alfred, the butler and special attendant, was like a beloved family member to Batman/Bruce Wayne. He was not a male lover. He was a servant. The only difference between Alfred and the Roman Centurion's servant is that Alfred wasn't a child. But, nevertheless, you can see how someone could deeply care for a servant, without that relationship being sexual.

I often hear people say "There's no gay agenda." *But if that's true, what reason could they offer for their willful dishonesty on this subject? If they're going to try to change the correctly used word "servant" in the Biblical story of the Roman Centurion, how can they explain not using the most common meaning of the word, "child; son or daughter in its place"? Certainly, it would make sense for a Roman Centurion to seek help for his son or daughter?*

And, if they aren't going to use the most common meaning of the word, why then would they skip the second, third, fourth, fifth, most common meanings of the word to arrive at the absolutely least common meaning of the word?

A meaning that still wouldn't say what they're trying to force it to say when applied to the passage?

If there's no "gay agenda" then why make up a fallacious argument while trying to insert homosexuality where it never existed?

In a nutshell, this leftist theory of Jesus "affirming a gay relationship" in the Bible has been completely blown out of the water. Not a shred of truth to it. Anyone claiming otherwise is depending on the ignorance of the person they're making the claim to, to keep them from knowing the difference.

■■

Now, on to the second fallacious claim in this double dose of theological nonsense: The false claim that "Jesus said people are born gay."

Now anyone possessing even a modicum of intellectual honesty has to know this to be false. *Why would Jesus ever say something that would make Him both a liar and a sinner in the same breath?* Well, He didn't. He didn't say anything of the sort. Not even close.

This nonsensical claim is derived from Jesus's teachings on marriage and divorce. Given the rather strict expectations that Jesus taught on marriage, and God's rules governing this sacred institution, someone in the group of men Jesus was teaching asked if it was even good to marry. Jesus went on to answer, expounding that marriage is not necessary to have a fulfilled life in Christ; and that there are some men who will never engage in marriage. He referred to these men as "eunuchs" which literally means an emasculated man. Eunuchs in Jesus's day did not engage in marriage. They also did not engage in sexual relations because they didn't possess the means to do so.

In speaking on this matter, Jesus referred to three specific types of eunuchs. A eunuch is a man who, at the time, would not engage in marriage or sexual relations. The first type of eunuch named by Jesus were those who were *"so born from their mother's womb."* This is the one definition that's been seized upon by the left, by homosexuals, and by atheist activists who falsely claim that this description means homosexuals. That Jesus was literally saying these are homosexuals who were "born that way".

That's a complete and total fabrication. One that makes Jesus a lost sinner.

Before we go further into examining this first type of eunuch, let's take a look at who the other two types of eunuchs mentioned by Jesus are. The second type of eunuchs mentioned by Jesus were the most common at the time, and throughout history. They make up the group that is most commonly meant when using the word "eunuch". These are the men "which were made eunuchs of men."

Is there anyone who doesn't know what we're speaking about here?

Just in case, let's state the obvious: these were emasculated male servants. In most cases, these were servants charged with looking after and assisting women in high society. The servants of Queens, Governesses, or other powerful or rich women. These servants would be emasculated so as to take away any chance of them fornicating, or trying to fornicate, with their charges. It also prevented the rape of these women by their male servants.

Notice that I didn't say they were simply "castrated"? The reason for this is that these men weren't simply just castrated. The word "eunuch" in the Bible actually refers to a man who has had both his male organ and his testicles removed, whereas "castration" as used today usually means a man who's only had his testicles removed. This is an important distinction. Especially in regard to this argument. You'll see why later.

The final type of eunuch mentioned by Jesus are the types I'll call "spiritual eunuchs". Jesus called these men those "which have made themselves eunuchs for the kingdom of Heaven's sake." Paul, and Jesus Himself, were two such spiritual eunuchs. Instead of pursuing marriage, and the sexual gratifications that come with it, they made themselves "eunuchs" by refusing to partake of either marriage, or sexual relations, in order to better serve God with singular focus. This wasn't a mandate from God, but a personal choice on their parts. And it was a choice that required a man of great faith, patience, perseverance, and fortitude to become a spiritual eunuch for God.

Now, as I said before, homosexual activists, atheists, and liberals have seized upon the first type of eunuch mentioned by Jesus and have wrongly ascribed the label "homosexual" to these men, thereby attempting to justify their belief that homosexuality isn't sin by claiming

Jesus said homosexuals were "born that way." However, this takes a strong mixture of willful deceit and abject ignorance to believe and push this notion. It makes Jesus a sinner, as well as a liar, in order to justify what God has called abomination.

Closer examination shows the glaring holes in this absurd allegation. For one thing, a "eunuch" in the example given by Jesus isn't simply a "castrated" male; in the traditional thought of what a castrated male is. Castration usually involves the removal of the testicles to lessen sexual desire in men. But that isn't what we're talking about. In the Bible, a eunuch is someone who has been completely emasculated. Meaning both the male organ and the testicles have been removed. Thus, these men will never engage in sexual relations. And that is an important distinction.

Now, when it comes to eunuchs who are "so born from their mother's womb", we aren't speaking of homosexuals at all. In most cases homosexuals are not emasculated, and therefore have the ability to engage in sexual relations, where a Biblical eunuch did not. This distinction alone, not to mention the fact that homosexuality is clearly condemned throughout the Bible, should tell us that this passage doesn't speak of homosexuals.

Remember, that a "eunuch" by Biblical definition was *not* a man who engaged in alternative, perverse sexuality. He was a man who didn't engage in, or have the capacity to engage in, sexual relations of *any* kind. Homosexuals in the Bible *were* capable of sex. A Biblical eunuch *was* not.

So, who were the eunuchs who were "born that way"?

Well, it really doesn't take much in the way of deep thought to come up with some easy examples. The eunuchs "from the womb" were men who were born with missing, underdeveloped, or malformed sex organs. Men born with severe physical disabilities or disfigurements which would preclude them taking part in marriage or sexual relations. Men born with severe mental retardation were "eunuchs from the womb." Or men born with genetic disorders and diseases which would also preclude them from marriage and sexual relations. Think Down Syndrome, cerebral palsy, or a myriad of other diseases which would effectively render a man a "eunuch from his mother's womb."

There's absolutely no way in which the term "eunuch" could imply a homosexual man in this passage of the Bible. Both the context of the passage, as well as common sense, would argue against adding such a specious definition to a word that never meant "gay."

We have to be careful what we ascribe to Jesus. If by adding words, or definition of words, which could never fit the narrative, we make Jesus a liar, or a sinner, or as in this case we make Him both, we also have corrupted Him, rendering Him incapable of becoming the sacrifice for our sins. In short, if this Jesus who said *"homosexuals are born gay"* existed, then our salvation does not. Now that's a terrible thought indeed.

Chapter 11:
"The Alt-Right Jesus"

So, I can't really even believe that I'm having to write this chapter. *Does anyone besides a handful of lifelong, backwoods Democrats in the deep-south really believe in this alt-right Jesus at all?* I debated with myself as to whether this chapter was even a necessity for this book, ultimately deciding to add it for posterity. I'm fairly well convinced that had I *not* added this chapter to the book, some would deride this work as only a hit-piece on liberalism. Not that they're going to refrain from doing that anyway. Make no mistake, they will. One group of trolls in my homosexual, liberal atheist "fan club" has already announced that they're just waiting for this book to be published so they can attack it with fake negative reviews. Just like they've done with the four Christian children's books that I've authored.

Suffice it to say, if your "Jesus" demands that you hate anyone, for any reason, he's not the real deal. If he favors one race over another, he's not legit. If he's a white supremacist, then he's not the Jewish carpenter who died on the cross two-thousand years ago for our sins. If he values you more than your neighbor, regardless of who you both are, he isn't worth mentioning. Not to mention he's not worth worshipping.

While the Bible is clear that Jesus isn't a socialist, a bleeding heart liberal, or an SJW (social justice warrior), He also isn't exactly a rubber stamp for alt-right politics either. Nor is He the founder of the Republican Party. Jesus wasn't, and isn't, particularly enamored with politicians and government leaders as a whole. And to say that there's a perfect political leader, much less a perfect political party is beyond absurd. There's no truth to that idea at all.

It's absolutely true that if we examine what Jesus stood for, and what both major political parties in America stand for, that one would have to say His positions are far closer to those of the Republican Party. That is, once you cut through the smoke and mirrors and the false claims to get to the heart of what each party *really* stands for. Talk is cheap. Results matter. A peek behind the curtain, often reveals the hidden truth.

Jesus is no respecter of persons. He doesn't care whether you're rich or poor, black or white, young or old, or what you've done in the past. He requires the same from you as He does from everyone else: Repent. Come to Him in faith, with a broken heart and a contrite spirit, and He will save your soul and heal what's broken.

Romans 2:10-16:

> [10] *But glory, honour, and peace, to every man that worketh good, to the Jew first, and also to the Gentile:*
> [11] *For there is no respect of persons with God.*
> [12] *For as many as have sinned without law shall also perish without law: and as many as have sinned in the law shall be judged by the law;*
> [13] *(For not the hearers of the law are just before God, but the doers of the law shall be justified.*
> [14] *For when the Gentiles, which have not the law, do by nature the things contained in the law, these, having not the law, are a law unto themselves:*
> [15] *Which shew the work of the law written in their hearts, their conscience also bearing witness, and their thoughts the mean while accusing or else excusing one another;)*
> [16] *In the day when God shall judge the secrets of men by Jesus Christ according to my gospel.*

The Bible also makes clear that in Jesus's eyes there's no distinction among the redeemed between one person and another. That the social caste systems of man doesn't matter to Him. In the days before Jesus came, and even in the early church, there were racial and social divisions just as there are today. But, we're told those divisions are not supposed to exist among the redeemed in Christ. In a time where the free man was valued more in social circles than the slave, when the man was valued more than the woman, and when the Jewish person was valued above the Gentile or Greek, Jesus saw no difference in any of those who'd received salvation.

Galatians 3:28:

> [28] *There is neither Jew nor Greek, there is neither bond nor free, there is neither male nor female: for ye are all one in Christ Jesus.*

This says it all. Among the redeemed, there is no caste system. No "levels". No "undesirables". No "this group is better than this other group". Jesus sees the free man as the same as the slave, the woman is equal to the man, all races are equal, and although the Jews are God's chosen, even the redeemed Gentile is equal to the redeemed Jew.

Therefore, any belief system that seeks to elevate the white race above any other race, is inherently wrong. *If Jesus didn't elevate His own people above that of the other races and peoples around them, why would He elevate white people above anyone else?*

In the end, all that matters is whether or not we're covered by the precious shed blood of the Lord Jesus Christ. When we stand before Him either as believers or non-believers, with all of our words, deeds, and even our thoughts, laid out naked before Him, we won't be separated by race, national origin, status in life, financial status, or any other divisions of man. We'll be separated as either the saved or the lost. The saved will receive their rewards according to their works after salvation, while the lost will receive the punishment for their deeds and their denial of Christ.

Summing up, it's hardly worth mentioning that the "Alt-right Jesus" is a fictional character. Anyone with even a modicum of Biblical knowledge already knows this. Yet for the sake of completion, there it is. He doesn't exist. He never existed. He's as fake as all the others described in the preceding chapters of this book.

Paul D. Little

Part Two:
The Real Jesus

Chapter 12:
Who Jesus Is

Ah, now we've come to the heart of the matter. Now that we've examined who Jesus is *not*, it's finally time to take a good look at who Jesus *is*. It's important to point out that since Jesus is God made flesh, it is highly unlikely that Jesus would side with any one person, agenda, or viewpoint one-hundred percent of the time. Being God and remaining free from sin, Jesus does not possess a thinking process that's skewed by sin, the way that of man is. The thinking process of even the most pious of Christians *is* affected by sin, as we all have the sin nature dwelling within us. We can't imagine a thought process that's free from that taint of sin, because we can never be free from sin totally. Not in this life.

That's why when we try to apply human logic to either God the Father, or God the Son, we'll always fall short in our analysis. We simply can't see things as He does, because our sin obscures and clouds our vision. This is one of the largest fallacies of non-believers when they start down the road of asking *"Why would God allow this to happen?"* or *"If He's real, why can't God just..."* They mistakenly attempt to apply the "wisdom" of man to the actions, plans, and thinking of God, which will never end up where they want it to.

With that said, we can see the *true* Jesus by reading and studying the Word of God, the Holy Bible. The Bible tells us that Jesus is the "Word made flesh". It only makes sense given this knowledge that if we want to learn more about Jesus, we need to spend much more time than most of us do immersed in the Bible. We also need to spend more time immersed in sincere prayer, so that we may have the wisdom to truly understand what we're reading.

So, who is Jesus?

*The **real** Jesus?*

- He's God made flesh, the living, breathing Savior who walked among men.
- He's the only begotten Son of the living God.
- He's the only man to ever live who was entirely free from sin.
- He's the risen Savior.
- He's the Messiah.
- He's the only way by which a person can get to Heaven.
- He's the perfect sacrifice.
- He's the sacrificial payment for our sins.
- He's the only one to ever be 100% God and 100% man at the same time.
- He's the only truly unbiased person to ever live.

In the coming chapters, we will address all of these aspects of Jesus, one by one.

Paul D. Little

Chapter 13:
Jesus, The God-Man Who Walked Among Us

Those who seek to deny Jesus have recently tested and tried a new tactic: disputing that Jesus ever lived. To deny that God actually walked among us as man. What was once considered an indisputable fact: that Jesus at the very least existed in human form, (even if people chose to believe that He was not the Son of God), is now being challenged by those who seek to deny Him. These deniers insist that Jesus is a nothing more than a myth; that the mortal man known as Jesus did not exist at all. This is a relatively new approach at trying to "disprove" Jesus. In the past, the Christ deniers would make the assertion that "While Jesus lived, He was simply a prophet, a good man, and a teacher."

This marks a remarkable change in tactics. Since the *"Jesus was just a man"* tactic hasn't done much to change our belief in Jesus, a new technique was required. The supposed "researchers" making this claim say that if Jesus had ever truly lived, other notable historical figures at the time would have surely made reference to such a person in their own writings. They assert that no such historical references can be found. They persist that a lack of such historical "evidence" must lead us to conclude that Jesus never really existed.

So, could that be true?
Could Jesus be just a myth?

Could He really be just an amalgamation of other historical and mythical personas, as the Christ-deniers claim?

No.

Not at all.

Jesus *did* walk among us as both a human being *and* God made flesh. The evidence is all there for anyone who wants to truly examine said evidence in a strictly objective light. There exists a wealth of evidence from Jewish sources (Sources who present the evidence in a not-so-surprisingly hostile fashion), Non-Jewish sources (Mostly Roman and Greek, many of which are also hostile in nature), and early Christian sources.

Let's take a look at the evidence that supports the purely historical account of Jesus's life. We'll start with some non-Jewish and non-Christian evidence that backs up the historical accounts of Jesus.

1. **Thallus:**

   Thallas was a Samaritan-born Roman historian who lived and worked in Rome around 52AD. While many of Thallus's original writings have been lost to us in the modern world, Julius Africanus, who was a reputable and noted second century Christian historian familiar with the writings of Thallus, quoted his works often. One passage of Thallus's writings that's of note relates to the darkness that spread over the earth at the time of Christ's crucifixion and His death on the cross. Thallus (who was neither a follower nor believer in the Lord Jesus Christ) thought to explain this darkness away as a solar eclipse. Julius Africanus writes: "On the whole world there pressed a most fearful darkness; and the rocks were rent by an earthquake, and many places in Judea and other districts were thrown down. This darkness Thallus, in the third book of his *History*, calls, as appears to me without reason, an eclipse of the sun. For the Hebrews celebrate the passover on the 14th day according to the moon, and the passion of our Savior falls on the day before the passover; but an eclipse of the sun takes place only when the moon comes under the sun. And it cannot happen at any other time but in the interval between the first day of the new moon and the last of the old, that is, at their junction: how then should an eclipse be supposed to happen when the moon is almost diametrically opposite the sun? Let opinion pass however; let it carry the majority with it; and let this portent of the world be deemed an eclipse of the sun, like others a portent only to the eye. Phlegon records that, in the time of Tiberius Caesar, at full moon, there was a full eclipse of the sun from the sixth hour to the ninth--manifestly that one of which we speak. But what has an eclipse in common with an earthquake, the rending rocks, and the resurrection of the dead, and so great a perturbation throughout the universe? Surely no such event as this is recorded for a long period. " (Julius Africanus, *Chronography*, 18.1). (48) (49)

It must be noted that even back then, much like today, there existed a movement by non-Christians to explain away the events surrounding Jesus's death on the cross as simply naturally occurring events. An effort to remove the supernatural aspects of these events and explain them as entirely natural. The fact that this noted historian is trying to explain away the Biblical account of the very real and documented darkness that enveloped the earth at the time of the crucifixion as a "natural event" shows that in fact Jesus existed; and the events surrounding His death on the cross are true.

It should also be noted that Thallus never once disputed the fact that Christ existed.

Not.

Even.

Once.

This can't be glossed over. A person typically doesn't try to disprove circumstances surrounding a living person, unless they *believe* that this person existed in the first place! He sought to explain away the darkness that accompanied Jesus's death on the cross, but he never denied the existence of Jesus.

Neither did Thallus dispute the crucifixion of Christ. Instead he focused on finding a natural cause for the accompanying darkness that was described in the Biblical account of the crucifixion. He sought to explain away the supernatural events surrounding Jesus's death on the cross. That would seem to point to his tacit belief that Jesus did in fact exist, and that He was in fact crucified.

315

Now, one of the most important facts to remember about the writings of Thallus is that they're widely believed to have been written between 50-100AD. That means they were written between seventeen to sixty-seven years after the events at Calvary. That's relatively a very short time from the actual historical events that are being discussed by Thallus.

For perspective on this: It's akin to discussing the events of Pearl Harbor, which occurred in 1941, between the years of 1958 and 2008. It's very hard to get the details of such a major and recent event wrong. We're now at nearly eleven years further along in history from Pearl Harbor than Thallus could've ever been from the events of the Cross. And that makes his writings all the more relative and important because the further away something is in history, the easier it is for the record to become skewed by personal biases and misinformation. The events of Jesus's death on the cross were still very, very fresh, from a historical standpoint, when Thallus wrote about them.

2. **Cornelius Tacitus** (c. A.D. 55-120):

    Tacitus was a Senator and respected Historian of the Roman Empire. Commonly referred to as "the greatest historian of ancient Rome", his most famous works are the Annals and the Histories. The Annals cover the period of time between 14AD and 68AD (the death of Nero) and the Histories cover the period of time between the death of Nero and 96AD. Tacitus wrote in regard to the presence of Christians in Rome and the history of Jesus:

    > *"But not all the relief that could come from man, not all the bounties that the price could bestow, nor all the atonements which could be presented to the gods, availed to relieve Nero from the infamy of being believed to have ordered the conflagration, the fire of Rome. Hence to suppress the rumor, he falsely charged with the guilt, and punished with the most exquisite tortures, the persons commonly called Christians, who were hated for their enormities. **Christus, the founder***

of the name, was put to death by Pontius Pilate,
procurator of Judea in the reign of Tiberius: but the
pernicious superstition, repressed for a time, broke out
again, not only through Judea, where the mischief
originated, but through the city of Rome also." (Annals
XV, 44) (45)

Notice in this account, Tacitus actually confirms the existence of
Jesus? He directly references Jesus's death on the cross. He confirms it
was Pilate who ordered the execution. He also references the
"pernicious superstition" that was subdued for a while in Judea and
Rome but later broke out on a much larger scale.
What was this "pernicious superstition"?
He was referencing the core belief of the death, burial, and
resurrection of the Lord Jesus Christ. The "superstition" he mentions
expressly refers to the resurrection. *How can so many people seeking to*
deny the existence of Christ by claiming that no "historical references"
exist at the same time ignore the words of the most famous Roman
historian of the same time period?
How can they explain away what he wrote about Jesus?
They can't. Jesus existed, just as surely as you or I do. Jesus *is*
the God man who walked among us. He lived. He still lives, and He will
live forevermore. And those of us who've found salvation at the cross
will live forevermore basking in His glory.

Chapter 14:
Jesus the Son of God

Almost everyone in the civilized world knows the story regarding the birth of Jesus Christ; even if they don't necessarily believe in it. Here, in America, and in many other countries around the world, hundreds of millions of people celebrate the birth of Jesus with a holiday called Christmas. Or many celebrate some version of the same holiday. The Bible tells us that Jesus was conceived by the Holy Spirit within the womb of a virgin girl named Mary. God sent an angel to tell Mary's soon-to-be-husband Joseph what was going to happen. He encouraged Joseph to be strong and faithful. Joseph listens and does as commanded of him by God the Father. He protects and shelters Mary from those who'd accuse her of wrongdoing, and he remains faithfully by her side. The baby is born and God sent His angels to proclaim the birth of Jesus throughout all the land.

Jesus was born in a manger and growing up, He lived a very humble life. The life of a mostly normal Jewish boy. He helped his earthly father, Joseph, as an apprentice carpenter, until His true ministry began in earnest around the age of thirty. During His childhood Jesus could often be found in the temples and synagogues asking questions of the rabbis and priests…and even teaching there at times. One account is given in which Jesus, being twelve years old, is found to be missing as His family is heading back home. When His frantic parents make their way back to town, they find Jesus teaching in the temple. At an early age He was already beginning His Father's work through His actions, deeds, and words.

It was at the age of roughly thirty that Jesus began the mission that was the true purpose for His life; His ministry as the Lord Jesus Christ. As the promised Messiah. After three years of His Ministry on earth, which included many miracles and great feats, Jesus's mission was completed in His sacrifice on the cross. For all who would hear, believe, repent, and accept Him as Lord and Savior, His death meant freedom from our sins. Including freedom from the wages, or consequences, of those sins.

Jesus is the forgiving, but *not* tolerant, Savior.

One fact that can be pointed to that lends credence to, and proves the divinity of, Jesus is His forgiving nature. I must stress emphatically, this is forgiving nature is *not* to be mistaken for a "tolerant" nature. As we looked at *"tolerance"* in making the case of who Jesus is *not,* the notion of "tolerance" in connection with Jesus is a false narrative.

Jesus was, and is, very forgiving as a loving Savior. Due to the time He spent in a physical human body (facing all of the same temptations, the same aches & pains, and the same afflictions that we also face), He has compassion on us in our struggles against temptation and sin. He was not and is *not* ever tolerant of sin and wrongdoing. He doesn't wink at sin. He doesn't accept sin.

By nature, mankind is *not* forgiving.

Not in the least.

Have you ever made your wife or your girlfriend mad?

If so, you know that forgiveness isn't a natural trait of mankind. It's something we have to work at.

In most cases we're selfish, self-serving, and very unforgiving toward others. It takes a lot of effort for us to be forgiving toward others…especially those who've unjustly wronged us. Earlier in this book, I presented a prime example of Jesus's all-encompassing, forgiving nature with the account of the adulteress found in the book of John. I made the case that while Jesus was forgiving of the woman's sins, He was *not* tolerant of her sins. He definitely wasn't tolerant that she should keep sinning. When Jesus was finished with her, He forgave her sins and admonished her to "go, and sin no more." To "tolerate" the sin, He'd have allowed her to go about her business, continuing on in her sin. In fact, I can confidently state that "tolerating" sin, would make Jesus guilty of that sin Himself. And we all know that He never sinned.

Another example of Jesus's forgiveness, a forgiveness that transcends that which man is capable of, can be found in the account of Zacchaeus. Zacchaeus was a deplorable tax collector who was despised among his own people. A criminal who was well known for cheating his fellow citizens by collecting more tax money than was due…and for using that surplus money for his own personal gain. He was a white-collar thief in other words. An embezzler. When Jesus met with Zacchaeus, He presented him with the Gospel. Zacchaeus believed in Jesus and repented. Jesus forgave his sins and granted him salvation, but likewise, He expected Zacchaeus's life to change. A tolerant Jesus would have tolerated the sin and would have allowed it to continue. A tolerant Savior would have allowed Zacchaeus to remain as he was prior to salvation. In this story we see the amazing forgiveness of the forgiving Savior, but we see that at the same time He was *not* tolerant of sin.

It should be noted that Zacchaeus *did* change when he received salvation in the Lord Jesus Christ. This change, this repentance, is the mark of true salvation. Not only did Zacchaeus give half of his riches to the poor, he also returned the ill-gotten gains he'd acquired back to those he'd cheated…fourfold. Meaning, he actually gave them back four times what he'd wrongfully taken from them in his selfish greed.

Only the true, the one, the only Son of God can accomplish such change in the heart of a wicked and greedy man. If one but looks, they'll easily find many such stories like that of Zacchaeus in modern day. Jesus is truly working miracles in the souls of men and women. Miracles that only the Son of God could bring about.

Chapter 15:
Jesus, The Sinless Savior

Jesus, the only man to ever live while being totally free from sin…that's hardly imaginable to us. Especially those of us who were once so deeply lost in sin. *I can't imagine never once having failed God, can you?*

Jesus was able to become our Savior simply because He was free from the taint and stain of sin. God demands a spotless sacrifice for the remission of sin. Prior to Jesus, for the Jews, a spotless lamb was used as a suitable sacrifice for the remission of sin. Unlike Jesus's sacrifice, which was permanent, a new lamb was needed periodically to remain in fellowship with God. Jesus became the spotless lamb for one and all; forever.

As the sinless Savior, Jesus couldn't fit with the narrative that some in these modern times would have us to believe. To remain free from sin, Jesus *couldn't* have any been the following:

- A man with long hair.
- Tolerate of sin.
- A political liberal.
- Affirming of homosexuality.
- A supporter of gay "marriage".
- A pro-abortionist.

- Or affirming of, supportive of, or encouraging of any other sins that would've made Him a sinner by default.

Jesus, as the perfect, spotless, sinless Lamb of God, became a *permanent* sacrifice for the remission of our sins. All we must do is accept Him, as He is, without trying to mold Him to *our* image. When we attempt to conform Jesus to us, He ceases to be the sinless Savior that He is and had to be. When we ascribe our personal thoughts, feelings, biases, and views to Jesus, we make Him a sin-stained and spotted lamb; a blighted offering that would never satisfy God.

Chapter 16:
Jesus, The Risen Savior

One thing that differentiates Christianity from all other major world religions is the Lord Jesus Christ Himself. Jesus, *is* the Risen Savior. Buddha is dead. Mohammed is dead. The Old Testament prophets are dead. Krishna is dead. All of those who've gone before and since Jesus are buried; both cold and dead in the grave.

Jesus *was* dead, but He took up His life after the third day and *is* alive again. He now sits on the right hand side of the Throne of God, awaiting the time when He shall return for His bride.

This is what allows us our home in Heaven. This is where our hope rests. Without a Risen Savior, we have nothing. No hope of salvation. No hope of eternal life. Without Jesus's resurrection, our faith would be as empty and dead as the founders and leaders of all the other world religions.

Jesus isn't buried in a tomb somewhere. You won't find His bones on this earth, although people have tried for two thousand years. You can search for ten thousand years, but you won't find His bones or His body...because He took those with Him when He ascended back to Heaven. He took His body with Him to await His father's orders to come get His bride.

One would think that if Jesus hadn't risen again on the third day, that the Jewish religious leaders and the Roman political leaders of the day would have presented His body to the public. They'd have been eager to show that Jesus was a fraud.

That only makes sense, right?

But of course, they instead claim that the Roman soldiers who were guarding the tomb fell asleep. That while the guards slumbered, the disciples made away with the body.

Of course!

That makes perfect sense!

(Sarcasm intended.)

In reality, it makes no sense whatsoever.

The Roman soldiers guarding the tomb would've never fallen asleep on the job. Typically, a Roman watch consisted of at least four guards. These watches would have rotated out in four hour shifts. The guards would've expected that someone might come along to steal the body. They had to believe that followers of Jesus would take the body, if possible, in order to stage a fake resurrection. That's the reason they were stationed there in the first place: to ensure that such a thing couldn't happen!

It must also be pointed out that given the unusual circumstances of the tomb which they were guarding, that it's highly likely that the Romans would've appointed more than one group of four soldiers to watch over the tomb. The Bible unfortunately doesn't give us the exact number of guards who were present. Still, as it was a Roman watch, we know there were at least four guards present. We also know that the Roman watch would have rotated out every four hours, giving the disciples very little chance to catch all four guards sleeping, within a small four hour window. They'd have had little chance to have pulled such a feat off.

And does anyone really believe the guards who were put there to prevent the tomb from being raided in the first place would be so entirely, grossly derelict in their duties as to all fall asleep on the job?

Could all four (possibly more) men have fallen asleep, at the same time?

And for how long?

Then there's that pesky, minute detail that a massive stone, one which must've weighed at least a ton, if not a few, blocked the entrance to the tomb. One would think that even the heaviest of sleepers would've heard that massive stone as it was slowly rolled away. The stone would've had to have been moved a significant distance in order to make room for at least two men to enter the tomb and abscond with a body that would've been heavy and stiffened in death.

Only a fool could believe that a group of four or more soldiers, sleeping nearby, wouldn't hear the huffing and puffing, the groaning, the straining, and the complaining of a group of men sufficient enough in numbers to move such a large stone. The screeching, scratching, and scraping of rock grinding against rock would've been enough to wake even the heaviest sleeper among the slumbering guards.

Only a fool could believe that such a heist was carried off without a hitch. Plus, in addition to the Roman watch, it's almost a sure thing that the Temple, the Jewish religious leaders, also had their own people present to watch over the tomb. After all, a resurrected Jesus would be an extreme threat to Judaism as a religious faith; thereby making the priests and rabbis themselves obsolete as religious leaders. It would be a huge oversight on their part not to have someone watching over the tomb as well.

It's quite conceivable that the entire area was on high alert for any signs of Christ's disciples and close followers. It's clear by Peter's repeated denial of Christ that the disciples were scared of being discovered and associated with Jesus. It's also clear by the fact that Peter was so easily recognized that the disciples were known and easily identified. The only reason for the disciples fearing being identified would be if they thought being recognized as a disciple would mean sharing Jesus's fate. I imagine that the disciples couldn't, or wouldn't, have gotten within a few miles of the tomb for fear of being noticed, recognized, identified, and apprehended.

The fact is that the soldiers did *not* fall asleep at the tomb.

The disciples never came near it.

No one made away with Christ's body.

No one breached His tomb.

No body belonging to Christ Jesus has ever been found.

No hidden tomb holding the bones of Jesus has ever been found.

None will ever be found.

Jesus didn't leave physical evidence of Himself on this earth in the form of a physical body.

Jesus did not leave behind a wife.

He did not leave behind a secret bloodline.

Jesus took all parts of His physical being to Heaven with Him; except for His blood that was shed on the cross.

What He *did* leave behind was the precious hope of eternal salvation. And, He left the requirement that this hope of eternal salvation be found in grace through faith, in those with a repentant heart and spirit. Faith and repentance being the operative words. Either one without the other is dead on arrival.

Jesus *is* the Risen Savior!

Chapter 17:
Jesus The Promised Messiah

Jesus *is* the promised Messiah…of that there can be no doubt. Jesus is the Messiah who prophesy in Old Testament spoke of. There is no other Messiah who has appeared before, or is yet to come after. If you're one of those who's holding out for another Messiah, you've been deceived.

Jesus *is* the Messiah spoken of in Isaiah 53:

> "*53 Who hath believed our report? and to whom is the arm of the LORD revealed?*
> *² For he shall grow up before him as a tender plant, and as a root out of a dry ground: he hath no form nor comeliness; and when we shall see him, there is no beauty that we should desire him.*
> *³ He is despised and rejected of men; a man of sorrows, and acquainted with grief: and we hid as it were our faces from him; he was despised, and we esteemed him not.*
> *⁴ Surely he hath borne our griefs, and carried our sorrows: yet we did esteem him stricken, smitten of God, and afflicted.*
> *⁵ But he was wounded for our transgressions, he was bruised for our iniquities: the chastisement of our peace was upon him; and with his stripes we are healed.*
> *⁶ All we like sheep have gone astray; we have turned every one to his own way; and the LORD hath laid on him the iniquity of us all.*

[7] He was oppressed, and he was afflicted, yet he opened not his mouth: he is brought as a lamb to the slaughter, and as a sheep before her shearers is dumb, so he openeth not his mouth.
[8] He was taken from prison and from judgment: and who shall declare his generation? for he was cut off out of the land of the living: for the transgression of my people was he stricken.
[9] And he made his grave with the wicked, and with the rich in his death; because he had done no violence, neither was any deceit in his mouth.
[10] Yet it pleased the LORD to bruise him; he hath put him to grief: when thou shalt make his soul an offering for sin, he shall see his seed, he shall prolong his days, and the pleasure of the LORD shall prosper in his hand.
[11] He shall see of the travail of his soul, and shall be satisfied: by his knowledge shall my righteous servant justify many; for he shall bear their iniquities.
[12] Therefore will I divide him a portion with the great, and he shall divide the spoil with the strong; because he hath poured out his soul unto death: and he was numbered with the transgressors; and he bare the sin of many, and made intercession for the transgressors."

Now, if this prophetic passage isn't speaking of Jesus, who's it speaking of?

Surely no one else has even come close to fulfilling or meeting these requirements. Not. Even. Close.

The Jewish people are typically quick to tell anyone who asks that the reason they reject Jesus as the Messiah is based on the following spurious claims, not necessarily in this order:

1. Jesus did not fulfill the messianic prophecies.
2. Jesus did not embody the personal qualifications of the Messiah.
3. Biblical verses referring to Jesus are "mistranslations".
4. Jewish belief is based on "national revelation", not individual testimony.

However, if we carefully scrutinize these claims, we can easily prove they're entirely wrong. We'll examine these claims individually and in depth. Some may seem common sense to most of us, however for the sake of argument, we must still cover all the bases.

The first claim that Jesus didn't fulfill the messianic prophesies is one that's blatantly false. The Jewish people believe that Jesus can't be the Messiah because, according to them, He hasn't fulfilled these prophecies *yet*...and no one else has...*yet*. So, they believe the Messiah is yet to come. They believe, wrongly I must add, *all* of the messianic prophesies must be fulfilled *prior* to the Messiah revealing himself.

However in my studies I've found no evidence to support that the promised Messiah must, or would, accomplish all of these things *before* revealing himself. Many of these prophecies are things that are yet to be fulfilled. Things that are set to happen *upon,* or immediately prior to, the second coming of Christ.

If one wanted to make the case that the second coming is when Christ is *truly* revealed to the entire world as the promised Messiah, I guess you technically could argue that. There will be no disputing His claim at that point, as all eyes will witness His glorious return to Earth. There will not be any unbelievers left at that point. The Bible says that every knee shall bow, and every tongue confess that Jesus Christ is Lord. In this manner, Christ *will* be revealed to all. (50)

However if the Messiah is only revealed to us at the end, that would defeat the entire purpose of His birth and ministry among us wouldn't it?

Wouldn't that defeat the purpose of grace through faith?

If Jesus appeared in the clouds, only at the end, and said "Here I am!" everyone would believe, because they'd seen Him with their own eyes. That's not faith. That would defeat the purpose of His sacrifice on the cross.

So, the argument that Jesus hasn't fulfilled the Messianic prophecies is entirely based upon the thinnest of hairline technicalities. I've searched far and wide and can't locate anything that states a specific requirement for fulfilling these prophecies before He is revealed.

So what are the "Messianic prophecies"?

Well, basically they're Biblical prophecies concerning the Messiah. The same prophecies, but ones that Jews and Christians hold a slightly different view of. According to the Jewish faith, these things must all be accomplished *before* the Messiah is revealed:

A. Building the Third Temple (Ezekiel 37:26-28).
B. Gathering all Jews back to the Land of Israel (Isaiah 43:5-6).
C. Ushering in an era of world peace, and end all hatred, oppression, suffering and disease. As it says: " And he shall judge among the nations, and shall rebuke many people: and they shall beat their swords into plowshares, and their spears into pruninghooks: nation shall not lift up sword against nation, neither shall they learn war any more." (Isaiah 2:4)
D. Spreading universal knowledge of the God of Israel, which will unite humanity as one. As it says: "And the LORD shall be king over all the earth: in that day shall there be one LORD, and his name one." (Zechariah 14:9).

See anything interesting there?

These are all things that are supposed to happen *after* the first part of the second coming of the Lord Jesus Christ. The rebuilt temple will be completed *after* the rapture. These are not things that must happen before the Messiah comes. Although it *is* the case that these things will take place before Jesus is revealed to all and all bow before Him as Lord.

The ushering in of world peace?

This takes place directly *after* the tribulation ends and Jesus defeats the enemies of God. There will be no "world peace" before that time, save for the three and a half years of false harmony under the rule of the Antichrist. The Bible doesn't teach anything different.

The gathering back of the Jews to the land of Israel?

That's been going on for decades. Displaced Jews have been returning to Israel in large numbers. Twenty-seven thousand Jews returned to Israel in 2017 alone. That's a pretty staggering number. Nowhere in the Bible does it say that this migration will be complete before the Messiah comes. Unless you're reading the second coming of Christ as the first appearance of the promised Messiah. (51)

The problem with the Jewish view of these events is that they've only read *half* of the book. They only have half of the story, because they haven't bothered to read the *entire* book. Had they, they'd readily accept Jesus as the Messiah and their Lord and Savior. I liken their view of the Bible to someone who's only read to the halfway point in a lengthy novel, or someone who's watched only half of a movie, and then decides that they know the full story. Their assumptions lead them to believe there's no need to view or read the rest of the story. The problem with this approach is that we're often wrong when we assume we know the ending.

How do I know that those pushing the "Jesus didn't fulfill the prophecies..." narrative haven't read the rest of the book?

Easy. I studied many, possibly a hundred or more, Jewish websites and sources. They all make the same uninformed claims, nearly verbatim. Some don't even bother to put these claims into their own words, but rather just copy and paste, word for word, from other websites and sources. I've read article after article titled "Why Jews reject Jesus as the Messiah", or similar tripe. Additionally, many of these sites and sources make the spurious claim that the Bible doesn't speak of a second coming of Christ at all! (50) (51)

What?

Yes. You read that correctly!

The same people who put forth the false claim that "Jesus didn't fulfill the prophecies..." also make the claim that the Bible doesn't speak of a second coming of Christ. They use this as grounds for disputing that He will fulfill these things upon His return.

This is a line taken directly from one such site:

> *"Christians counter that Jesus will fulfill these in the Second Coming. Jewish sources show that the Messiah will fulfill the prophecies outright; in the Bible no concept of a second coming exists." (*51)

Read the second half of the book people!

The fact that a group would actually dispute that the second coming is mentioned in the Bible is hard to believe. Especially when at least forty-four verses exist that deal with the second coming of Christ! (52)

What more evidence do you need that someone hasn't read the second, and most important, part of the Bible?

So, is this mistake simple ignorance?

Or is it something more nefarious?

Something like the willful intent to mislead others regarding Christ?

Here are just a few of the more important verses from the Bible regarding the second coming of Christ:

Acts 3:19-21:

"[19] Repent ye therefore, and be converted, that your sins may be blotted out, when the times of refreshing shall come from the presence of the Lord.
[20] And he shall send Jesus Christ, which before was preached unto you:
[21] Whom the heaven must receive until the times of restitution of all things, which God hath spoken by the mouth of all his holy prophets since the world began."

1 Thessalonians 4:15-17:

"[15] For this we say unto you by the word of the Lord, that we which are alive and remain unto the coming of the Lord shall not prevent them which are asleep.
[16] For the Lord himself shall descend from heaven with a shout, with the voice of the archangel, and with the trump of God: and the dead in Christ shall rise first:
[17] Then we which are alive and remain shall be caught up together with them in the clouds, to meet the Lord in the air: and so shall we ever be with the Lord."

Titus 2:12-14:

"[12] Teaching us that, denying ungodliness and worldly lusts, we should live soberly, righteously, and godly, in this present world;
[13] Looking for that blessed hope, and the glorious appearing of the great God and our Saviour Jesus Christ;
[14] Who gave himself for us, that he might redeem us from all iniquity, and purify unto himself a peculiar people, zealous of good works."

Revelation 1:7-8:

"⁷ Behold, he cometh with clouds; and every eye shall see him, and they also which pierced him: and all kindreds of the earth shall wail because of him. Even so, Amen.
⁸ I am Alpha and Omega, the beginning and the ending, saith the Lord, which is, and which was, and which is to come, the Almighty."

Revelation 22: 12-13:

"¹² And, behold, I come quickly; and my reward is with me, to give every man according as his work shall be.
¹³ I am Alpha and Omega, the beginning and the end, the first and the last."

Those verses are crystal clear in meaning. Jesus *is* coming again! To deny that the Bible mentions the second coming of Christ is akin to denying that the earth revolves around the sun!

So, in summing up, on point one, they've been squarely refuted and definitively proven wrong. Strike that point.

■■

Now, let's examine the second point that the deniers of Christ as the Messiah hold up:

Their claim is that Jesus *"didn't embody the personal qualifications of the Messiah"*...

And just like claim #1 above, this point is also patently false.

This claim, however, is based upon a three-part fallacy. To debunk this claim, we must take each point and dissect it separately. The Jews break this claim into three separate parts:

    A. The Messiah as a Prophet
    B. A descendant of David
    C. Torah observance

Let's begin by examining all three of these points separately.

The first part of this fallacy is utterly insane claim that Jesus wasn't the *"The Messiah as a Prophet"*.

Umm...

Hello?

Jews claim that the Messiah will be the greatest prophet of all time...and guess what?

Jesus was the greatest prophet of all time!

They follow up this denial of Jesus as a prophet by claiming that *"Prophecy can only exist in Israel when the land is inhabited by the majority of world Jewry."* (53) (54)

Interesting argument. I can't find that claim anywhere in my Bible. I can't find a single point wherein the Bible claims that prophecy is limited to and only valid "when the majority of the world's Jews reside in Israel".

Furthermore, if we believe that God is who He claims to be, why would we handicap Him with such artificial limitations?

Isn't this nothing more than teachings of the Pharisees?

A point must be inserted here regarding the Pharisees. Many people misunderstand the Pharisees of Biblical times and why they were so despised in the Bible. It wasn't just that they held fast to Jewish law and applied it in the strictest of senses. It wasn't just that they rigidly held to Biblical religious teachings, without ever allowing for grace. No, the biggest problem with the Pharisees is that they *added to* what the Bible said, including making up their own rules and structures. They took what the Bible said, added to it and created new rules for others to live by that weren't necessarily Biblical. Then they persecuted those who didn't follow their new brand of legalistic, rigid, believe-ism that was free from grace.

In examining the claim, above, you can see what I mean. These Jewish leaders and sources have added a false "rule" to the Bible...where none such existed before. Jesus can't be excluded as a Prophet simply because someone made up a nonexistent rule about when and how prophesy can legitimately exist in Israel.

This seems to be nothing more than a belief that someone pulled from thin air and applied as "truth". Thus it must be discarded. In summing up, Point A of this three point fallacy is nothing but abject conjecture at best. Attempting to discount Jesus as a Prophet based on non-Biblical criteria is a fool's game.

I can think of no finer example of why Jesus had such disdain for the Pharisees and religious leaders of His time. Not much has changed in the last two thousand years on this front it would seem. We see modern day Pharisees creating their own gospels today, most of the time in the names of "inclusiveness" and "tolerance". (I have to also point out that Jews are returning home in record numbers these days! A sure sign of Jesus's impending return.) (55)

■■■

Now, on to point B, the second leg of this fallacious claim: This claim states that "since Jesus isn't descended from David on His father's side, He can't be the promised Messiah". Again, this is an erroneous argument based on nothing more than arbitrary conditions set forth by man, not by God. Here's a couple of reasons why this claim is false:

1. Both Mary and Joseph were direct descendants of David.
2. While Jews typically trace their bloodlines only through the father's family, there's no earthly father for Jesus, thus an exception must be made, and only His earthly parent's bloodline must be used. That means we must trace His heritage through His mother's bloodline. That makes Mary's bloodline of extreme importance. (56)

In examining this claim, we must keep in the forefront of our knowledge that Jesus was the exception to a *lot* of normal rules. He's the only man to ever have existed without a natural, mortal man as His father. There's no human DNA contributed from a father's side in His case. This is what made Jesus both 100% God, while He's also 100% man.

Now, considering Joseph's heritage, Joseph was a direct descendant of David. Yet, he was also a direct descendant of Jeconiah. Having the blood of Jeconiah in his veins precludes Joseph from the throne of David because an heir to the throne would have to be descended from David; while also _not_ having the blood of Jeconiah in his heritage. This would've kept Joseph from the throne. It would also have kept Jesus from the throne…if, and only if, Joseph had been Jesus's biological father. This is one of the reasons why Jews deny Jesus as the Messiah. They disbelieve the virgin birth, denying that God is the father of Jesus. Thus, they believe Joseph to be His biological father and therefore, claim that Jesus couldn't sit on the throne because of tainted blood of Jeconiah.

Here's where the Bible lays out the curse against Jeconiah, in Jeremiah 22: 21-30:

> *21 I spake unto thee in thy prosperity; but thou saidst, I will not hear. This hath been thy manner from thy youth, that thou obeyedst not my voice.*
>
> *22 The wind shall eat up all thy pastors, and thy lovers shall go into captivity: surely then shalt thou be ashamed and confounded for all thy wickedness.*
>
> *23 O inhabitant of Lebanon, that makest thy nest in the cedars, how gracious shalt thou be when pangs come upon thee, the pain as of a woman in travail!*
>
> *24 As I live, saith the LORD, though Coniah the son of Jehoiakim king of Judah were the signet upon my right hand, yet would I pluck thee thence;*
>
> *25 And I will give thee into the hand of them that seek thy life, and into the hand of them whose face thou fearest, even into the hand of Nebuchadrezzar king of Babylon, and into the hand of the Chaldeans.*
>
> *26 And I will cast thee out, and thy mother that bare thee, into another country, where ye were not born; and there shall ye die.*
>
> *27 But to the land whereunto they desire to return, thither shall they not return.*
>
> *28 Is this man Coniah a despised broken idol? is he a vessel wherein is no pleasure? wherefore are they cast out, he and his seed, and are cast into a land which they know not?*
>
> *29 O earth, earth, earth, hear the word of the LORD.*
>
> *30 Thus saith the LORD, Write ye this man childless, a man that shall not prosper in his days: for no man of his seed shall prosper, sitting upon the throne of David, and ruling any more in Judah."*

Here's the crux of the issue: Because Jesus didn't share the actual blood of Joseph, He didn't share the taint of the blood of Jeconiah either. He wasn't under the curse that would have disallowed Him from sitting on the throne of David.

What the Jewish people who deny Jesus Christ as the Messiah fail to realize is that God Himself appointed Joseph to be Jesus's father. That decree is as good as having the actual blood of David following through His veins on His paternal side...without the taint of Jeconiah that Joseph would've also passed down. Jesus *is* of the lineage of David. Both through His mother and His appointed father's side.

More than that, Jesus has the actual blood of God flowing through His veins! That gives Him the birthright to every throne on both the earth and in Heaven!

■■■

Offered by some of these websites and resources as more "proof" that Jesus can't be the Messiah is this little nugget:

> *"According to Jewish sources, the Messiah will be born of human parents and possess normal physical attributes like other people. He will not be a demi-god, nor will he possess supernatural qualities."* (57)

Umm...I'd like to ask the following question: What "Jewish sources"?

That begs questioning. This could mean anything from the unconfirmed ravings of a wild man to the conjecture of a young school child. *Literally any Jewish person saying something about anything could be cited as a possible "Jewish source", couldn't they?*

What sources are we speaking of?

Unnamed sources?

Who comes up with this stuff?

The mainstream media?

How can one possibly vet the veracity of a source that's as ambiguous as the ubiquitous "Jewish sources?

Sounds like the same "unnamed sources" who spread disinformation via the mainstream media today. President Trump can take some solace in the fact that Jesus was the target of smear campaigns by "unnamed sources" long, long before he was. And while Trump is no Jesus by any means, the "unnamed sources" who're attacking him daily share a kinship with those who did the same to Jesus: they're also of their father, Satan.

Unnamed "Jewish sources" isn't a credible resource for making this kind of claim. Claims based on unnamed, unverifiable, and unknown sources must always be discarded by anyone possessing a modicum of intellectual honesty.

Does anyone reading this **truly** *believe that if one were debating a Jewish man and they said "Well, according to 'Christian sources'..." that what followed would be accepted as a valid argument?*

Of course not!

One might as well say, "Well, according to my Uncle Steve..."

It's traditional to quote the *actual* sources, rather than levying such a vague reference when attempting to sway someone to your viewpoint. I'm sorry that I don't buy into the "according to Jewish sources" rhetoric. The arrogance to intimate that unnamed "Jewish sources" somehow carry more weight than other, *specified* sources speaks volumes about how deeply the desperation runs in some Jews to reject Jesus. It's deeply ingrained.

Remember next time someone challenges you on a claim, just cite your "anonymous, unnamed sources" to win the argument. This reminds me of a time when I debated a man who claimed to be a liberal *and* a Christian at the same time. He claimed that Jesus was liberal in nature and would've supported all manner of modern day sin and modern-day political liberalism. He kept citing "biblical scholars" in trying to bolster his arguments. When I attempted to pin him down by asking for *specific* biblical scholars who espoused the same things he was presenting as "truth", he couldn't provide these "scholars". I wonder how many people he swayed to his viewpoints with his *"Biblical scholars say..."* argument? I doubt there were many.

Furthermore, the entire statement above is riddled with numerous inaccuracies. Take a look this part of that phrase: "*...and possess normal physical attributes like other people.*"

Did anyone ever make the claim that Jesus didn't "possess normal physical attributes"?

Where has that ever been argued? By anyone? Ever?

I've certainly never heard any Christian making any such claim. In fact, the Bible is quite clear that Jesus's appearance and "physical attributes" weren't just "normal", but that He didn't possess *any* physical traits as to make Him remarkable or desirable to others. In other words, as far as "normal physical attributes" go, He was very much an average man.

340

The Jewish statement goes on to state *"He will not be a demi-god, nor will he possess supernatural qualities"*... Yeah. Let's examine that logic for a moment.

First, let's get this straight...Jesus wasn't a "demi-God". The Bible makes no such claim. Jesus was and *is* God made flesh, not a mythological demi-god. A demi-god by definition is:

Demi-god:

Noun: a being with partial or lesser divine status, such as a minor deity, the offspring of a god and a mortal, or a mortal raised to divine rank.

That doesn't describe Jesus. The Bible says He's part of God, and equal to Him. Part of the Holy Trinity, each part equal with the other two. He *is* God. So, in a sense, part of their claim is true. The Messiah was never prophesied as a demi-god. Jesus wasn't a demi-god either, so this part of their claim only supports, rather than detracts from the claim of Jesus as Messiah.

Now, let's look at the second half of that statement. Here we see full-on cognitive dissonance on display. *Why?* Easy. Look at their own stated beliefs on what the Messiah will accomplish. They state on the one hand *"nor will he possess supernatural qualities"* and then go on to describe how He will accomplish that which can only be accomplished by...wait for it...wait for it...supernatural qualities!

*How could anyone **not** possessing supernatural qualities ring in world peace?*

*How could anyone **not** possessing supernatural qualities reveal God to the entire world?*

*How could anyone **not** possessing supernatural qualities cause the Jewish people to reassemble in Israel en masse?*

The second point of this three point fallacy is done. Stick a fork in it.

▪▪

So, now we move on to point C...

The claim here doesn't require much effort to debunk at all. This is something I think my ten year-old son could've tackled in my stead. The claim being thrust upon us is that Jesus *can't* be the Messiah.

Why?

Because Jews claim that the Messiah will enforce and bring about strict adherence to the Torah. They further claim that Jesus supposedly "contradicts" the Torah in many instances. Included in this false accusation is the claim that by proclaiming Himself the Messiah, and the Son of the Living God, that Jesus has attempted to seduce the Jewish people into following a false God.

Offered as "proof" of this claim are the following verses;

Deuteronomy 13:1-4

> *"13 If there arise among you a prophet, or a dreamer of dreams, and giveth thee a sign or a wonder,*
> *² And the sign or the wonder come to pass, whereof he spake unto thee, saying, Let us go after other gods, which thou hast not known, and let us serve them;*
> *³ Thou shalt not hearken unto the words of that prophet, or that dreamer of dreams: for the LORD your God proveth you, to know whether ye love the LORD your God with all your heart and with all your soul.*
> *⁴ Ye shall walk after the LORD your God, and fear him, and keep his commandments, and obey his voice, and ye shall serve him, and cleave unto him."*

This passage doesn't say what they claim at all. This passage is about false prophets rising up to try to seduce the Jews into following a false God. Jesus didn't ask anyone to follow a false God. He asked them to follow the God of the Torah. The same God who blessed the Jewish people and made a covenant with them in the first place.

Jesus *is* the God of the Torah, therefore He can't be asking Israel to follow a false God. Nor does this passage speak anything about *"strict adherence to the Torah"*. It does mention that we're to *"walk after the Lord you God, and fear him, and keep his commandments..."*, which ironically is exactly what Jesus tells us, and them, to do.

They seem to try to make the same case that those who follow the "hyper-grace" heretical doctrine do. They seemingly believe that Jesus, in claiming to have fulfilled the law, did away with the law. As we examined before, Jesus advocated no such thing. He made it abundantly clear that He came to fulfill the law, but that while the law has been fulfilled, we're still to try to keep the law. In fulfilling the law, He simply became our atonement for breaking the law. That's all. He made it clear that the law will not pass away, until the end, when peace will reign under His rule.

It would seem that their own arguments are based solely in ignorance of what the New Testament says about Jesus. They claim that the Messiah will demand strict adherence to the Torah and the case can be made that Jesus does just that. By no means did Jesus say we are free to sin at will. We just no longer have to perform rituals and sacrifices for the remission of sins as Jesus became the sacrifice for all time.

Now, that we've demolished this three point fallacy, let's move on to debunking the rest of the claims that Jesus can't be the Messiah.

■■

Now, this third rationale for why Jesus can't be the Messiah hinges on allegations of Biblical "mistranslations". This, I've found, is a go-to defense for anyone and everyone possessing a desire to dispute Biblical claims.

Want to excuse homosexuality?
Call the passages condemning it "mistranslations".
Want to dispute that women can't be spiritual leaders over men in church?
Call the Biblical passages condemning that "mistranslations".
Want to dispute the need to tithe?
You guessed it! Call the passages emphasizing tithing "mistranslations".

Claiming the ubiquitous "mistranslation" is an easy excuse for attempting to dispute Biblical truth. It's a lazy debate tactic meant to end the conversation on the topic at hand, rather than to further discussion thereof. It's the go-to tactic of the corrupt, the lazy, and the intellectually dishonest.

An example conversation on a Biblical topic that I had with a person who subscribes to the "mistranslations" myth follows.

Me: "Well, you know the Bible says that's a sin."

Who Stole Jesus

Her: *"That's your interpretation."*

Me: *"I didn't offer you my interpretation. I quoted the Bible to support the claim that this is a sin."*

Her: *"Well, that's a mistranslation of the original scriptures!"*

Me: *"Says who?"*

Her: *"Biblical scholars."*

See the problem here?

No matter what's said, the "mistranslation" lie effectively ends the conversation. It's akin to shouting, "You're wrong!", and walking away. Most people living today will never lay eyes on the original scriptures, written in the original languages. So instead of trusting in the accuracy of the preserved Word of God, instead, they rely on Google theology. Theology posted most often by those who are no more qualified in the field than those who often cite these Google Theologians as "scholars". The fact remains that most often when someone claims, *"That's a misinterpretation!"* in order to justify their sins, you can rest assured they're usually wrong.

It should come as no surprise that the Jews who wish to dispute Christ as the Messiah would also use this as a go-to excuse for discrediting His claim to the throne. This outlandish claim of Biblical "mistranslations" regarding Jesus is a two-part fallacy that we'll explore next.

■■

The first part of this fallacy hinges on the virgin birth. Jews dispute the virgin birth that's recorded in the Bible, which, if false, would deny Jesus the right to the throne of David. It would also deny Jesus's divinity as well as His ability to become a suitable sacrifice for the remissions of our sins.

They base their dispute of the virgin birth upon the Hebrew word "alma". This is the Hebrew word used to describe Mary. Their claim can best be paraphrased as this: *"The Bible doesn't claim that Mary was a virgin. The word 'alma' means a 'young girl'."* Here's where we see what might make a difference, if we're talking about modern society that is. However, you can't frame this argument through the prism of our societal views today. Nor can it be viewed through the modern cultural norms of today, which are vastly different from the cultural norms of ancient times.

For example: If we speak of a young girl of Mary's age today, sadly, there's only about a twenty-five percent, or less, chance she'd be assumed to be a "virgin". However if you go back to ancient times, a Hebrew "young girl" of this age would absolutely be assumed to be a virgin. Especially considering that they'd likely stone her to death for *not* being a virgin. There's greater than a ninety-eight percent chance that any "young woman" referenced when the Old Testament was written would be a virgin.

Now, while the Jews who reject Jesus are quick to point out that "alma" *could* also mean a young woman who was "married", there's by no means any indication that's the case most of the time.

Further complicating their claim that "alma" doesn't mean virgin is that early translators, both Hebrew and Greek alike, believed "virgin" to be the proper translation in the context it was used. The Gospels themselves were originally written in Greek, not Hebrew. The Greek word "Parthenos" was used to describe Mary and it *does* unequivocally mean "virgin". And lastly, you have common law and usage of the word "alma" at the time; in which it was assumed, unless otherwise noted that an "alma" is a virgin and thereby virtuous.

Also of note is that Mary said, when told she'd be carrying Jesus, *"How shall this be, seeing I know not a man?"*…the meaning of which is very clear. The word "know" in this usage literally meaning carnal, or sexual activity. Basically, (in modern English) she would've proclaimed, "But, I've never even had sex!" (Luke 1:34)

Thus, their claim of "misinterpretation" of verses referencing the virgin birth are wholly wrong.

Notice a trend here?

None of their arguments are holding water thus far. Not even under the minutest scrutiny.

■■■

Now, on to the next false argument regarding the easily claimed, but not so easily proven, ubiquitous, "misinterpretation". This argument involves Isaiah 53, which is the prophecy of the coming Messiah. The claim made by modern Jewish leaders is that Isaiah 53 doesn't really speak of the Messiah at all, but rather speaks of Israel; or rather the entirety of the Jewish people as a whole.

What?

This claim makes less sense than turning off a light in order to make the room brighter! In fact, this claim is about as sane as the leftists who claim that Planned Parenthood, and easy access to abortions, actually *decreases* the abortion rate.

It's nonsensical drivel at best.

Let's examine Isaiah 53 for ourselves to see if we can possibly comprehend where this argument originates and if it holds water. I've bolded certain key phrases or passages for emphasis.

Isaiah 53:

*"53 Who hath believed our report? and to whom **is the arm of the LORD revealed?***
*2 For he shall grow up before him as a tender plant, and as a root out of a dry ground: **he hath no form nor comeliness; and when we shall see him, there is no beauty that we should desire him.***
3 He is despised and rejected of men; a man of sorrows, and acquainted with grief: and we hid as it were our faces from him; he was despised, and we esteemed him not.
4 Surely he hath borne our griefs, and carried our sorrows: yet we did esteem him stricken, smitten of God, and afflicted.
5 But he was wounded for our transgressions, he was bruised for our iniquities: the chastisement of our peace was upon him; and with his stripes we are healed.
6 All we like sheep have gone astray; we have turned every one to his own way; and the LORD hath laid on him the iniquity of us all.
*7 **He was oppressed, and he was afflicted, yet he opened not his mouth: he is brought as a lamb to the slaughter, and as a sheep before her shearers is dumb, so he openeth not his mouth.***
8 He was taken from prison and from judgment: and who shall declare his generation? for he was cut off out of the land of the living: for the transgression of my people was he stricken.

⁹ And he made his grave with the wicked, and with the rich in his death; because he had done no violence, neither was any deceit in his mouth.

¹⁰ Yet it pleased the LORD to bruise him; he hath put him to grief: when thou shalt make his soul an offering for sin, he shall see his seed, he shall prolong his days, and the pleasure of the LORD shall prosper in his hand.

¹¹ He shall see of the travail of his soul, and shall be satisfied: by his knowledge shall my righteous servant justify many; for he shall bear their iniquities.

¹² Therefore will I divide him a portion with the great, and he shall divide the spoil with the strong; because he hath poured out his soul unto death: and he was numbered with the transgressors; and he bare the sin of many, and made intercession for the transgressors. "

Is there any logical context by which we can see this passage from the viewpoint of it being about the Jewish people as whole or Israel as a nation?

I'm having trouble finding any contextual reference for viewing this passage as speaking of a nation, or a race of people as a whole. That's not Biblical at all. In fact, context seems to make it very clear that this scripture speaks of a single, autonomous person; not a group of people. Not a nation of people. It is clear it references *one* person. It's the *Lord Jesus Christ* that Isaiah 53 speaks of.

Let's examine why Isaiah 53 *can't* be speaking of a nation, or a collective group of people by dissecting the scriptures.

- *"and to whom is **the arm of the LORD** revealed? "*: Take a look at the phrase highlighted in bold type. This clearly indicates a person; an autonomous, living individual. In modern English, we'd call this type of person a "right hand man". It's hard to swallow that this reference could be an allusion to a nation, or a collective group of people. It's specifically speaking about The Lord Jesus Christ as "the arm of the Lord". In other words, just as your arm is an extension of your body, Jesus is an extension of God; a part of God Himself.

- Consider this, the Jewish people argue that Isaiah 53 refers to Israel or the Jewish people as a whole. But notice this quote: *"**he hath no form nor comeliness; and when we shall see him, there is no beauty that we should desire him.**"* This again appears readily evident that the passage speaks of an individual, not a collective group. I've referenced this verse elsewhere in this book. It only makes sense that God had the foresight to ensure that no one would be desirous of the Messiah as a mortal man. A literal and quite frank interpretation of this scripture in modern English: *"He will be a homely man. Not someone who'd spark lust in others."* Now, unless those arguing that this scripture speaks of the Jewish people as a "collective group" believe that Isaiah 53 in effect calls all Jewish people ugly, then they have a real issue with their exegesis here.

- Now, with regard to verses three and four, I could see how these descriptions *could* be applied to the Jewish people and Israel as a nation. Certainly the Jews have been made to suffer greatly throughout history. There's certainly existed an undercurrent of antisemitism in America and a direct hatred of Jews throughout the world for decades. The crimes against the Jewish people in WWII will forever be a stain on human history. No other race of people and no other country has ever faced as much hatred on a national level. No other nation has been surrounded with neighboring nations who'd love to see their citizenry wiped out completely. With that said, while these particular verses (verses 3 & 4 of Isaiah 53) *could* feasibly fit the nation and people of Israel, these scriptures do *not* actually speak of them. In order for these verses to apply in this manner, the rest of Isaiah 53 would also have to equally apply to the Jewish people and Israel as a nation...and it does not.

- Now, in examining verses five and six:

> *"But **he** was wounded for our transgressions, **he** was bruised for our iniquities: the chastisement of our peace was upon **him**; and with **his** stripes we are healed. ⁶ All we like sheep*

*have gone astray; we have turned every one to his own way; and the LORD hath laid on **him** the iniquity of us all."*

There's really no way that we can make these passages fit either the Jews as a collective people or Israel as a nation. Everyone knows that throughout history the Jews have been unfairly despised and hated by the rest of the world. That much is 100% true. The Jewish people, and the nation of Israel, itself have suffered greatly at the hands of those who would wipe them out simply for existing. This should simply increase our faith as it fits with what the Bible says about Israel for turning its back on Him. What we cannot see is Israel, or the Jewish people, being wounded and chastised for *our* sins; the sins of all other peoples and nations. Nor has any of the evil that's befallen Israel and the Jewish people served to "heal" us as verse 5 proclaims.

The Bible is quite clear that any punishment of the nation of Israel that's been allowed by God has been because of Israel's rebellion against God. There is zero Biblical evidence of God punishing the Jews because of the sins of the Gentiles. None at all. In fact, the Bible is quite clear that the Jewish people and the nation of Israel are *favored* by God above all others. Verse six says that the sins of *all* have been laid upon "him". This couldn't possibly mean the nation of Israel or the Jewish people as a whole, again for the reasons cited above. God wouldn't punish His chosen people for the sins of the Gentile nations. There's nothing at all scriptural about Israel, or the people thereof, being punished in the place of, or as a substitutionary sacrifice for, the Gentiles. All scriptural teachings in both the Old and New Testaments would prove otherwise.

Consider what Jesus Himself said to a Gentile woman who came to Him seeking healing for her daughter...

> *"25 Then came she and worshipped him, saying, Lord, help me. 26 But he answered and said, It is not meet to take the children's bread, and to cast it to dogs." (Matthew 15:25-26)*

Does this sound like God would punish those who Jesus called the "children" because of the sins of those He called "dogs"?

- Verse 7 also makes clear that it's Jesus, not Israel or the Jewish people being spoken of. Let's take a look: *"⁷ He was oppressed, and he was afflicted, yet he opened not his mouth: he is brought as a lamb to the slaughter, and as a sheep before her shearers is dumb, so he openeth not his mouth."* Let me ask you, does this sound like Israel to you? While I do **not** share this opinion, the most common grievance we hear about modern day Israel is that they're too quick, and too strong, in their decisive action against terrorist groups and the rogue nations that launch attacks against them. That hardly sounds like the lamb suffering oppression, affliction, and death without opening his mouth or fighting back. Israel isn't about to become the "silent, meek lamb" for anyone.

- The argument by some in the Jewish community that Isaiah 53 references Israel, or the Jewish people as a group, gets even more ridiculous the further one delves into the chapter. Let's examine what verse 8 says:

    "⁸ He was taken from prison and from judgment: and who shall declare his generation? for he was cut off out of the land of the living: for the transgression of my people was he stricken." ...

    Now, while Jews have certainly faced imprisonment and judgment, the people as a whole, the nation of Israel, has never been "cut off out of the land of the living". That would mean there are none left. Jesus was "cut off out of the land of the living" when He died on the cross for our sins. Again, this verse speaks of the substitutionary death of Jesus on the cross for the transgressions of man, not the death of Israel or the extinction of the people thereof. Pay close attention to the last line of this verse… *"for the transgressions of my people"*... Now, we must ask, who makes up the "my people" who are referenced in this passage? *Israel.* The Jewish people themselves are the "my people" of this passage. So, in attempting to apply the logic that this chapter speaks of Israel as a nation or a people, then this passage would make absolutely no sense at all. It would literally be declaring that God made Israel the sacrifice for the sins of Israel; that they died to pay for those sins, but that this somehow was also salvation for Israel. *If the Jewish people all died to pay the price for the sins of the Jewish people, how are there Jewish people alive today? How can one become the sacrifice for one's own sin?*

- Verse 9 only continues to illustrate this point: *"⁹And he made his grave with the wicked, and with the rich in his death; because he had done no violence, **neither was any deceit in his mouth.**"*…Israel hasn't made their grave with anyone; neither the wicked nor the rich. The nation and people exist…and thrive to this day. *Notice the last line in this verse?* There's been one, and only one, man who walked this earth who's never been guilty of deceit: The Lord Jesus Christ. While I staunchly support Israel, I can tell you that no nation on earth could ever truthfully claim that they've never been deceitful. Show me a Jewish person who's never lied (other than Jesus) and show me a nation who's never lied, and I will show you a liar.

- At this point, verses 10, 11, & 12 really shouldn't have to be broken down much farther. It's abundantly clear from verses 1-9 that this chapter of Scripture cannot be speaking of anyone but the coming Savior, the Messiah, the Lord Jesus Christ. It's abundantly clear that there's no way by which a serious, thinking individual can reach the conclusion that this chapter speaks of a nation or a group of people as a whole. The entire narrative is crystal clear. It speaks of one person and one person only. It speaks of a person who became the sacrifice for the sins of all others. It speaks of one person who bore the shame, the rejection, the persecution, and the pain of all of us. It speaks of the Lord Jesus Christ.

So, we see emphatically the claim that *"Isaiah 53 has been misinterpreted"*, is again, just another false flag. There's simply no truth to this argument. Even if one believes Isaiah 53 was "misinterpreted" there's no way to make this chapter of Scripture say what those who reject Jesus as the Messiah claim that it says.

You just can't get there from here, as the old saying goes.

■■■

Point #4 that the Jews use to foster the claim that Jesus isn't the Messiah rests upon the spurious claim of being the only religion founded on "National Revelation". They claim that all other religions rely only on "personal revelations" to the believer. In this claim, Jewish religious leaders make the claim that the Torah says that it wasn't just Moses who received the Ten Commandments and revelation from God, but that it was the entire Jewish Nation who heard the voice of God…at the same time.

They then go on to claim that no other religion in the world was founded by God speaking to an entire nation of people at once. Now, part of the claim about God speaking to all of Israel is true. He did speak to them all on Mount Sinai. They perceived the fire, the lightening, the trumpet, and the thunder of His voice, but it's not clear that they heard, or comprehended, His voice and His words themselves. For posterity, I have to point out that He did in fact reveal Himself to Moses *first, making this a* "personal revelation". But, let's take their "National Revelation" claim at face value. This still doesn't make their claim of being the only religion based upon "National Revelation" true. Not if we pull the curtain aside a little.

Why?

Because God, as Jesus, didn't just speak to a single nation or people, He traveled among many nations and peoples proclaiming the Word of God...as the living Messiah. Jesus spoke to the Jews, the Gentiles, the Greeks, and the Romans alike. He revealed Himself as God everywhere He went. Jesus reached *all* people who would hear Him. Far more people heard His message during His travels than the number of people who could possibly have been present at the foot and foothills of Mount Sinai.

Furthermore, Jesus was revealed to the entire Jewish nation also. He suffered, bled, and died on the cross in front of their very eyes after they rejected him as the Messiah. The earthquake that announced His death was felt by the entire Jewish nation and the surrounding lands. The earth encompassing darkness that preceded His death on the cross was a "planetary revelation".

So, this claim of the only religion featuring a "National Revelation" doesn't hold water upon close examination.

Beyond that, the claim of Judaism being based solely upon "National Revelation" is also patently false. In Exodus Chapter 19, we see that Moses was given the Commandments and the Word of God. Contrary to their claim, we do not hear that the entire nation of Israel heard the entire conversation. This matter isn't even the slightest bit unclear. Moses unequivocally received these things from God and was directed to instruct the Jewish people on them.

Verses 18-19 of Exodus chapter 20 says that the people of Israel were so scared of the thundering, the lightning, the loud trumpet of God, and the fire on the mountain that they moved from the base of the mountain to a place much farther away. They didn't want to hear God's voice and trembled in fear to do so.

> [18] *And all the people saw the thunderings, and the lightnings, and the noise of the trumpet, and the mountain smoking: and when the people saw it, they removed, and stood afar off.*
>
> [19] *And they said unto Moses, Speak thou with us, and we will hear: but let not God speak with us, lest we die.*

Why would God command Moses to instruct the people of Israel on His Commandments, if the nation of Israel as a whole had already heard Him?

We see in the chapter that Moses kept traveling from the top of the mountain where God was, to the foothills of the mountain where the people hid from God's presence. He had to do so because the Commandments and the Word of God was revealed to Moses first; directly contradicting the claim of "National Revelation". Let's look at verses 20 and 21 of Exodus chapter 20.

> *²¹ And the people stood afar off, and Moses drew near unto the thick darkness where God was.*
>
> *²² And the LORD said unto Moses, Thus thou shalt say unto the children of Israel, Ye have seen that I have talked with you from heaven.*

Why would God have to instruct Moses on what to say to the people if they heard it for themselves?

Personal revelation, rather than "National Revelation" was how Judaism started, despite the claims to the contrary. See what Exodus 19:3-6 says about what led up to the events described above:

> *"And Moses went up unto God, and the LORD called unto him out of the mountain, saying, **Thus shalt thou say to the house of Jacob, and <u>tell</u> the children of Israel;**
> ⁴ Ye have seen what I did unto the Egyptians, and how I bare you on eagles' wings, and brought you unto myself.*
> *⁵ Now therefore, if ye will obey my voice indeed, and keep my covenant, then ye shall be a peculiar treasure unto me above all people: for all the earth is mine:*
> *⁶ And ye shall be unto me a kingdom of priests, and an holy nation. **These are the words which thou shalt <u>speak unto the children of Israel.</u>***

(The bolding and underlining in this passage was added by me for emphasis.)

This passage makes it clear that it's Moses who's having a *personal revelation* from God. God instructs Moses on what to say to the people of Israel...thereby doing away with the claim of Judaism originating with "National Revelation". It was only after Moses had a few back and forth personal conversations with God that God decided to reveal Himself to the nation of Israel as a whole. (Exodus 19:16)

So, while there was eventually a "National Revelation" of sorts that happened, Judaism itself actually began with what can only be called a *personal revelation*. The very thing that Jews today decry as non-valid when it comes to religion. So, by their very own criteria, Judaism isn't a valid religion either.

I'll also reiterate again, that Jesus's ministry and travels represents not just a "National Revelation" but an international one as well.

■■■

The last claim that the Jewish people make as to why they reject Jesus is that they're still waiting for the Messiah...the Messiah who already came and wasn't recognized by His own!

How sad is that?

Even sadder still is that in making the claim that they're still seeking their Messiah, they lament the current condition of society, while pushing the need to remain faithful to the Torah. Yet most of them long, long ago departed living a lifestyle that's anything resembling what the Torah taught.

They don't realize that what they're truly waiting for isn't the coming of the Messiah; they're waiting for the *Second Coming of the Messiah*. Even more tragic, is that they don't realize that all of the things they cite as conditions for the appearance of the Messiah are actually signs of things that are set to happen immediately before, or shortly after, Second Coming of Jesus Christ. The temple reconstruction, the Jewish people re-inhabiting the ancestral lands of Israel and making it thrive, the ushering in of true world peace, etc.

Most tragic of all is that when they meet the promised Messiah in person, and finally recognize Him for who He is, it won't be a happy reunion for them. They won't be pleased to hear what their Messiah has to say to them. Even as their knees bow and their tongues confess that Jesus Christ *is* Lord, they'll tremble in fear at the knowledge that they've allowed themselves to be led astray. They'll find that very Messiah they've repeatedly rejected on such spurious grounds is now the

Messiah that they bow and tremble before. Only they'll tragically find that their reluctant acceptance of who He is comes too late to save them from their sins and the terrible fate that awaits all who reject the risen Savior. (58) (59)

What a said day this will be for not only the Jewish nation, but for the majority of the people of this world. It will be a day of great joy for the redeemed, and a day of mourning followed by an eternity of horror for the lost.

Jesus *is* the Messiah.

Jesus *is* the risen savior.

Chapter 18:

Jesus: The Only Means By Which We Can Get To Heaven

The title of this chapter says it all. Jesus is the only means by which we can get to Heaven. There's no disputing it. There's no shortcuts, no alternate means, no different path to Heaven. There's one route and one route only to get to this much sought after destination.

Being a "good person" won't grant us eternal life.

Keeping the Commandments to the best of our ability won't save us.

Feeding the poor and clothing the naked won't save us from Hell.

Believing in a higher power or a nameless, faceless God won't save our souls.

Buddha doesn't have the power to save.

Mohammed doesn't have the power to save us either.

There's nothing within our own power that can save us. No belief in any other deity will keep us from perishing. We can't work our way into Heaven. We can't buy our way into God's grace. We can't observe any special rituals that will allow us entry therein. Church membership won't cut it. Singing in the choir won't open the doors of Heaven to us. Even tithing isn't a magical key to the pearly gates.

Jesus Himself said it best:

> *"Jesus saith unto him, I am the way, the truth, and the life: no man cometh unto the Father, but by me."* (John 14:6)

This makes it abundantly clear that there's no other way, no other method, no works, and no other paths that will get you to Heaven. You must come by and through Jesus or not at all. The road to salvation is grace through faith in the Lord Jesus Christ, submitting to Him with a repentant heart.

Paul D. Little

Chapter 19:
Jesus: The Perfect Sacrifice

Jesus is the perfect sacrifice. The spotless Lamb of God. That's the only reason that Jesus was able to become the propitiation for our sins. That's the only way we can become free from the wages of sin, and why we have access to the throne of God.

No other sacrifice would do.

It's because of Jesus's sinless nature that His shed blood can offer salvation for all. With God, only perfection will do when it comes to salvation...and perfection can only come through a sinless sacrifice. It is Christ's shed blood that makes us perfect when we could never be perfect on our own...for the purposes of salvation. We'll remain imperfect sinners until such time as Christ returns and the curse is broken. But Christ's virtue and His shed blood hides our sin from the sight of God.

Jesus was able to do what no other sacrifice could: He satisfied the need for a sacrifice...not for just a season, but for all time. We only need be covered by the blood once. Once salvation is obtained, it's eternal. It cannot be lost, or this would indicate that His sacrifice was not sufficient. Not perfect. Incomplete.

It's because of Jesus being the perfect, sinless sacrifice, the spotless Lamb of God that we know He can't be the embodiment of many of the counterfeit Jesus personas revealed within this book. To be one of those "Jesus's", He couldn't also be the sinless Savior.

359

Jesus *is* the perfect sacrifice. He needed nothing other than His shed blood to complete the plan of salvation. Nothing can be added, nothing can be taken away. He finished the work of salvation on the cross so that all who would believe may partake of the free pardon of sin.

Chapter 20:
Jesus: The Payment For Our Sins

Jesus, or rather His shed blood, His life itself, *is* the payment for our sins. We need no other sacrifice. We need nothing else by which to become a Child of God. It's Jesus and Jesus alone who allows us to have a home in Heaven.

We don't need anything else.

In fact, there's nothing else that will do. We don't need a priest. We don't need a special ritualistic prayer. We don't need the blessing of an earthly Pastor or spiritual leader. We don't need "last rites" administered by a man who is no less and no more a sinner than we are.

We cannot pay for our sins with good deeds or kindness. We cannot pay for our sins with a simple "I'm sorry." We cannot pay for our sins by any means other than the one that God's provided for us.

We need the shed blood of Jesus and salvation by grace through faith in the Lord Jesus Christ with a repentant heart. Without that, there's no payment for the remission of our sins and we'll never see Heaven.

See Ephesians 2:8-9:

> [8] *For by grace are ye saved through faith; and that not of yourselves: it is the gift of God:*
> [9] *Not of works, lest any man should boast.*

A common misconception is that you can be good enough to get into Heaven. But being "a good person" is a work. It's admirable, but it's not a pass to Heaven. The seams of hell are straining, nearly ready to burst, with the souls of the lost who were by all accounts "good people" in life. No one is good enough for Heaven, that's why our Savior had to pay the price we could never pay.

God has made a way by which we can join Him in His Heavenly home, and we cannot get there by any other means. Jesus is that way. His blood paid the otherwise unpayable debt.

Chapter 21:

Jesus: 100% God While Also Still 100% Man

This can be a daunting concept to wrap our heads around. Jesus was a man...and yet He was, and is, also God. That sounds like a contradiction, and yet it's not.

Jesus was fully man. He hungered the same way we hunger. He felt pain in the same way we feel pain. He grew cold, tired, hot, and lonely, the same way we experience those sensations. He experienced *all* the things that we do on a daily basis. He ate. He slept. He thirsted. He even feared.

Think about that for a moment: Jesus felt everything that you've felt, and yet He also overcame it all so that He could be the sacrifice for our sins. He's the only man who never sinned. As God made flesh, Jesus uniquely knows what it is like to struggle as a human, yet also have the power to forgive us for our failures at the same time.

Mohammed was only one-hundred percent man.

Buddha was only one-hundred percent man.

All other spiritual leaders are dead and buried and were also only one-hundred percent man. None of these men could even save their own souls, much less yours or mine. Jesus is the only one who is both man and God fully...and that's the reason we can trust in Him to forgive and save our souls.

Jesus was not a Demi-god. He was not half man, half God. He was and is God. Part of the Holy Trinity. Equal partners with God the Father, and The Holy Spirit. And it's for this reason that we are able to

be saved if we but call upon His name, with a repentant heart. (60) (61)
(62)

Chapter 22:
Jesus: The Only Unbiased Person To Ever Live

Jesus is the only person in the world who ever lived who never held personal biases. The *only* person to ever have lived a life wherein each person who He came across meant the same to Him. Each person He encountered held the same value to Him.

Let's face it, no matter how "nonjudgmental" we consider ourselves, *everyone* has at least some deeply held personal biases. No honest person can claim that there's not someone, or possibly even groups of people, that we just don't like; even though we may have valid reasons for that dislike. It's simply human nature.

Are we more favorably biased towards the ones we love and our close friends?

Of course we are.

Are we more biased towards the people in our lives who treat us the best?

Of course we are!

With Jesus, personal bias, or favoritism, doesn't come into play. Jesus spoke kindly with the Samaritan woman at the well. He treated her the same as He treated everyone else; although the Samaritans were generally despised by the Jews. This woman herself showed deep surprise when Jesus asked her to draw some water from the well for Him. She basically asked Him "Wait, you want a drink of water…from me? A Samaritan?"

John 4:9:

⁹ Then saith the woman of Samaria unto him, How is it that thou, being a Jew, askest drink of me, which am a woman of Samaria? for the Jews have no dealings with the Samaritans.

Jesus not only spoke to the woman, He shared the Gospel plan of salvation and He offered it freely to her. You see, not only was she a Samaritan, she was also a serial adulteress. Someone the likes of who most of us wouldn't have wanted anything to do with. She'd already had five husbands and the man she was currently in a relationship with wasn't one of those five.

Even Jesus's disciples were surprised, nay shocked, to see Jesus sitting with this woman, talking as if they were old friends. Although they didn't comment on this openly, the Bible says they "marveled" to see Him speaking with her in such a manner.

John 4:27:

"²⁷ And upon this came his disciples, and marvelled that he talked with the woman: yet no man said, What seekest thou? or, Why talkest thou with her?

The Samaritan woman received salvation that day. She also went back to the town giving testimony of Jesus to all who would listen to her. I've no doubt that because of her testimony, many others of Samaria also received Jesus and the free pardon of sin.

How exciting is that?

It just sends shivers down my spine to think of such a compassionate, loving Savior. One who looks past the sin, the outer, as well as inner layers, the dirt and grime, and sees a precious soul under our vile outer shells of humanity. The ability that only He possesses to see through the mess we make of ourselves to the inner soul itself.

Let's step back for a minute and see how truly amazing this one seemingly simple interaction truly is. Here's a woman who's from a race of people who were largely despised by the world. Not only is this woman of a people who were despised and shunned, she's one of the worst of worst among the citizens of Samaria. She's a serial adulteress. She's a cheater for sure, possibly a serial liar as well. While the Bible doesn't tell us anything more about her character, I think it wouldn't be a stretch to surmise that she was probably an unsavory character all the way around.

If we're honest with ourselves, in His shoes, most of us would have passed by on the other side of the road. We'd have turned away from the woman at the well, as quickly as we could. Maybe we'd avert our eyes, pretending not to see her. Most of us wouldn't have given her the time of day. We definitely wouldn't have greeted her with the loving compassion that Jesus did.

But notice this: Jesus didn't just speak to the woman at the well...He actually *waited* for her to arrive. Let that sink in. In His foreknowledge of things to come, Jesus planned ahead and waited for this woman to come to Him. A person that the majority of us would have ignored, or even worse, might have mocked, shunned, or scorned.

He waited for her to arrive! To come to Him. He planned on meeting her. If that doesn't touch your soul, nothing will. *(And I have to say, if you haven't be born again, Jesus is also waiting for you to arrive at the well of life. Will you meet Him there?)*

You see, Jesus didn't let bias stand in the way of His mission to offer salvation to all who'd accept Him. He didn't let His disgust at her filthy sins cloud His vision. He didn't let her sins kept Him from seeing beyond them to her wounded inner soul.

Think about something for a moment here. Think of the most sexually promiscuous person you know. Consider most sin-riddled person you've ever encountered in your life. Then consider this: If you're aware of the extent of this person's sins that are *known* to you, how much more sin does this person have hidden that you *don't* know about? I'd venture to say what you know about them is the tip of a very large iceberg.

Now consider that Jesus sees *all* sin in a person's life. *That's pretty deep, huh?* He knows those things that's common knowledge about us, all the things that others around us know; but He also knows all those things that we hide from others. He knows all of our secrets. Our secret thoughts. Our secret deeds. Our secret hearts. While this adulterous woman was probably reviled even among the Samaritan people for her proclivity to sin, Jesus knew even more about her sin than everyone else around her could possibly ever know. He saw even into the depths of her blackened heart and her vilest thoughts and imaginations.

This woman whose *known* sins would keep most of us away from her, was still precious to the Lord who even knew that much more about her sins than anyone else living ever could.

What compassion!

What unbiased love!

Remember, even the disciples when they came upon Jesus ministering to the Samaritan woman were inwardly amazed that He was speaking with her. None voiced their open disproval, but again, the Bible tells us that they "marveled" at this act of compassion. In other words, the disciples largely reacted much like we would have.

What's more, Jesus used this woman greatly. He allowed her to go back to town proclaiming that the Messiah had come. She gave a powerful testimony of an all-knowing, all-caring savior! Jesus does the same today: some of the most powerful personal testimonies come from those who were once lost in the deepest pools of sin until Jesus saved them. Some of those we'd be least likely to associate with prior to salvation have some of the most compelling personal testimonies.

Can you imagine the other citizens of this town upon hearing how this woman, who was an outcast even amongst her own, chief among sinners in that region, met the Messiah and instead of facing scorn and rejection, she was shown love and mercy? The others in Samaria clamored for Jesus and asked Him to stay among them. So, He dwelt with them for two full days. I can only imagine that many a soul was saved in those two days, largely due to the testimony of a social pariah.

Jesus turned a broken vessel into an instrument of love. He took a person who was a useless sinner to most, and made her a useful tool for God. He repaired a broken and empty vessel and filled it with love and purpose.

Who but Jesus could do this?

∎∎∎

We see further evidence of Jesus's unbiased love in His conversion of Saul. Like most of us would be tempted to feel today, I'm sure that some of the early believers in Christ would've loved to have seen something truly awful befall Saul. Here's a man who was a very zealous Jew. One who was dead set on rooting out and destroying Christianity, its converts, and especially its preachers and prophets.

Here's a man who took great pride and joy in having the followers of Jesus imprisoned and destroyed. A man who'd been present at, and responsible for, the execution of many Christians.

This was a man who most would say was worthy of a painful death…and yet Jesus saw through that, and just like in the case of the woman at the well, Jesus used this deeply flawed and imperfect man to accomplish His will. Instead of giving him what he deserved, Jesus handpicked Saul to preach His Word. He converted, rather than destroyed him. He waited for Saul on that road to Damascus. Saul who bore letters of arrest in hand. He waited for a lost sinner to come to Him. He gave Saul a new name, a new life, a new passion, and a new purpose.

Only an unbiased and all-loving Savior could do that.

Jesus, the only unbiased person in the world, is the only one who can save us from the wrath of God the Father. Because of our sins, we're well deserving of that wrath. He's the only one who can help. Because of His all-powerful compassion and His unbiased love, all we need to do is ask in repentance and faith.

.

Chapter 23:
Jesus: The Way of Salvation

So, now that we know who Jesus is, because we first ruled out who He isn't, the next logical question is *"How do I obtain salvation?"*

If you're not sure of your salvation, then this is, without doubt, the most important chapter in this book. If you only take one chapter to heart, make it this one. Even if you believe you're sure of your salvation, if you claim salvation by any other means than what's described here, you need to strongly consider these words. In fact, you need to consider these words as if your very life depends on it because, spiritually speaking, it just might.

You might have begun reading this book thinking that you've come to Jesus by another means. You might have trusted in baptism alone. Or you might have trusted in the faith of your parents to carry over to you. Or you might have trusted that your church membership would carry you through to Heaven.

Perhaps you've trusted in your good works, your kindness, or your generosity. Or perhaps you've believed that keeping the two specific commandments that Jesus mentioned is enough to see you through. Perhaps you've bought into the "scales of righteousness" belief, wherein you believe that as long as your good deeds outweigh your bad, that you'll be fine. Or maybe there's some other reason that you feel some doubt about your salvation.

Maybe you've never known Jesus at all.

It's not too late.

That's the good news.

As long as your lungs still fill with air, as long as your brain still functions, as long as your heart still beats, you can have a personal relationship with Jesus. A relationship that's the only way to get to Heaven.

So what must you do to obtain the free pardon of sin?

Nothing really. Except believe. Have faith. Feel sorrow for your sins, for failing God, and be willing to allow Jesus to help you turn from them.

Remember when you were a child?

Remember that simple child-like faith that you had in Santa Claus?

Remember how you just knew, without even the slightest doubt, that if you behaved and did what your parents asked, that Santa Claus would visit your home in the dead of night on Christmas Eve, and you'd be greeted the next morning with the things you'd asked for?

Remember the simple, unwavering faith that you had in the tooth fairy? That as long as you placed that tooth under your pillow, that the next morning, the tooth would be gone while a reward waited in its place?

That's the kind of faith that salvation requires. The difference is that you'll not be disappointed with Jesus as you were when you discovered that Santa and the Tooth Fairy weren't real. Because it doesn't get more real than Jesus. You'll never outgrow Him.

Believe with a repentant heart that Jesus is the only begotten Son of God; that He died on the cross for the remission of your sins; that He rose again on the third day; and that He awaits in Heaven, even now, for His Father's command to return for His believers.

What's a repentant heart?

That's easy. It's a sorrowful spirit. It's a heart that acknowledges your lost condition, your separation from God, because of the sins you've committed. It's a contrite spirit. It's a heart that's willing to allow Jesus to help you turn from your sins and begin a new life. It's a heart that seeks a new life and a new beginning in Christ.

A repentant heart is the key to salvation. Simple belief without a contrite spirit doesn't work. Faith without a repentant heart is dead on arrival.

While salvation can't be boiled down to just a simple, formulaic prayer, if the repentant heart exists and it's accompanied by true belief, then salvation comes easily. A simple prayer such as this is all that needs to be said. God can already see and read your heart. In fact, He knows your heart better than you do.

What follows is a simple example of a prayer that can be offered. Often referred to as a "sinner's prayer". There are no right or wrong words, if the prayer comes from an earnest, sincere, and repentant heart. Remember, God knows your heart, the words matter much less than your intent and your faith:

> *"Lord Jesus, please forgive me. I know that I'm a lost sinner and that I cannot save myself. I confess my sins and that they've caused me to be separated from you. I want to turn from those sins and need your help to do so. By faith I gratefully receive your gift of grace and salvation. I am ready to trust you as my Lord and Savior. Thank you, Lord Jesus, for your sacrifice on the cross. I believe you are the Son of God who died on the cross for my sins. I believe you rose from the dead on the third day. Thank you for bearing my sins and giving me the gift of eternal life. I believe your words are true. Come into my heart, Lord Jesus, and be my Savior. Amen."*

Note, as stated above, your prayer doesn't need to be these exact words. Any prayer uttered in the right spirit, with the right heart, that contains a message similar to this will work. It just needs to be heartfelt with true faith in Jesus.

After you receive salvation, it's usually followed with a believer's baptism. And attending a Bible-believing, Bible-preaching church is essential to a believer's life and growth in Christ.

That's what salvation is all about. That's the real relationship with Jesus. That's all that's needed to go from a lowly sinner, to a repentant child of God. It's so simple and yet so many perish because they wouldn't submit to Jesus.

How sad is it to have your sins already paid for, and yet fail to redeem your salvation?

Yet, so many people don't redeem what they already have waiting for them. How many people would have a winning lottery ticket worth tens of millions, or an inheritance worth millions, just waiting to be collected and then fail to go and claim it? No one. Not a single person. *(Note: I don't play the lottery and I don't condone or endorse gambling.)*

Salvation is worth more than either of these, more than all the millions in the world, and yet so many people leave it unclaimed. It's heartbreaking to know this, and yet people die lost every day. All while already having their sin debts paid in full.

Don't die lost today!

If there's any doubt in your mind as to the condition of your soul, you can take the steps above. Or, seek out the counsel of a qualified pastor, preacher, or minister who belongs to a Bible-believing, Bible-preaching church. They can lead you down the right path and answer any lingering questions you might have. One thing is for sure, you need to do something.

You can't afford not to.

Afterword

Thank you for taking the time to read my book. This body of work is a culmination of many years of writing, research, prayer, Bible study, an undying love for the Lord, as well as a burden for the lost.

Jesus has been a huge part of my life since I got saved twenty-seven years ago. He's been with me through thick and thin, even during the times that I haven't been entirely faithful to Him. What a wonderful Savior we have who's so faithful and just to forgive us for all our sins and unrighteousness. We don't deserve what He did for us on the cross, but I'm so glad that He accomplished His Father's will.

Jesus loves you and is unwilling that any should perish, but that all should have everlasting life. I pray that all who are reading this will one day join me in the chorus up in Heaven singing eternal praises to our King.

Until that time, may God Bless you and keep you!

I sincerely hope that this book has been a help to you in some small way. I'd love to hear your thoughts on it. Please reach out to me with questions, comments, or other author inquiries to whostolejesus@gmail.com.

Paul D. Little

October 16th, 2019

Paul D. Little

Citations

1. https://news.gallup.com/poll/224642/2017-update-americans-religion.aspx

2. Matthew 16:23 *"²³ But he turned, and said unto Peter, Get thee behind me, Satan: thou art an offence unto me: for thou savourest not the things that be of God, but those that be of men."*

3. http://www.activistmom.com/blog/auburn-high-school-students-petition-against-teachers-lgbt-pride-flag-in-classroom/ Posted 08/23/2017

4. https://www.christianpost.com/news/pregnant-single-woman-fired-from-church-job-for-not-marrying-childs-father-says-she-might-sue-132638/

5. Luke 8:1 *"¹And it came to pass afterward, that he went throughout every city and village, preaching and shewing the glad tidings of the kingdom of God: and the twelve were with him, ²and certain women, which had been healed of evil spirits and infirmities, **Mary called Magdalene, out of whom went seven devils,** ³and Joanna the wife of Chuza Herod's steward, and Susanna, and many others, which ministered unto him of their substance.*

6. https://www.washingtonpost.com/local/on-easter-mary-magdalene-will-be-maligned-as-a-prostitute-except-she-wasnt/2017/04/13/4e5d502a-2067-11e7-be2a-

3a1fb24d4671_story.html?noredirect=on&utm_term=.54c11
5ea4251

7. Matthew 18:6 *"⁶ But whoso shall offend one of these little ones which believe in me, it were better for him that a millstone were hanged about his neck, and that he were drowned in the depth of the sea. "*

8. Deuteronomy 22:25-26 *"²⁵ But if a man find a betrothed damsel in the field, and the man force her, and lie with her: then the man only that lay with her shall die. ²⁶ But unto the damsel thou shalt do nothing; there is in the damsel no sin worthy of death: for as when a man riseth against his neighbour, and slayeth him, even so is this matter:*

9. http://www.dailymail.co.uk/news/article-3234361/Texas-professor-bans-students-saying-God-Bless-class.html

10. https://praisephilly.com/2647262/professor-bans-college-students-from-saying-bless-you-in-class/

11. http://eagnews.org/students-revolt-after-prof-bans-saying-god-bless-you-in-class/

12. https://www.voanews.com/a/oregon-same-sex-marriage-wedding-cake/4183943.html

13. https://www.christianitytoday.com/news/2018/june/jack-phillips-masterpiece-cakeshop-wins-supreme-court-free-.html

14. https://www.usatoday.com/story/opinion/2018/08/16/jack-phillips-despite-my-supreme-court-victory-im-still-under-attack-column/996588002/

15. https://www.adflegal.org/enough-is-enough?mwm_id=337016133021&gclid=EAIaIQobChMI14efgf334QIVBrjACh1Rpwl7EAAYASAAEgIagfD_BwE

16. https://www.adflegal.org/detailspages/blog-details/allianceedge/2017/08/28/make-me-a-cake-for-my-.-.-.-divorce-party

17. http://www.bpnews.net/44570/colo-tells-bakers-ok-to-refuse-bible-cakes

18. https://books.google.com/books?id=-VgaAAAAYAAJ&pg=PR3&source=gbs_selected_pages&hl=en#v=onepage&q&f=false

19. http://webstersdictionary1828.com/Dictionary/marriage

20. http://www.slate.com/articles/news_and_politics/jurisprudence/2009/04/noah_webster_gives_his_blessing.html

21. https://books.google.com/books?id=-VgaAAAAYAAJ&pg

22. http://www.nytimes.com/2008/12/21/opinion/21kristof.html

23. https://en.wikipedia.org/wiki/List_of_mayors_of_Atlanta

24. https://www.investors.com/politics/editorials/how-decades-of-democratic-rule-ruined-some-of-our-finest-cities/

25. http://www.sheknows.com/entertainment/articles/973497/stacey-dash-told-to-kill-herself-over-romney-endorsement

26. http://www.frontpagemag.com/fpm/147677/how-left-keeps-blacks-line-stacey-dash-chapter-mark-tapson

27. *"Pay no attention to that man behind the curtain"*…this is what the Wizard, in The Wizard of Oz, yells as Dorothy's dog, Toto, pulls the curtain back to reveal that the Wizard is merely a normal man and not at all what he seems. Many culturally references have come from this scene, such as the phrases "pulling back the curtain" and "the curtain was pulled back", or "the person behind the scenes".

28. https://www.forbes.com/sites/jerrybowyer/2011/11/23/occupy-plymouth-colony-how-a-failed-commune-led-to-thanksgiving/#3db783876dfe

29. https://www.politifact.com/virginia/statements/2016/jun/13/dave-brat/dave-brat-us-labor-participation-rate-lowest-70s/

30. https://www.washingtontimes.com/news/2013/mar/28/food-stamp-president-enrollment-70-percent-under-o/

31. https://www.investors.com/politics/editorials/food-stamps-disability-welfare-medicaid-enrollment/

32. https://abcnews.go.com/WNT/story?id=130391&page=1

33. https://www.theverge.com/2016/3/24/11297128/matthew-doyle-arrest-muslim-tweet-brussels

34. https://www.christianpost.com/news/christian-street-preachers-found-guilty-of-abuse-for-quoting-bible-saying-jesus-only-way-to-god-176317/

35. https://www.washingtonpost.com/national/religion/houston-subpoenas-pastors-sermons-in-gay-rights-ordinance-case/2014/10/15/9b848ff0-549d-11e4-b86d-184ac281388d_story.html

36. https://www.nytimes.com/1989/10/13/us/rape-and-incest-just-1-of-all-abortions.html

37. https://www.abortionfacts.com/facts/8

38. http://www.life.org.nz/suicide/suicidekeyissues/abortion-and-suicide/

39. https://www.huffingtonpost.com/richard-schiffman/why-people-who-pray-are-heathier_b_1197313.html

40. https://www.heritage.org/poverty-and-inequality/report/air-conditioning-cable-tv-and-xbox-what-poverty-the-united-states

41. http://amazinghealth.com/13.06.24-identical-twin-studies-prove-homosexuality-is-not-genetic

42. https://concernedwomen.org/images/content/bornorbred.pdf

43. https://www.uua.org/beliefs/what-we-believe

44. Matthew 6:7 *"But when ye pray, use not vain repetitions, as the heathen do: for they think that they shall be heard for their much speaking."*

45. Numbers 6:2-8 *"2 Speak unto the children of Israel, and say unto them, When either man or woman shall separate themselves to vow a vow of a Nazarite, to separate themselves unto the LORD:-3 He shall separate himself from wine and strong drink, and shall drink no vinegar of wine, or vinegar of strong drink, neither shall he drink any liquor of grapes, nor eat moist grapes, or dried.4 All the days of his separation shall he eat nothing that is made of the vine tree, from the kernels even to the husk.5 All the days of the vow of his separation there shall no razor come upon his head: until the days be fulfilled, in the which he separateth himself unto the LORD, he shall be holy, and shall let the locks of the hair of his head grow.6 All the days that he separateth himself unto the LORD he shall come at no dead body.7 He shall not make himself unclean for his father, or for his mother, for his brother, or for his sister, when they die: because the consecration of his God is upon his head.8 All the days of his separation he is holy unto the LORD."*

46. Numbers 6:13-20 *"13 And this is the law of the Nazarite, when the days of his separation are fulfilled: he shall be brought unto the door of the tabernacle of the congregation:14 And he shall offer his offering unto the LORD, one he lamb of the first year without blemish for a burnt offering, and one ewe lamb of the first year without blemish for a sin offering, and one ram without blemish for peace offerings,15 And a basket of unleavened bread, cakes of fine flour mingled with oil, and wafers of unleavened bread anointed with oil, and their meat offering, and their drink offerings.16 And the priest shall bring them before the LORD, and shall offer his sin offering, and his burnt offering:17 And he shall offer the ram for a sacrifice of peace offerings unto the LORD, with the basket of unleavened bread: the priest shall offer also his meat offering, and his drink offering.18 And the Nazarite shall shave the head of his separation at the door of the tabernacle of the congregation, and shall take the hair of the head of his separation, and put it in the fire which is under the sacrifice of the peace offerings.19 And the priest shall take the sodden shoulder of the ram, and one unleavened cake out of the basket, and one unleavened wafer, and shall put them upon the hands of the Nazarite, after the hair of his separation is shaven:20 And the priest shall wave them for a wave offering before the LORD: this is holy for the priest, with the wave breast and heave shoulder: and after that the Nazarite may drink wine."*

47. https://www.bibletools.org/index.cfm/fuseaction/Lexicon.show/ID/G3816/pais.htm

48. https://www.neverthirsty.org/about-christ/historical-quotes/thallus/

49. http://christianthinktank.com/jrthal.html

50. http://www.aish.com/jw/s/48892792.html

51. https://jewsforjudaism.org

52. http://ipost.christianpost.com/post/44-bible-verses-about-second-coming-of-jesus-christ-besides-the-gospels

53. http://www.aish.com/jw/s/48892792.html

54. https://www.simpletoremember.com/articles/a/jewsandjesus/

55. https://onenewsnow.com/culture/2018/04/14/tens-of-thousands-of-jews-returning-to-israel

56. https://www.blueletterbible.org/faq/don_stewart/don_stewart_185.cfm

57. http://www.aish.com/jw/s/48892792.html

58. Isaiah 45:23 *"²³ I have sworn by myself, the word is gone out of my mouth in righteousness, and shall not return, That unto me every knee shall bow, every tongue shall swear."*

59. Romans 14:11 *"¹¹ For it is written, As I live, saith the Lord, every knee shall bow to me, and every tongue shall confess to God."*

60. Matthew 28:19 *"Go ye therefore, and teach all nations, baptizing them in the name of the Father, and of the Son, and of the Holy Ghost:"*

61. John 10:30 *"I and [my] Father are one."*

62. 1 John 5:7 *"For there are three that bear record in heaven, the Father, the Word, and the Holy Ghost: and these three are one."*

About The Author:

Paul D. Little is an author, a preacher, a motivational speaker, a dedicated husband, and a doting father. When he's not spending time with his wife and their four children, he's reading, writing, or working in the ministry. To date, he's authored five books, including four Christian children's books, *The Christmas Chips, Titus Meets The Easter Bunny, Sam and Luke Discover Thanksgiving, and Savannah's Valentine*. All four children's books contain the Gospel message and are great ways to share the good news of Christ with children.

Currently, he is penning two new books, *Silas's Independence Day* (a Christian children's book), and *The Reaping* (a novelization of the real events surrounding the rapture and the aftermath thereof, told by a fictional witness).

He can be reached for questions, comments, booking requests, and speaking engagements through his personal Facebook page, or through his email whostolejesus@gmail.com. He'd love to hear from you, so drop him a line today!

www.ingramcontent.com/pod-product-compliance
Lightning Source LLC
Chambersburg PA
CBHW021212090426
42740CB00006B/189